INTERNATIONAL INVESTMENT LAW AND THE ENERGY TRANSITION

The global energy sector is in flux, transitioning from reliance on fossil fuels to clean energy sources at an unprecedented pace. This book explores the complex interplay between this transition and international investment law.

The book navigates the tension between attracting crucial and expensive investments in clean energy and protecting a state's right to regulate its energy sector for environmental and other reasons. It analyses how international treaties and investment arbitration tribunals are evolving to address these challenges, examining how the scope of investment protection is being redefined and how the delicate balance between stability and regulatory flexibility is being recalibrated. The book delves into this complex landscape, exploring how established legal frameworks, especially international investment law, grapple with the unique characteristics of renewable energy, critical minerals and rapidly evolving technologies.

While offering a roadmap for the current energy transition, the book also identifies unanswered questions. It paves the way for further discussion on critical mineral supply chains and the future of international investment law in a transformed energy landscape.

Global Energy Law and Policy: Volume 10

Global Energy Law and Policy

Energy policy and energy law are undergoing rapid global transformation, characterised by the push in favour of decarbonisation. The 2015 Sustainable Development Goals, the Paris Agreement and COP26 on international climate and energy action have forged a consensus for a pathway to a universal just transition towards a low-carbon economy for all states and all societies.

This series publishes conceptual work that help academics, legal practitioners and decision-makers to make sense of these transformational changes. The perspective of the series is global. It welcomes contributions on international law, regional law (for example, from the EU, US and ASEAN regions), and the domestic law of all states with emphasis on comparative works that identify horizontal trends, and including transnational law. The series' scope is comprehensive, embracing both public and commercial law on energy in all forms and sources and throughout the energy life-cycle from extraction, production, operation, consumption and waste management/decommissioning. The series is a forum for innovative interdisciplinary work that uses the insights of cognate disciplines to achieve a better understanding of energy law and policy in the 21st century.

Recent titles in this series:

Decarbonisation and the Energy Industry
edited by Tade Oyewumni, Penelope Crossley, Frédéric Gilles Sourgens and Kim Talus

The Global Energy Transition: Law, Policy and Economics for Energy in the 21st Century
edited by Peter D Cameron, Xiaoyi Mu and Volker Roeben

The Law and Governance of Mining and Minerals: A Global Perspective
by Ana Elizabeth Bastida

National Climate Change Acts: The Emergence, Form and Nature of National Framework Climate Legislation
edited by Thomas L Muinzer

Governing the Extractive Sector: Regulating the Foreign Conduct of International Mining Firms
by Jeffrey Bone

Stability and Legitimate Expectations in International Energy Investments
by Rahmi Kopar

Land Law and the Extractive Industries: Challenges and Opportunities in Africa
by Victoria R Nalule

China's Global Energy Expansion: A Regulatory Assessment
by Xiaohan Gong

Critical Minerals, Sustainability, and the Energy Transition in the Global South: A Justice Perspective
by Susan Nakanwagi

International Investment Law and the Energy Transition
edited by Rahmi Kopar and Volker Roeben

International Investment Law and the Energy Transition

Edited by
Rahmi Kopar
and
Volker Roeben

• HART •
OXFORD • LONDON • NEW YORK • NEW DELHI • SYDNEY

HART PUBLISHING

Bloomsbury Publishing Plc

Kemp House, Chawley Park, Cumnor Hill, Oxford, OX2 9PH, UK

1385 Broadway, New York, NY 10018, USA

Bloomsbury Publishing Ireland Limited, 29 Earlsfort Terrace, Dublin 2, D02 AY28, Ireland

First published in Great Britain 2025

A catalogue record for this book is available from the British Library.

Library of Congress Cataloging-in-Publication data

ISBN: HB: 978-1-50998-322-3
ePDF: 978-1-50998-324-7
ePub: 978-1-50998-323-0

Typeset by Compuscript Ltd, Shannon

TABLE OF CONTENTS

CONTRIBUTORS

Crina Baltag: Associate Professor of International Law, Stockholm University, Attorney-at-Law, and Arbitrator

Crina Baltag is Associate Professor in International Arbitration at Stockholm University and qualified attorney-at-law, with over 20 years of extensive practice in international dispute resolution. Crina has been appointed as arbitrator in numerous arbitrations under the rules of the ICC, LCIA, SIAC, SCC, FAI, VIAC, CAM-CCBC etc, as well as in ad hoc arbitrations, and she acts as expert in various international commercial and investment arbitrations. Crina publishes extensively on current international arbitration topics, in particular on energy-related ones.

Peter D Cameron: LLB (Hons), PhD (Edinburgh), FCIArb, Fellow of the Royal Society of Edinburgh, Barrister (England and Wales), Associate Tenant at Landmark Chambers in London, Professor of International Energy Law and Director of the Centre for Energy, Petroleum and Mineral Law and Policy at the University of Dundee

Peter Cameron is one of the world's leading authorities in the specialist field of energy law. He sits as arbitrator in complex, high-value, cross border disputes at the International Centre for Settlement of Investment Disputes (ICSID) and the International Court of the International Chambers of Commerce (ICC). He is the author of the leading textbook, *International Energy Investment Law*, 2nd edn (Oxford University Press, 2021) and editor-in-chief of the journal, *Global Energy Law and Sustainability*. He is on the list of practitioners in International Arbitration at the Vienna International Arbitration Centre (VIAC).

Elena Cima: PhD, Senior Lecturer, University of Geneva

Elena Cima is a Senior Lecturer in Public International Law at the University of Geneva, where. She teaches courses on international environmental and climate law, energy law, and investment law. She is the Director of the University of Geneva's Summer School in International Law and International Humanitarian Law. Elena holds a PhD in International Law from the Geneva Graduate Institute, a Bachelor of Laws from the University of Milan and an LLM degree from Yale Law School.

Penelope Crossley: Professor of Law, Sydney Law School, and Solicitor of the NSW Supreme Court

Penelope Crossley is a Professor of Energy Law at Sydney Law School. She is an international expert in the complex legal issues associated with the Energy Transition, including renewable energy and energy storage law, and electricity market governance. Penelope is known for her sustained engagement with industry and government stakeholders, and for developing recommendations that have been directly adopted into law, international policy documents, and consumer guides.

Ylli Dautaj: Visiting Associate Professor, Penn State Law, and Managing Partner, DER Juridik, PhD

Ylli Dautaj currently teaches as a Visiting Associate Professor at Penn State Law. He was previously a lecturer at Brunel University London and a Teaching Fellow at Durham Law School. Furthermore, Ylli practices out of Stockholm, Sweden, at DER Juridik. He represents clients in both litigation and arbitration. He focuses his practice on energy disputes, eg oil, gas, renewable, nuclear, etc.

Can Eken: Assistant Professor in Commercial Law, Durham Law School, Durham University

Can Eken is an assistant professor at Durham Law School, Durham University, and deputy director of the Durham International Dispute Resolution Institute (DIDRI). His research and teaching mainly focuses on international commercial arbitration, investment law and third-party funding. Can is admitted to practice law as an attorney in California, Turkey, and as a solicitor in England and Wales. He is also a Fellow of the Chartered Institute of Arbitrators. He was a visiting scholar at Stanford University and the Max Planck Institute in Luxembourg.

Martin Jarrett: Doctor of Laws (Summa Cum Laude), Graduate Diploma of Legal Practice, Bachelor of Laws (First Class Honours), Bachelor of Arts, Solicitar and Barrister in New South Wales, Australia, Senior Research Fellow at Max Planck Institute for Comparative Public Law and International Law, Honorary Fellow at University of Western Australia, and Adjunct Lecturer at Goethe University Frankfurt

Martin is a qualified Solicitor and Barrister (New South Wales, Australia) and holds the following degrees; Graduate of Laws (summa cum laude); Graduate of Diploma of Legal Practice; Bachelor of Laws (with first class honours); and Bachelor of Arts. He currently works as a Senior Research Fellow at the Max Planck Institute for Comparative Public Law and International Law, and also holds positions at the University of Western Australia (honorary fellow) and Goethe University Frankfurt (adjunct lecturer).

Rahmi Kopar: Assistant Professor in Private International Law at Ankara Yildirim Beyazit University Faculty of Law, PhD (CEPMLP, Dundee), LLM (Vienna)

Rahmi Kopar is an assistant professor at Ankara Yildirim Beyazit University in Türkiye where he teaches Private International Law, International Investment Law, International Arbitration, and Energy Law. He has arbitration experience under ICSID, ICC, SIAC, LCIA, and ISTAC rules. He is a qualified lawyer in Türkiye and was admitted to Istanbul Bar in 2011.

Volker Roeben: Dean of Durham Law School and Professor of International Law, Dr Iur Habil, LLM (UC Berkeley), LLM (College of Europe)

Volker is also a visiting professor at the China University of Political Science and Law in Beijing, a docent at the University of Turku, and an associate at the Centre for Energy, Petroleum and Mineral Law & Policy of the University of Dundee. Formerly, Volker was senior research fellow at the Max Planck Institute for Comparative Law and Public International Law, and a professor at Swansea University and the University of Dundee. He has served as legal adviser at the Energy Charter Secretariat.

Islambek Rustambekov: Acting-Rector at Tashkent State University of Law and Professor at the Private International Law Department and Cyber Law Department at Tashkent State University of Law, Doctor (DSc) of Law at Tashkent State University of Law, PhD in Law at Tashkent State University of Law, LLM in International Commercial Law at University of Salford Manchester, LLM in Private International Law at Tashkent State University of Law, LLB in Law at Tashkent State University of Law

Islambek Rustambekov is the Acting-rector and Professor of Private International Law and Cyber Law at Tashkent State University of Law. He is an accomplished arbitrator and mediator, listed in multiple international arbitration centres including ICSID, HKIAC, AIAC, and others. With over 200 publications and numerous roles in legal reform projects, Rustambekov has significantly contributed to the fields of international dispute resolution, arbitration, and mediation in Uzbekistan.

ABBREVIATIONS

AIP	Agreement in Principle
BITS	Bilateral Investment Treaties
CAFTA-DR	Dominican Republic – Central America Free Trade Agreement
CBA	Community Benefit Agreements
CDP	Community Development Plan
CETA	Comprehensive Economic and Trade Agreement
COP	Conference of the Parties
COPINH	The Civic Council of Popular and Indigenous Organisations of Honduras
ECT	Energy Charter Treaty
EIA	Environmental Impact Assessment
EMA	Energy Market Authority
ESF	The World Bank's Environmental and Social Framework
ESG	Environmental, Social, and Governance Investing
ESMP	Environmental and Social Management Plan
FDI	Foreign Direct Investment
FET	Fair and Equitable Treatment
FPIC	Free, Prior, and Informed Consent
GATT	General Agreement on Tariffs and Trade
GDP	Gross Domestic Product
GFC	Global Financial Crisis
GHG	Greenhouse gases
HRIA	Human Rights Impact Assessment
IACHR	Inter-American Commission on Human Rights

IBA	International Bar Association
ICA	International Commercial Association
ICC	International Chamber of Commerce
ICESCR	The International Covenant on Economic, Social, and Cultural Rights
ICSID	International Centre for Settlements of Investment Disputes
IEA	International Energy Agency
IEIL	International Energy Investment Law
IIA	International Investment Agreement
IIL	International Investment Law
IISD	International Institute for Sustainable Development
ILO	International Labour Organisation
IPCC	Intergovernmental Panel on Climate Change
IPFSD	Investment Policy Framework for Sustainable Development
ISDS	Investor-State Dispute Settlement
ITA	International Trade Association
NAFTA	North American Free Trade Agreement
NAAEC	North American Agreement on Environmental Cooperation
NDC	Nationally Determined Contributions
NEPA	The National Environmental Policy Act
NOC	National Oil Company
OECD	The Organisation for Economic Cooperation and Development
OPA	Ontario Power Authority
PRI	Principles for Responsible Investment
REIPPPP	The Renewable Energy Independent Power Producer Procurement Programme
SCC	Stockholm Chamber of Commerce
SDG	The United Nations Sustainable Development Goal
SEC	Securities and Exchange Commissions

REIO	Regional Economic Integration Organisation
TFEU	Treaty on the Functioning of the European Union
UN	United Nations
UNCITRAL	United Nations Commission on International Trade Law
UNCTAD	United Nations Conference on Trade and Development
UNDRIP	United Nations Declaration on the Rights of Indigenous People
UNFCCC	United Nations Framework Convention on Climate Change
UNGP	The United Nations Guiding Principles on Business and Human Rights
USMCA	United States-Mexico-Canada Agreement
VCLT	Vienna Convention on the Law of Treaties
WTO	World Trade Organisation

TABLE OF CASES

TABLE OF LEGISLATION

Statutes

Treaties

Other

Introduction

RAHMI KOPAR AND VOLKER ROEBEN

In this series of publications, the volume entitled *The Global Energy Transition*, published in 2019, started the enquiry into what impact the energy transition would have on global energy law and policy. Energy transition remains a shorthand expression for a global shift from dependence on a high-carbon base for growth to a low-carbon energy system. In *The Global Energy Transition*, it was proposed that this shift has been generating three trends in the evolution of global energy law, a term understood as comprising international law, regional laws and domestic laws. First, whilst energy had been largely decentralised in the high-carbon world, there now is a trend to establish centralising international law-based global governance. This extends a set of multilateral international law regimes to energy, which include the international law regimes of climate change based on the UN Framework Convention and the Paris Agreement, world trade based on the WTO and free trade agreements, and the oceans based on the UN Convention on the Law of the Sea. It also generates new principles such as access for all to modern energy services and solidarity. A second trend is for competition and regulation to assume a greater role in the sector, primarily as a matter of domestic and regional law world-wide but with dissemination of concepts and formation of principles shared between these legal orders. Third and finally, international energy investment law is changing.

International energy investment law (IEIL) is the branch of international law that promotes, facilitates, and protects investments in transboundary energy projects. It forms a sectoral international legal regime because international rules are underpinned by binding dispute settlement. This book analyses out how the transitioning from the fossil fuel, high-carbon landscape to a new low-carbon energy system is changing international energy investment law. That change occurs along two vectors.

The first vector of change relates to the objective itself of a transition towards low-carbon energy, and away from fossil fuels, which should be just and orderly. This change takes place outside of international energy investment law proper but with effect for it. It is a multilateral process of formalising and authorising the transition objective at UN level and for all states. The objective of transitioning to a low-carbon energy system was arguably first formalised in Sustainable Development Goal 7 of the 2030 UN Agenda for Sustainable Development, which provides that all should have access to modern energy services and sets out a target to increase the share of renewables in the global energy supply by 2030. This formalisation in the 2030 Agenda remains non-binding. In a second step, the UN climate change regime has both concretised the transition objective and conferred legal authority on it. Acting under the Paris Agreement, a binding treaty with near-universal membership, the meeting of Parties adopted the First Global Stocktake decision in December 2023. In that decision, the Parties commit to an orderly and just transition away from fossil fuels. They also set a target of increasing the share of renewables by 30 per cent. This decision not just expressly formalises the energy transition objective, it also confers legal authority on the transition objective. The decision reflects an agreement of the Parties in relation to the Paris Agreement, which, under Article 31(3)(a) of the Vienna Convention on the Law of Treaties, has to be taken into account in interpreting the obligations of Parties under this treaty. They, thus, only comply with that stocktake by accepting the transition objective. It obligates Parties in an economy-wide manner, creating an impetus for legal change of all international legal regimes from the sea to trade. International energy investment law is such a regime, which needs to be aligned with the transition objective through the available instruments of legal change. The work of the prominent scholars and practitioners assembled here therefore discusses instruments of legal change to align this regime with the transition priority: treaty reform-work and arbitral practice. These instruments will now be considered more closely.

I. Treaty Law

International energy investment law is mostly a branch of international law based on treaty and customary international law, although contracts between states and investors under domestic law are also a source of it. The large number of investment treaties are of a bilateral nature, the so-called BITs, while the Energy Charter Treaty (ECT) is the only multilateral investment treaty dedicated to energy. The ECT covers promotion and protection of investments and the settlement of related disputes. In addition, it covers trade in energy, transit in the energy sector, and environmental cooperation. Concluded in 1994, ECT 1.0 was designed to protect investments in oil and gas in another Party rather than the state of nationality of the investor. Most energy investment arbitrations internationally to this date have been brought under the ECT regime. As a result, the Treaty has been the subject of intense scrutiny by Parties as to its alignment with the transition priority, culminating in intensive reform (modernisation) work. As the energy transition takes hold, Parties have embarked on a process of amending the Treaty to protect low-carbon energy investments and at the same time phase out the protection of fossil fuels investments (ECT 2.0). This amendment process is governed by the customary law of treaties, codified in the 1969 Vienna Convention on the Law of Treaties (VCLT). The VCLT determines whether Parties can amend that Treaty, withdraw from their obligations, and how it is interpreted.

II. Investor-State Dispute Settlement

International energy investment law forms an institutionalised international legal regime because the treaty law is underpinned by binding dispute settlement, the investor-state dispute settlement (ISDS). This is a mechanism for settling disputes between investors and host-states pertaining to the protection of energy investments. It relies on a decentralised network of arbitral tribunals without any formal hierarchy, but which are engaged in a discourse on or at least mutual observation of practice. This makes it possible to settle individual disputes and, at the same time, to develop international investment law in the transition era through convergent practice across all tribunals.

Decisions made by the arbitral tribunals have a significant transformative effect both on state and foreign investor behaviours. States choose to be more reluctant towards granting incentives to foreign investors during this energy transitions phase. Foreign investors on the other hand look for more creative ways to protect their existing or future investments against potential host state intervention. The existence of change is one of the very little-known parameters in this relationship. However, none of the parties (host state or the investor) favour the change since it encourages further obscurity. The investor-state dispute settlement mechanism provides a clarification to the blurry scene of the energy transitions.

The contributions to this volume reflect this unifying approach to legal change. This, therefore, becomes the basic organisation of the book, which is divided into two main parts: (1) treaty, and (2) arbitral practice.

III. Part 1: Change Through Treaty

The contributions in Part 1 present an analysis of the ECT reform, which is driven by the climate and energy security agenda. It consists of four chapters:

1. Crina Baltag, The Right to Regulate and the Energy Charter Treaty: A Developing Narrative

Crina Baltag analyses the balance between a host state's right to regulate and the investors' need for protection in the Energy Charter Treaty, which has been one of the salient topics of international investment law recently. This becomes more the case in the global energy transition due to the pressing need for states to change their laws and in a sector with long investment durations. The right to regulate is an expression of state sovereignty. However, the limits of this right are not clear. Should a state bear any liability towards foreign investors if it uses its right to regulate and affect the investor detrimentally? Baltag discusses this question and attempts to provide an answer from the perspective of the recent ECT modernisation process. She concludes that the modernised ECT addresses the right to regulate issue suitably and will contribute towards the climate change mitigation goals.

2. Elena Cima, Old Wine in New Bottles: An Environmental Account of the Modernisation of the Energy Charter Treaty

Elena Cima provides a contextual account of the ECT modernisation. As she notes, many other agreements completed during the same period took climate change or environment issues into account. Even though there are a few references to environment within the ECT, the part that governs international investments does not refer to climate or environment at all. Reflecting on the modernisation process, Cima argues that the reform studies do not seem to be capable of answering ongoing climate challenges. There is no doubt that there are several developments in this regard however large gaps remain within the context of Article 24 of the ECT. Cima criticises the 'exception-based model' approach favoured by the ECT modernisation process since it places investment protection hierarchically above a host state's pursuit of environmental objectives. Cima concludes that these developments would have been considered modern 25 years ago while a more concrete stance is needed today.

3. Ylli Dautaj, The Energy Charter Treaty 2.0: Promoting and Protecting Energy Investments in an Era of Sustainable Development

Ylli Dautaj analyses the modernisation of the Energy Charter Treaty. He touches upon the recent debate on the legitimacy concerns about the investment treaty regime before delving into the ECT modernisation process. He argues that the ECT 2.0 will be the most important instrument in the energy transition. Protecting fossil fuel investments and transitioning to clean energy are not mutually exclusive and the ECT 2.0 can accomplish this. To this effect he analyses two scenarios: a world with the ECT 2.0 and another without one. After conducting this comparison, Dautaj concludes that the ECT 2.0 does not interfere with a state's ability to regulate to accelerate the energy transition, offers a flexibility regime, and narrows down the substantive protection standards offered to investors.

4. Martin Jarrett, The Investment Protection Status of Fossil Fuel-Related Investments in the Energy Charter Regime

Martin Jarrett approaches this debate from the perspective of the states that have expressed their intention to withdraw from the ECT. These states do not accept the investment protection scope that fossil fuel investments will receive both under the current ECT and the proposed modernised one. Jarrett then explores three different routes that these contracting states might take under the law of treaties: staying in the ECT 1.0, withdrawing from it, or accepting the ECT 2.0. Since withdrawing from the ECT would not mean much for existing investments due to the sunset clause that provides another 20 years of protection after the withdrawal, Jarrett explores the possibility of concluding inter-se agreements between withdrawing states to prevent investment claims based on fossil fuels by investors of another party to the inter-se agreement. For this purpose, he delves into the Vienna Convention on the Law of Treaties. He concludes that an inter-se agreement would be permissible under Article 41 of the VCLT. However, investors might easily overcome this by only restructuring their ownership status and moving their nationality to a state that is still a party to the ECT. He concludes that among the choices of staying in the ECT 1.0, withdrawing from it, or adopting the ECT 2.0, the latter would be the best option for a Party wishing to reduce the protection that it grants for fossil fuel investments.

IV. Part 2: Change Through Investor-State Dispute Settlement

This Part discusses change through investment law and investor-state dispute settlement, again driven primarily by the climate change agenda. The social dimension of the energy transition and its interaction with investment law is also analysed within this Part. It comprises four chapters.

5. Can Eken and Volker Roeben, Turkey's Energy Charter Treaty Investment Arbitration Map: An Analysis of Arbitral Tribunal positions on unmeritorious applications

While there is a widespread concern regarding energy investment arbitrations constraining the space for state action, Can Eken and Volker Roeben highlight the trend that unmeritorious applications are dismissed at an early stage. They use investment arbitration cases brought under the Energy Charter Treaty against Turkey as a case study. They provide a doctrinal analysis of these six cases and relevant rules in the ECT and Bilateral Investment Treaties (BITs) to understand the approaches that arbitral tribunals took in these cases, finding that this line of cases demonstrates that a host state can successfully defend unmeritorious arbitrations brought against it at the procedural stage. These findings go beyond the Turkey-related case study. Since similar provisions and energy policies can replicate themselves in other cases and jurisdictions, they are broadly relevant to understating the limits of investment protection under the Treaty in the energy transition.

6. Peter Cameron, International Dispute Resolution and the Energy Transition Rollercoaster

Peter Cameron enquires into the potential of the energy transition to generate investment disputes. He notes that the energy transition is a product of ambitious policy aims, not market requirements. Although states are the driving forces behind it, funding for the transition needs to come from the private sector. Both the roles of the state and that of private capital will increase simultaneously, which might be disruptive. He then identifies three directions in which the energy transition is generating legal disputes in the energy sector: the state role in energy transition requires an increased level of scrutiny which will change the dynamics of the relationship between investors and states; the reliability of the legal guarantees offered to investors will be questioned; and the types/scales of investors active in the sector will change. Altogether, these will bring new types of disputes arising from both the already existing and future investments. Cameron then provides examples from recent disputes, arising from biofuels, geothermal, critical minerals, and mandatory phase-outs, and envisages that these types of disputes might overhaul the classic oil and gas disputes in this new transition phase. He concludes that the pace of the policy changes on the government side to satisfy the requirements of the energy transition era will lead to increasing disputes.

7. Penelope Crossley, Future Developments in Investor-State Disputes in the Renewable Energy Sector: From Fair and Equitable Treatment to the Rise of Protectionism and Sovereign Supply?

Penelope Crossley analyses the evolution of investor-state disputes in the renewable energy sector. She underlines the need for clean energy investments if the world is to achieve net zero by 2050. This, COVID-19 and then Russia's invasion of Ukraine have motivated states globally to move towards renewable energy and domestic resources. Regulatory support mechanisms and incentive schemes are playing an important role in this regard. However, the problem with these regulatory incentives has been that they lacked the flexibility to adapt to changing market conditions. They did not include any time or budgetary limitations or sunset clauses, which led to the recent boom in renewable energy investment disputes. Crossley then refers to the recent Spanish renewable energy disputes. She contends that the Spanish cases led other states around the world to be more careful in this regard and take certain measures to prevent potential cases in the future. However, some states have been deploying regulatory instruments and protectionist trade policies to bolster the domestic renewable energy sector, and to counter China's dominance as a critical technology and raw material supplier of the world, including the Inflation Reduction Act (US), Green Transformation Strategy (Japan), Solar PV Incentive II (India), RepowerEU Plan (EU), and Uyghur Forced Labor Protection Act (US). Crossley provides a comprehensive analysis of the regulatory mechanisms introduced by the US. Finally, she stipulates that the next wave of investment disputes will focus on securing the access to critical minerals and rare earth metals which are necessary for renewable energy technologies.

8. Islambek Rustambekov, The Intersection of Human Rights and Energy Transition: Exploring the Social Dimensions of Energy Transition and the Potential Impact on Vulnerable Communities

Islambek Rustambekov approaches the energy transition problem from its social dimension and highlights the potential conflicts between foreign investors and public interest. He explores the intricate relationship between international investment law, human rights, and the energy transition. He suggests that ISDS can be employed as an effective mechanism to manage the social aspects of the energy transition. The need for immediate reforms in investment law to align it with human rights principles and sustainable development goals is emphasised throughout the chapter. While explaining potential human rights abuse types during the energy transition phase, Rustambekov relies on several case studies and explains the lessons learned. One of the key issues underlined in the chapter is the importance of participatory decision-making and targeted support for vulnerable communities.

V. Cross-cutting Issues: Energy Transition and the System of International Energy Investment Law

Other than these two main strands, there are also several issues, problems and solutions that cut across treaty and dispute settlement. These common matters relate to the internal system of international investment law, which retains its function of attracting investment, but where standards are being readjusted to permit states to regulate the sector of low-carbon energy.

This book considers how the energy transition changes international energy investment law. The preceding parts have analysed the instruments of treaty amendment and convergent practice of the several individual arbitral tribunals that effectuate this change. These instruments form what may be called the external system of IEIL. Treaty-makers and arbitral tribunals that control these instruments then face a common challenge: reform the established law in such a way that the energy transition objectives are achieved, without compromising the rationale of providing stability to long-term transboundary investment. As the contributions to Parts I and II of this book demonstrate, both treaty-makers and arbitral tribunals grapple with this problem, and the various solutions they offer, whilst they may differ in detail, can be arranged within and affect the internal system of international energy investment law.

This internal system of IEIL provides orientation, underpins, and holds together the different manifestations of rules and interpretive awards. Key elements of this internal system are the relationship with wider international law, the overall rationale, the scope *ratione materiae* and *ratione personae*, the right to regulate of the host state, and the standard for balancing that right with the rights of the investor. These elements constitute a standard of legality for host state measures affecting an energy investment. The consequence of a breach of that standard is the right of the investor to receive compensation. Is this internal system flexible enough to adapt to the move in the energy source from high to low-carbon?

It is a characteristic of this internal system that it relates IEIL to the wider international law binding on States Parties. In the carbon era, this wider international law had primarily been the permanent sovereignty over natural (fossil fuel) resources, guaranteeing to each host state the exclusive competence to exploit these and then trade on the global market. In the contemporary era, energy governance becomes more centralised, with the wider international law enshrining a community interest in energy and the energy transition. This community interest manifests itself in the global climate regime binding for virtually all states.

This regime establishes the common concern of all states for the global climate. It leads to the temperature goal enshrined in the Paris Agreement of holding global warming to well below 2°C. This can only be achieved if the share of low-carbon energy in the global energy mix is increased and that of fossil fuels correspondingly reduced. This international law is complemented by the common policy aim of all states to secure the supply of energy, where many states now seek to substitute low-carbon energy for fossil fuels in that quest. Finally, the UN Agenda 2030 establishes a new interest to ensure the access of all individuals to sustainable energy. International energy investment law relates to and aligns with these wider changes. Alignment is in particular secured through the VCLT. In this respect, Article 31(3)(c) VCLT provides that the interpretation of each investment treaty needs to account for other relevant rules of international law applicable to the Parties. These are the rules of the universally applicable UNFCCC and the implementing Paris Agreement, whose obligations are in turn concretised by decisions of the meeting of the parties to that treaty (Article 31(3)(a) VCLT).

The rationale of international energy investment law is to enable transboundary investment. Clearly the underlying energy resource that attracts investment is very different in the low-carbon scenario from any fossil fuels that were dominant when the rationale was first formed. That begs the question whether the function of the law remains relevant. As several contributions to this volume highlight, the very function of this branch of international law serves the transition objective well. The transition depends on private, often transboundary investment in low-carbon energy resources and infrastructure. This investment requires the legal certainty that international energy investment law provides. Thus, the rationale of international energy investment law and ISDS – ie, attracting investments – is retained for the new law-carbon based energy investments. For host-states to be able to attract foreign investment, there needs to be international protection for the investor. This applies with the same force to low-carbon investment as it has applied traditionally to investments in fossil fuels.

The scope *ratione materiae* of international energy investment law determines what investments can fall under the protection of this law. The *ratione materiae* scope now extends to the low-carbon energy forms and the underpinning architecture, rather than fossil energy. This applies throughout the low-carbon supply chain, starting with the critical minerals needed for energy storage and the EV rollout. This extension can be effectuated by treaty or by interpretation. It allows host-states to prioritise investments in low-carbon energy. At the same time, the fossil fuel investments can be removed from the protective scope of IEL through treaty amendment within the boundaries of the law of treaties. Such retrenchment of the protective scope could potentially also be the result of arbitral interpretation of the unchanged law, under Article 31(3)(c) VCLT. From the scope of protection *ratione personae* unmeritorious claims are removed. This does offer host states additional protections.

The right to regulate empowers the host state to a certain extent without compensation. What emerges as a consensus in treaty and arbitral practice is that, very importantly, the right to regulate of host states protects the legitimate interest they may pursue in regulating, thereby interfering with the investments; including through existing support policy, but possibly not simply protectionist objectives. But where are the boundaries and how to balance with the right of the investor to stability, a line that demarcates the investor a right to be compensated for any losses of the state's measures? The fundamental question may have remained unanswered for some time but it now comes to the fore in the energy transition, as states engage in more complex regulation over time than they did in the high-carbon era.

There is thus a balance to be struck between stability and regulatory flexibility. There are no absolutes. Rather, the intensity of the interference with the expected stability will be balanced with the weight of the public interest in changing the regulatory environment. In short, there is a proportionality test and non-discrimination scrutiny of the host state's action.

The implication is that the internal system of IEIL, formed for the fossil fuel economy, is both robust and flexible enough to absorb the transition impetus and the specific characteristics of the low-carbon energy system, marked by decentralised resources, infrastructure, novel and maturing technologies, strong government involvement, and a supply chain covering generation, transmission and consumption but anchored in critical minerals. In this sense, international energy investment law advances the transition by increasing low-carbon investment. The resulting change thus takes place within the system of international energy investment law. This internal, unwritten system provides the rationalising effect, guaranteeing the investor a level of protection and scrutiny of the rationality of public policy decisions. It also formulates an outer limit to states' policy decisions.

PART 1

Change Through Treaty

1

The Right to Regulate and the Energy Charter Treaty: A Developing Narrative

CRINA BALTAG

A discussion on the right of the state to regulate in the public interest and the transition to a cleaner energy can only occur when it is understood that, on one hand, there will be a greater role of the state during the energy transition, and that, on the other hand, there will also be a greater need for private capital. As a result of the November 2022 Sharm el-Sheikh Climate Change Conference (COP 27), the Sharm el-Sheikh Implementation Plan recognises that there is an 'urgency to rapidly transform energy systems … including by accelerating clean and just transitions to renewable energy'. However, it also accepted the reality that 'USD 4 trillion per year needs to be invested in renewable energy up until 2030 to be able to reach net zero emissions by 2050, and that, furthermore, a global transformation to a low-carbon economy is expected to require investment of at least USD 4–6 trillion per year'.[1]

I. The Right to Regulate

The right to regulate is undoubtedly an expression of state sovereignty. Internal state sovereignty can be defined as the state's right and obligation to regulate in public interest. This is triggered by the fact that states have the obligation to take positive action to ensure that human rights are complied with.[2] In *Urbaser v Argentina*, the arbitral tribunal held that '[i]ndeed, the enforcement of the human right … represents an obligation to perform. Such obligation is imposed upon States'.[3] Equally,

[1] UNFCCC, 'Sharm el-Sheikh Implementation Plan' (COP 27, November 2022), available at unfccc.int/documents/624444 at [9] and [30], footnotes omitted.

[2] See the Preamble of the Universal Declaration of Human Rights, proclaimed by the United Nations General Assembly in Paris on 10 December 1948, which states that 'Whereas Member States have pledged themselves to achieve, in co-operation with the United Nations, the promotion of universal respect for and observance of human rights and fundamental freedoms.'

[3] *Urbaser S.A. v Argentine Republic*, ICSID Case No. ARB/07/26, Award at [1210].

the state also expresses external state sovereignty, this being the right to enter into international treaties and commit to certain obligations which may directly shape their sovereignty. This includes the obligations that states commit to in order to promote and protect foreign investments.

Most of the old generation international investment treaties reflect upon the right of a state to regulate, either by not expressly providing for this right, or by enforcing rights only upon investors. The new generation of international investment treaties require a more active role from states in regulating investments on their territories, as opposed to just promoting and protecting them.[4]

A point of consensus is that arbitral tribunals are in agreement that the right to regulate is a sovereign right of the state, even when this is not expressly provided for in an international investment treaty. For example, the tribunal in *Marfin v Cyprus* explained that the sovereign right to regulate is a customary international law right.[5]

By exercising the right to regulate, it can be argued that the state needs to have a legitimate objective that acts in the public interest and which is clearly motivated.[6] Furthermore, most arbitral tribunals would assess the state's measure in order to determine whether the measure was non-discriminatory, in conformity with due process, transparent,[7] reasonable and proportional. When it comes to the burden of proof, if the right to regulate is viewed as an exception to the protection offered by international investment treaties, then the state must prove that all the above-mentioned conditions are met. However, if the right to regulate is viewed as a principle of international law, and therefore as an expression of state responsibility, then the burden of proof would fall on the investor.[8]

The key question, which so far has split the arbitral tribunals, remains, if the state has the right to regulate and it does so under the test deemed to be applicable by the arbitral tribunal and under the relevant treaty, will the state still have to pay compensation to the investor? In other words, by lawfully exercising the right to regulate, is the state exempt from any liability towards the investor? Ultimately, the answer would determine who takes the risk when a state amends its laws and regulations to serve the public interest. The arbitral awards offer little guidance

[4] See C Baltag, *From investment promotion and protection to investment regulation* (Columbia FDI Perspectives, No. 293, 14 December 2020).

[5] *Marfin Investment Group v The Republic of Cyprus*, ICSID Case No. ARB/13/27, Award at [827].

[6] *AES Summit Generation Limited and AES-Tisza Erömü Kft v The Republic of Hungary*, ICSID Case No. ARB/07/22, para 10.3.30. Also, *Gold Reserve Inc. v Bolivarian Republic of Venezuela*, ICSID Case No. ARB(AF)/09/1 at [667].

[7] *Mamidoil Jetoil Greek Petroleum Products Societe S.A. v Republic of Albania*, ICSID Case No. ARB/11/24 at [657]: 'The Tribunal holds that it was within the realm of Respondent's sovereign power to adopt the Land Use Plan for Durres, change the zoning regulations and prohibit the unloading of petroleum cargo. The measures pursued a legitimate objective of public policy, were carried out in a transparent way, were proportionate and not arbitrary, and did not lead to unreasonable instability, as developed below.'

[8] See *Les Laboratoires Servier, S.A.A., Biofarma, S.A.S., Arts et Techniques du Progres S.A.S. v Republic of Poland*, UNCITRAL, Award at [584].

when it comes to the distinction between the legitimate and compensable right to regulate, and the legitimate and non-compensable right to regulate. In *Eco Oro v Colombia*, an arbitration concerning an open-pit mining project in Colombia which was postponed and affected by state biodiversity regulations, the arbitral tribunal held that while the state had the right to regulate under Canada-Colombia Free Trade Agreement, and that the right to regulate was lawfully exercised, it still owed compensation to investors.[9] The *Eco Oro* case reaches a similar conclusion to the tribunal in *Infinito Gold v Costa Rica*.[10] However, it comes into conflict with the decision of the tribunal in *David Aven v Costa Rica*, under the Dominican Republic–Central America Free Trade Agreement (CAFTA-DR), in which the arbitral tribunal denied compensation and reasoned that the rights of investors are subordinate to the right of the state in order to ensure that public interest is respected and enforced.[11]

II. The Energy Charter Treaty: Modernisation and the Right to Regulate

The current version of the Energy Charter Treaty (ECT)[12] does not have a specific provision on the right of the Contracting Parties to regulate. Despite this, nothing has prevented arbitral tribunals from balancing the legitimate expectations of the investors against the right to regulate of the Contracting Parties.[13]

However, the ECT is currently undergoing modernisation. In November 2018, the Energy Charter Conference approved the list of topics for the modernisation of the ECT.[14] These topics included, among others, the definitions of 'investment', 'investor', of the right to regulate, of the Fair and Equitable Treatment, indirect expropriation, the denial of benefits, sustainable development and corporate social responsibility etc. The successful conclusion of the modernisation discussions was

[9] *Eco Oro Minerals Corp. v Republic of Colombia*, ICSID Case No. ARB/16/41, Decision on Jurisdiction, Liability and Direction on Quantum at [698].

[10] *Infinito Gold Ltd. v Costa Rica*, ICSID Case No. ARB/14/5, Award at [781].

[11] *David R. Aven and Others v Republic of Costa Rica*, ICSID Case No. UNCT/15/3, Award at [688].

[12] The Energy Charter Treaty was signed on 17 December 1994 and entered into force on 16 April 1998. The references in this chapter are made to the version printed in (1995) 34 International Legal Materials 373–454.

[13] *Charanne and Construction Investments v Spain*, SCC Case No. V 062/2012, Award at [493]: 'Although RD 661/2007 and RD 1578/2008 were directed to a limited group of investors, it does not make them to be commitments specifically directed at each investor. The rules at issue do not lose the general nature that characterizes any law or regulation by their specific scope. To convert a regulatory standard into a specific commitment of the state, by the limited character of the persons who may be affected, would constitute an excessive limitation on power of states to regulate the economy in accordance with the public interest.' See also Dissenting Opinion of Samuel Wordsworth QC in *RWE Innogy GmbH and RWE Innogy Aersa S.A.U. v Kingdom of Spain*, ICSID Case No. ARB/14/34 at [48]–[49].

[14] Energy Charter Secretariat, Report by the Chair of the Subgroup on Modernisation, Brussels, 27 November 2018, CCDEC 2018 21 NOT.

announced on 24 June 2022, with the Contracting Parties to the ECT reaching an agreement in principle.[15] While the text of the modernised ECT was expected to be approved at the Energy Charter Conference on 22 November 2022,[16] the future of a modernised ECT is uncertain, given the position of some European Union Member States that plan to exit the ECT.[17]

It must be taken into consideration that the modernisation process happened behind closed doors, with few official and general statements being made by the Modernisation Group and the European Union on the progress of discussions. Nonetheless, drafts of the ECT for discussion surfaced in the public domain and provided some understanding of the approach of the Contracting Parties to the topics addressed in the process.[18]

In the November 2020 draft of the modernised ECT, a new provision on the right of the Contracting Parties to regulate in public interest was introduced. The provision provided for the following:

> Acknowledging the rights and responsibilities of the Contracting Parties to regulate investments within the territories of their States in order to meet their own policy objectives.
>
> 1. The Contracting Parties reaffirm the right to regulate within their territories to achieve legitimate policy objectives, such as the protection of the environment. including combatting climate change. protection of public health. social services. public education, safety, public morals, social or consumer protection, privacy and data protection, or the promotion and protection of cultural diversity.
> 2. For greater certainty, the provisions of Part Three of the Treaty shall not be interpreted as a commitment from a Contracting Party that it will not change the legal and regulatory framework, including in a manner that may negatively affect the operation of investments or the investor's expectations of profits.
> 3. For greater certainty and subject to paragraph 4, a Contracting Party's decision not to issue, renew or maintain a subsidy
>   (a) in the absence of any specific commitment under law or contract to issue. renew, or maintain that subsidy: or
>   (b) in accordance with any terms or conditions attached to the issuance, renewal or maintenance of the subsidy
> 4. shall not constitute a breach of the provisions of Part Three of the Treaty.
>
> For greater certainty, the provisions of Part Three of the Treaty shall not be construed as preventing a Contracting Party from discontinuing the granting of a subsidy or

[15] Energy Charter Conference, *Finalisation of the negotiations on the Modernisation of the Energy Charter Treaty*, (Brussels, 24 June 2022) www.energychartertreaty.org/modernisation-of-the-treaty/.

[16] ibid.

[17] J Tropper, 'Withdrawing from the Energy Charter Treaty: The End is (not) Near' (*Kluwer Arbitration Blog*, 4 November 2022).

[18] The author is aware of at least two working drafts leaked into the public domain: (i) Energy Charter Secretariat, *Report of the Modernisation Group on Progress Made in Fulfilling the Negotiations Mandate*, 31st meeting of the Energy Charter Conference, 16 December 2020, CC699; and (ii) Energy Charter Secretariat, *Agreement in Principle on the Modernisation of the Energy Charter Treaty*, Ad-hoc Meeting of the Energy Charter Conference, 24 June 2022, CC 750 Rev.

> requesting its reimbursement, where such action is necessary to comply with obligations imposed upon the Contracting Party concerned by an international agreement establishing a Regional Economic Integration Organisation or been ordered by a competent court, administrative tribunal or other competent authority or as requiring that Contracting Party to compensate the investor therefore.[19]

It is to be noted that this version of the provision on the right to regulate appears to address to the wave of investment arbitrations against Spain and the other EU Member States in regards to the changes in tariffs for solar energy, implementing EU measures.[20] Paragraph four of this provision provides that, where the Contracting Party to the ECT is discontinuing the granting of a subsidy or is requesting its reimbursement and where such action is necessary to comply with obligations imposed by a Regional Economic Integration Organisation, the measure will not be in breach of Part Three of the ECT concerning investment promotion and protection.[21]

The June 2022 modernised ECT provision on the right of the Contracting Parties to regulate is considerably reduced to the following:

> The Contracting Parties reaffirm the right to regulate within their territories to achieve legitimate policy objectives, such as the protection of the environment, including climate change mitigation and adaptation, protection of public health, safety or public morals.[22]

[19] Energy Charter Secretariat, *Report of the Modernisation Group on Progress Made in Fulfilling the Negotiations Mandate*, 31st meeting of the Energy Charter Conference, 16 December 2020, CC699.

[20] See eg *Isolux Netherlands, BV v Kingdom of Spain*, SCC Case V2013/153; *Eiser Infrastructure Limited and Energía Solar Luxembourg S.à r.l. v Kingdom of Spain*, ICSID Case No. ARB/13/36 etc. See also the ECT statistics: www.energychartertreaty.org/cases/statistics/.

[21] See the similarity of this provision with those in recently concluded bilateral investment treaties (BITs):

> Article 3
>
> Investment and regulatory measures
>
> 1. The provisions of this Agreement shall not affect the right of the Parties to regulate within their territories through measures necessary to achieve legitimate policy objectives, such as the protection of public health, safety, environment or public morals, social or consumer protection or promotion and protection of cultural diversity.
> 2. For greater certainty a Contracting Party's decision not to issue, renew or maintain a subsidy
>   a. in the absence of any specific commitment under law or contract to issue, renew or maintain that subsidy; or
>   b. in accordance with terms or conditions attached to the issuance, renewal or maintenance of the subsidy,
>
> does not constitute a breach of the provisions of this Agreement.
>
> Nothing in this Agreement shall be construed as preventing a Contracting Party from discontinuing the granting of a subsidy or requesting its reimbursement where such measure is necessary in order to comply with international obligations between the Parties or has been ordered by a competent court, administrative tribunal or other competent authority, or requiring that Contracting Party to compensate the investor therefor. (Hungary-United Arab Emirates BIT, entered into force on 10 April 2022).

[22] Energy Charter Secretariat, *Agreement in Principle on the Modernisation of the Energy Charter Treaty*, Ad-hoc Meeting of the Energy Charter Conference, 24 June 2022, CC 750 Rev.

However, this provision would be read together with the proposed amendments to Article 13 on expropriation. The proposed paragraph four of Article 13 provides that:

> Except in rare circumstances when the impact of measure or series of measures is so severe in light of its purpose that it is manifestly excessive, non-discriminatory measures by a Contracting Party that are designed and applied to protect legitimate policy objectives, such as public health, safety and environment (including with respect to climate change mitigation and adaptation), do not constitute indirect expropriation.

The proposed paragraph four clarifies that measures taken by the Contracting Parties to the ECT to protect legitimate policy objectives, including climate change mitigation and adaptation, that are non-discriminatory and not manifestly excessive, will not constitute indirect expropriation. Consequently, Contracting Parties will not owe compensation for implementing such measures. The proposed provision is in line with the provisions implemented in the new generation of international investment agreements.[23]

Furthermore, a new proposed paragraph in the Preamble of the modernised ECT acknowledges 'the inherent rights of the Contracting Parties to regulate investments within their territories in order to meet legitimate and public policy objectives'.[24]

III. The Energy Charter Treaty: Modernisation and Climate Change Mitigation

In line with the suggested provisions which guarantee the right of the Contracting Parties to regulate in the public interest, including the protection of environment, climate change mitigation and adaptation, the modernised ECT also proposes the inclusion of specific assurances for the transition to a clean energy and the observance of international commitments.

Article 1(5) defining the 'Economic Activity on the Energy Sector', read in conjunction with the suggested amendments to Annex NI to the ECT, provides for a phase out of the promotion and protection of fossil fuel investments.[25]

The preamble of the ECT proposes the inclusion of specific reference to the Rio Declaration on Environment and Development and Agenda 21 of 1992, the ILO Declaration on Fundamental Principles and Rights at Work of 1998,

[23] See eg Article 7(2)(c) of the Hungary-United Arab Emirates BIT: 'For greater certainty, non-discriminatory measures that the Contracting Parties take for reason of public purpose which are taken in good faith, which are not arbitrary, and which are not disproportionate in light of their purpose, shall not constitute indirect expropriation'.

[24] Energy Charter Secretariat, *Agreement in Principle on the Modernisation of the Energy Charter Treaty*, Ad-hoc Meeting of the Energy Charter Conference, 24 June 2022, CC 750 Rev.

[25] ibid.

the Ministerial Declaration of the UN Economic and Social Council on Full Employment and Decent Work of 2006, the ILO Declaration on Social Justice for a Fair Globalisation of 2008, the UN 2030 Agenda for Sustainable Development of 2015 with its Sustainable Development Goals and the 2015 Paris Agreement and the United Nations Framework Convention on Climate Change.[26]

In addition to these provisions, the modernised ECT draft addresses 'Climate Change and Clean Energy Transition', which emphasises the 'urgent need of pursuing the ultimate objective of the United Nations Framework Convention on Climate Change (UNFCCC) the purpose and goals of the Paris Agreement in order to effectively combat climate change and its adverse impacts, and committed to enhancing the contribution of trade and investment in energy-related sectors to climate change mitigation and adaptation, each Contracting Party reaffirms its commitments to: (a) effectively implement its commitments and obligations under the UNFCCC and the Paris Agreement.'[27]

It can be concluded that the draft modernised ECT suitably addresses the right of Contracting Parties to regulate, which is necessary for implementing the measures to either phase out fossil fuel investment or/and incentivise investments in renewable energy. Furthermore, the modernised ECT draft appears to align the ECT to the climate change mitigation efforts, by including provisions on the withdrawal of the protection to fossil fuel investments, as well as provisions that expressly reference the international commitments that are addressing environmental protection and the fight against climate change.[28]

[26] ibid.
[27] ibid.
[28] The paper's final draft is dated 5 March 2023.

2

Old Wine in New Bottles: An Environmental Account of the Modernisation of the Energy Charter Treaty

ELENA CIMA*

I. Introduction

The Energy Charter Treaty (ECT) was not designed to be an environmental, let alone a climate treaty. It was conceived to create a commonly accepted foundation on which to develop inter-governmental cooperation between Eastern and Western Europe after the Cold War, and it was precisely in the energy sector that such cooperation was deemed crucial in the early 1990s. It developed into the key sector for climate change mitigation that since the adoption of the ECT in 1994 has undergone a profound and drastic transformation.

Therefore, once the modernisation of the ECT was announced in 2017, it came as no surprise that many thought and hoped that the ECT's investment provisions would be brought in line with the climate goals of the Paris Agreement. However, the modernisation process, which was concluded on 24 June 2022 with an agreement in principle, tells a different story, where any improvement made with regards to the environment or the climate only appears to be an improvement when compared against the original text of the ECT. In reality, it is obsolete and outdated when framed within the broader international investment law landscape.

In order to provide an 'environmental' account of the outcome of the modernisation process, this chapter is divided into five Sections. After this brief introduction, Section II traces the evolution of the energy sector since the adoption of the ECT, and the emergence of the climate crisis as the underlying force for

* Lecturer, University of Geneva. PhD (Geneva Graduate Institute), LLM (Yale Law School), LLB (University of Milan).

revising and updating the investment provisions of the ECT. Section III describes the years of the ECT negotiations as a period characterised by the emergence of sustainable development and of the climate crisis, showing the reluctance of the ECT negotiators to integrate these environmental concerns into the text of the treaty, unlike other contemporary trade and investment negotiations. Section IV provides a critical analysis of the 'environmental' outcome of the modernisation process, describing how it is nothing more than the repackaging of old concepts and regulatory techniques. Finally, Section V provides some final conclusions.

II. Treaties as 'Living Instruments': The Importance of Reforming the ECT[1]

International law can be seen as a reflection of international society, which explains the dynamic and evolutionary nature of international law. International treaties, one of the sources of international law, possess the same critical trait. Often described as 'living instruments', treaties have to operate for decades into the future, and therefore cannot be interpreted and applied 'as though they were frozen in time' when they were concluded.[2] Whilst the 'living instrument' metaphor was initially used with reference to treaties constitutive of international organisations – such as the United Nations (UN) Charter – it is now used in regards to a wide range of law-making treaties in many areas of international law.[3] Nearly 30 years have passed since the initial drafting of the ECT and a lot has changed over the course of these three decades. In the 1990s, the energy sector was characterised by centralised energy supply systems that were largely based on fossil fuels, and energy issues mostly revolved around questions of price, availability of supply, and security. Today, energy policies – and the energy foundations that support the world economy – are being entirely reshaped by climate change and global warming, and are increasingly focused on renewable energy and energy efficiency and conservation – a transformation that has been defined 'as far-reaching as when civilisation moved from wood to coal and then on to oil and natural gas.'[4] Energy markets have changed, the economic relations between the countries that negotiated the treaty have changed, investment patterns have changed, and last but not least, climate change has become a pressing emergency.

[1] This section is based, in part, on a previous publication of the author: E Cima, 'Retooling the Energy Charter Treaty for Climate Change Mitigation: Lessons from Investment Law and Arbitration' (2021) 14(2) *JWELB* 75–87.

[2] Case Concerning Gabčikovo-Nagymaros Project (Hungary/Slovakia) (1997) ICJ Rep. 7, pp 114–15 (Separate Opinion of Vice President Weeramantry).

[3] AD McNair, 'The Functions and Differing Legal Character of Treaties' (1930) 11 *BybIL* 100, 112.

[4] D Yergin, *The Quest. Energy Security and the Remaking of the Modern World* (Penguin Press, 2011) 494, 425.

A. Lisbon 1994: The Origins of the ECT

The strategic importance of the energy sector, its economic and geo-political repercussions, and its unique characteristics led to the signing of a multilateral treaty on trade, transit and investment in the energy sector: the ECT.[5] The latter was opened for signature in Lisbon on 17 December 1994, after three years of intense negotiations.[6] The provisions of the ECT reflect the historical, political, and economic environment of the early 1990s – characterised by the redrawing of the political map of Eastern Europe and the former Soviet Union – and were designed to respond to the specific needs and concerns of the countries involved in the negotiations at the time. At the time, the end of the Cold War offered an unprecedented opportunity to overcome the previous economic divisions between Eastern and Western Europe, and it was precisely in the energy sector that cooperation was deemed crucial.[7] This was because it would have secured democratic restructuring as well as an accelerated economic recovery in Eastern Europe and the former Soviet Union.[8]

In fact, the adoption of the ECT represented the successful culmination of a series of discussions on how to develop inter-governmental energy cooperation between Eastern and Western Europe, and established a commonly accepted foundation on which to build and develop such cooperation. Concretely, the establishment of a common legal framework to cooperate on energy trade, transit and investment was in the interest of all the parties involved. Eastern European countries hoped to obtain easier access to Western capital, expertise and technology, and to reduce their one-sided dependency on the Russian Federation. Russia was rich in energy resources – in particular oil and gas – but needed Western capital to secure stable exports. West European countries, finally, hoped to secure access to Eastern European markets for their energy industries and to secure long-term energy flows from the former Soviet Union as they were desperate to reduce their dependence on Middle Eastern oil and to diversify their energy supply mix.[9]

[5] E Cima, 'Investment Arbitration in the Energy Sector: Past, Present and Future' in T Schultz and F Ortino (eds), *Oxford Handbook on International Arbitration* (Oxford University Press, 2020) 815, 823; E De Brabandere, 'The Settlement of Investment Disputes in the Energy Sector' in E De Brabandere and T Gazzini (eds), *Foreign Investment in the Energy Sector. Balancing Private and Public Interests* (Martinus Nijhoff Publishers, 2014) 135; K Hobér, 'Overview of Energy Charter Treaty Cases' in M Scherer (ed), *International Arbitration in the Energy Sector* (Oxford University Press, 2018) 175.

[6] For a comprehensive analysis of the negotiations that led to the adoption of the Treaty, see TW Wälde (ed), *The Energy Charter Treaty: An East-West Gateway for Investment and Trade* (Kluwer Law International, 1996).

[7] A Konoplyanik and TW Wälde, 'Energy Charter Treaty and its Role in International Energy' (2006) 24(4) *JERL* 523, 524.

[8] Final Act of the European Energy Charter Conference, SF/EECH (17 December 1994) 4.

[9] J Doré, 'Negotiating the Energy Charter Treaty' in Wälde (n 6) 138, 139; Konoplyanik and Wälde (n 7) 524.

The ECT would allow for such a trade-off: it would guarantee Western European countries' access to energy sources in the former Soviet Union,[10] protecting their investments in these strategic but volatile industries, while, at the same time, granting Eastern European countries and Russia access to Western markets.[11] At the same time, it would send an important political message, as the ECT was the first multilateral trade instrument that the Eastern European states and the former Soviet Republics had the opportunity to negotiate during the post-communist era.[12] The result of these negotiations was a binding multilateral instrument aimed at promoting 'long-term co-operation in the energy field, based on complementarities and mutual benefits.'[13]

B. The Evolution of the Energy Sector

Undoubtedly, the ECT was in every respect a product of its time, having been proposed and negotiated as a solution to all problems that Eastern and Western Europe could possibly face in the energy sector at the time. It was not just supposed to provide answers, but it was also supposed to provide them quickly,[14] and it reflected the energy industry as it existed in the early 1990s. However, the never-ending succession of events, crises and opportunities over the past three decades have significantly changed the face of the energy sector. For its part, the ECT was never supposed to remain 'frozen in time'. Rather, as pointed out by the Energy Charter Conference in its 2009 Rome Statement, it was always supposed to reflect new developments and challenges in international energy markets.[15]

When it was adopted in 1994, the ECT was aimed at promoting 'long-term co-operation in the energy field.' At that time, such 'long-term cooperation' was needed to ensure energy security and to set standards for the energy market economy. In doing so, it had been designed to address and protect investments in the energy industries as they existed in the 1990s, and which included 'oil and gas upstream investment … building of long-distance oil and gas pipelines, electricity transmission grids, [and] acquisition and expansion of existing electricity and gas distribution and supply systems.'[16] International energy governance between the 1970s and the 1990s reflected the energy sector as it existed at the time, with the creation of the International Energy Agency to ensure importing countries'

[10] T Roe and M Happold, *Settlement of Investment Disputes under the Energy Charter Treaty* (Cambridge University Press, 2011) 9.

[11] TW Wälde, 'Investment Arbitration Under the Energy Charter Treaty – From Dispute Settlement to Treaty Implementation' (1996) 12(4) *Arbitration International* 429, 430. Cima (n 5) 824.

[12] Doré (n 9) 138.

[13] The Energy Charter Treaty (1995) 34 ILM 360 (ECT), Article 2.

[14] Doré (n 9) 153.

[15] Energy Charter Conference, Joint Statement (9 December 2009) 2.

[16] Wälde (n 11) 431.

access to oil and the International Atomic Energy Agency to focus on nuclear energy. However, this sector, under many respects, looks very different today; renewables are becoming a significant and growing part of the energy mix. Investment in renewables and in low-carbon energy technologies has become crucial and has increased dramatically.[17] As a matter of fact, the energy industry has never witnessed such a strong emphasis on innovation, know-how, and technological change.[18]

It is not just the energy market that has evolved over the last three decades. Investment activities and patterns have changed, prompted by a multitude of drivers, including technological change, evolving consumer preferences and domestic policies. Policies affecting the energy sector are motivated by a range of objectives, such as ensuring affordable energy supply, improving energy security, delivering universal energy access and reducing air pollution.[19] However, the main driver is the urgent and pressing need to tackle climate change.

C. The Climate Challenge

Today, as a part of the strategy to mitigate climate change, it has become fundamental to phase out the reliance on fossil fuels and to scale up renewable energy sources. However, there is still a massive investment gap between the current levels and the levels needed to have a significant and positive impact on climate change mitigation. If the international community is to achieve the goals set forth in the Paris Agreement and to keep global warming well below 2°C, significant investments in renewable energy will be required over the next few decades, and even more will be required to reach the more ambitious target of 1.5°C and to adapt to climate change.[20]

In this context, foreign investment in sectors with strategic importance for climate change mitigation – such as renewable energy and energy efficiency – can positively contribute to the transition to a low-carbon economy. Similar to other economic instruments, investment schemes can be seen as instrumental to climate change mitigation, as clearly framed in the UN 2030 Agenda for Sustainable Development.[21] The Agenda explicitly acknowledges the positive role that foreign investments can play in enabling and facilitating the achievement of several sustainable development goals (SDGs), including the transition

[17] IEA, Press Release, 'Record Clean Energy Spending Is Set to Help Global Energy Investment Grow by 8% in 2022' (22 June 2022).

[18] Yergin (n 4) 554.

[19] International Energy Agency, *Perspectives for the Energy Transition. The Role of Energy Efficiency* (OECD/IEA, 2018) 15.

[20] Paris Agreement to the United Nations Framework Convention on Climate Change, 12 December 2015, TIAS No 16-1104 (Paris Agreement) Article 2.1(a).

[21] Transforming Our World: The 2030 Agenda for Sustainable Development, 25 September 2015, A/RES/70/1 (2030 Agenda).

to a low-carbon economy.[22] SDG 7, on ensuring access to affordable, reliable, sustainable and modern energy for all, contains the pledge to enhance, by 2030, 'international cooperation to facilitate access to clean energy research and technology, including renewable energy, energy efficiency and advanced and cleaner fossil-fuel technology, and promote investment in energy infrastructure and clean energy technology.'[23]

The critical role of foreign investment – and of investment policies and norms – towards climate change mitigation has been emphasised in the context of several Conferences of the Parties (COPs) to the United Nations Framework Convention on Climate Change (UNFCCC), including COP 26 which took place in 2021 in Glasgow and COP27, which was recently concluded in Sharm El-Sheik. Along the same lines, the latest report of the Intergovernmental Panel on Climate Change (IPCC) acknowledged the important contribution of investment in low-carbon technologies and infrastructure, which has been facilitated by appropriate policies and regulations.[24]

However, the latest IPCC Report acknowledges the existence of significant gaps and shortcomings in the development of international legal norms, which, despite improvements in the overall international governance of energy, seem to still be largely concerned with promoting further development of fossil fuels:

> A large number of bilateral and multilateral agreements, including the 1994 Energy Charter Treaty, include provisions for using a system of investor-state dispute settlement (ISDS) designed to protect the interests of investors in energy projects from national policies that could lead their assets to be stranded. Numerous scholars have pointed to ISDS being able to be used by fossil-fuel companies to block national legislation aimed at phasing out the use of their assets.[25]

III. No Space for the Environment in the ECT

The critical role of the energy sector for climate change mitigation was already clear in the early 1990s. In 1990 the IPCC published its very first Report, where it emphasised the importance of relying on cleaner energy sources and technologies

[22] See MM Mbengue, 'Facilitating Investment for Sustainable Development: It Matters for Africa' (2018) 222 *Columbia FDI Perspectives on Topical Foreign Direct Investment Issues*; KP Sauvant and H Mann, 'Making FDI More Sustainable: Towards an Indicative List of FDI Sustainability Characteristics' (2019) 20 *JWIT* 916; S Schacherer and RT Hoffmann, 'International Investment Law and Sustainable Development' in M Krajewski and RT Hoffmann (eds), *Research Handbook on Foreign Direct Investment* (Edward Elgar, 2019) 563–95.

[23] 2030 Agenda, SDG 7.A (emphasis added).

[24] IPCC, *Climate Change 2022. Mitigation of Climate Change. Summary for Policymakers* (2002) paras B.5 and E.4.3.

[25] ibid 14–81. See K Bos and J Gupta, 'Stranded Assets and Stranded Resources: Implications for Climate Change Mitigation and Global Sustainable Development' (2019) *Energy Res. Soc. Sci.* 56; K Tienhaara, 'Regulatory Chill in a Warming World: The Threat to Climate Policy Posed by Investor-State Dispute Settlement' (2018) 7(2) *Transnatl. Environ. Law* 229–50.

to reduce carbon dioxide emissions.[26] Two years later, the UNFCCC was adopted, establishing the legal and institutional framework necessary to ensure international cooperation aimed at climate change mitigation.[27] The UNFCCC had been signed in Rio de Janeiro at the end of the Rio Conference on Environment and Development, the second UN conference on the global environment, which crystallised the key principles of international environmental law.[28] All these events produced significant impacts in several areas of international law, including international economic law. Many trade and investment agreements adopted during the 1990s have integrated climate and environmental concerns into their substantive standards of protection, and so has the practice of trade and investor-state dispute settlement.[29] Both have started to evolve towards a more climate-friendly direction. However, the same cannot be said for the ECT, whose original text seems to have largely overlooked the environmental developments of the 1990s.

A. The 'Sustainable Development' Decade

In 1970, former United States (US) President Richard Nixon declared that the 1970s would be the 'environmental decade',[30] and he was right. The 1970s were marked by the first revolutionary environmental law-making initiatives, both at a national and international level. Instead, the 1990s could be defined as the 'sustainable development' decade, when considering the paradigm-shifting role played by this concept well beyond environmental law and governance.[31]

The notion of sustainable development represented the cornerstone of the discussions that allowed an ad hoc commission to prepare the second international environmental conference, which was organised under the auspices of the UN in Rio de Janeiro in 1992. To head the commission, the UN Secretary General deliberately chose a political leader who has traditionally been associated

[26] IPCC, *Policymaker Summary of Working Group III (Formulation of Response Strategies)*, 118.

[27] United Nations Framework Convention on Climate Change, 9 May 1992, 1771 U.N.T.S. 107, 31 I.L.M. 849 (UNFCCC).

[28] United Nations Conference on Environment and Development, Rio de Janeiro, Brazil, 3–14 June 1992, Rio Declaration on Environment and Development, U.N. Doc. a/conf.151/26/Rev.1 (Vol. i), Annex i (Aug. 12, 1992) (Rio Declaration).

[29] See eg T Gazzini, 'Bilateral Investment Treaties and Sustainable Development' (2014) 15 *JWIT* 929; P Muchlinski, 'Negotiating New Generation International Investment Agreements. New Sustainable Development Oriented Initiatives' in S Hindelang and M Krajewsky (eds), *Shifting Paradigms in International Investment Law* (Oxford University Press, 2016) 43; MM Mbengue and S Schacherer, 'The "Africanization" of International Investment Law: The Pan-African Investment Code and the Reform of the International Investment Regime' (2017) 18 *JWIT* 441; C Titi, 'The Evolution of Substantive Investment Protections in Recent Trade and Investment Treaties' (2018) *RTA Exchange. International Centre for Trade and Sustainable Development & Inter-American Development Bank.*

[30] R Nixon, 'Statement about the Environmental Policy Act of 1969' (1 January 1970). See WH Jr. Rodgers, 'The Most Creative Moments in the History of Environmental Law: "The Whats"' (2000) *U Illinois L Rev* 1.

[31] For a survey of different opinions regarding the origin of the term 'sustainable development', see C Brighton, 'Unlikely Bedfellows: The Evolution of the Relationship Between Environmental Protection and Development' (2017) 66 *ICLQ* 209, 222.

with the notion of sustainable development, Norway's Prime Minister at the time, Gro Harlem Brundtland. Drawing on the past intellectual concept of 'Spaceship Earth',[32] the report produced in 1987 by the so-called Brundtland Commission – the Brundtland Report – managed to integrate economics with environmental protection for the very first time by showing 'what conservation might mean for economic policy, [and] how misguided economic policy could degrade the environment.'[33] The notion of sustainable development inspired the negotiations of the UN Rio Declaration on Environment and Development which, adopted in 1992, declared that 'States should cooperate to promote a supportive and open international economic system that would lead to economic growth and sustainable development in all countries, to better address the problems of environmental degradation.'[34]

The Rio Conference led to the adoption of another important instrument, the UNFCCC – the very first international law instrument dealing with climate change mitigation. The Framework Convention had been built on the work conducted by the scientific community and, in particular, by the IPCC, which had been established in 1988 and had just released its first Assessment Report. The latter recognised the importance of foreign investment as one of the ways in which the private sector could contribute to cooperative climate change mitigation efforts.[35] Inspired by the work of the IPCC and by the Rio negotiations, the UNFCCC explicitly incorporates the notion of sustainable development and reiterates that the international economic system should be aimed at achieving and ensuring sustainable development.[36]

It was against this backdrop that a number of trade and investment agreements, including the ECT, were negotiated in the early 1990s. However, while other trade and investment negotiations that took place during the same years were deeply affected by all these environment and climate-related developments, the negotiators of the ECT seemed to be working in isolation and seemed to be immune to the 'sustainable development fever'.

B. The Influence of Sustainable Development on Trade and Investment Treaty-Making

The introduction of this new overarching principle changed the rules of the game for both international economic law and environmental law.[37] In regards to the

[32] KE Boulding, 'The Economics of the Coming Spaceship Earth' in H Jarrett (ed), *Environmental Quality in a Growing Economy* (John Hopkins University Press, 1966) 3–14.

[33] D Pearce et al, *Blueprint For A Green Economy* (Earthscan, 1990) xii.

[34] Rio Declaration, Principle 12. For references to sustainable development, see also Principles 1, 3 and 4.

[35] IPCC (n 26).

[36] UNFCCC, Article 3.5.

[37] E Cima, *From Exception to Promotion. Re-Thinking the Relationship between International Trade and Environmental Law* (Brill, 2021) 153.

former, this principle shifted the focus away from economic growth plain and simple. The term 'development' reflects 'some set of desirable goals or objectives for society'[38] which undoubtedly include but are not limited to economic growth. It refers to a process of transformation which combines economic growth with broader social and cultural changes, to enable individuals to achieve a certain 'quality of life' and realise their full potential.[39] At the same time, 'the dimension of sustainability brings the recognition that [growth and] development must … adhere to the physical constraints imposed by ecosystems, so that environmental considerations have to be embedded in all sectors and policy areas.'[40]

Several negotiations around that time were deeply influenced by this change of paradigm. One example is provided by the Uruguay Round of trade negotiations, which led to the establishment of the World Trade Organisation (WTO).[41] Until 1995, the multilateral trade regime coincided with the General Agreement on Tariffs and Trade (GATT), which had been adopted in 1947.[42] While the preamble to the GATT identified as the core objective of the Agreement 'raising standards of living, ensuring full employment and a large and steadily growing volume of real income and effective demand,'[43] the WTO, influenced by the Brundtland Report and the emergence of this new paradigm, was asked to pursue the much broader objective of 'sustainable development, seeking both to protect and preserve the environment.'[44] Thus, the growth and development promoted by the trade regime would have to be sustainable, and trade rules themselves should not undermine domestic and international efforts towards securing the environmental pillar of sustainable development.[45]

The negotiations of the North American Free Trade Agreement (NAFTA), which took place between 1991 and 1994, were similarly influenced by the events of the 'sustainable development decade.'[46] Significantly, on 4 October 1992 Clinton gave a major speech on NAFTA where, while expressing his general support for the agreement, he also recognised its deficiencies.[47] In particular, he expressed concerns regarding environmental protection and declared that he would not sign legislation implementing NAFTA until new 'supplemental agreements' had

[38] Pearce et al (n 33) xii.

[39] N Carter, *The Politics of the Environment: Ideas, Activism, Policy* (Cambridge University Press, 2018) 211.

[40] ibid 212. Cima, From Exception to Promotion (n 37) 153.

[41] Marrakesh Agreement Establishing the World Trade Organization, 15 April 1994, 1867 U.N.T.S. 154 (WTO Agreement).

[42] General Agreement on Tariffs and Trade, 30 October 1947, 61 Stat. A-11, 55 U.N.T.S. 194 (GATT).

[43] GATT, Preamble.

[44] WTO Agreement, Preamble.

[45] Cima (n 37) 154.

[46] North American Free Trade Agreement, US-Can.-Mex, 17 December 1992, 32 I.L.M. 289 (1993) (NAFTA). See CL Deere and DC Esty (eds), *Greening the Americas. NAFTA's Lessons for Hemispheric Trade* (MIT Press, 2002).

[47] B Clinton, 'Expanding Trade and Creating American Jobs', at North Carolina State University (4 October 1992) in (1993) 23 *Envtl L* 683. See Candidate Bill Clinton's Proposal for Supplemental Agreements on NAFTA, in R Dabell and M Henfeld (eds), *Beyond NAFTA, The Western Hemisphere* (Oolichan Books, 1993) 192.

been negotiated with Mexico and Canada regarding these issues.[48] As a result, besides the adoption of an environmental side-agreement – the North American Agreement on Environmental Cooperation (NAAEC)[49] – NAFTA Chapter 11, which deals with investment protection, has integrated several environmental provisions.

For instance, Article 1114 incorporates a key environmental law principle – the principle of non-regression – which requires countries not to lower their environmental standards in order to attract foreign trade and investment. The Article was motivated by the fears of environmentalists that NAFTA would create a pollution haven along the Mexican side of the border with the United States, contributing to Mexico's environmental degradation by driving US and Canadian companies to relocate to Mexico. At the same time, this would encourage both the United States and Canada to lower their own environmental standards in order to keep their companies at home, thus creating a snowball effect.[50]

C. The Reluctance of the ECT to Incorporate Environmental Considerations

The ECT was negotiated during the same years as NAFTA, the first half of the 1990s. While the ECT was being negotiated, the Rio Conference on Environment and Development was taking place, the UNFCCC was being adopted, and the international community was being made aware of the need to transition towards a low-carbon economy. Yet, the space devoted to these considerations – environmental protection, climate change mitigation, renewable energy, energy efficiency and conservation – remains very limited in the text of the ECT as it was adopted in 1994.

There are two places, in the text of the treaty, where one can find a reference to these considerations. The first one is the Preamble, which recalls 'the United Nations Framework Convention on Climate Change, the Convention on Long-Range Transboundary Air Pollution and its protocols, and other international environmental agreements with energy-related aspects.'[51] The second one is Article 19, titled 'Environmental Aspects', which 'provides the essence of the environmental dimension of the Energy Charter Treaty.'[52] However, while the

[48] See S Charnovitz, 'The NAFTA Environmental Side Agreement: Implications for Environmental Cooperation, Trade Policy, and American Treatymaking' (1994) 8 *Temple Int'l & Comp L J* 257.

[49] North American Agreement on Environmental Cooperation, US-Can.-Mex. 32 I.L.M. 1482 (1993).

[50] JE Bailey, 'Free Trade and the Environment–Can NAFTA Reconcile the Irreconcilable' (1992) 8 *Am U J Int'l L & Pol'y* 839, 867. R Housman and PM Orbuch, 'Integrating Environmental and Labor Concerns in the North American Free Trade Agreement: A Look Back and a Look Ahead' (1993) 8(4) *Am U Int'l L Rev* 719, 732.

[51] ECT, Preamble.

[52] P Vajda et al, 'Article 19: Environmental Aspects' in R Leal-Arcas (ed), *Commentary on the Energy Charter Treaty* (Edward Elgar, 2018) 269, 271.

provision mentions several key environmental law principles – sustainable development, precaution, polluter-pays – and acknowledges the role played by cleaner fuels and technologies, it does not technically belong to the investment protection portion of the treaty. This means inter alia that it is not a provision that can be raised in the context of an investor-state dispute. In fact, unlike the dispute resolution clauses of other investment treaties that refer to 'any' or 'all' disputes concerning an investment,[53] Article 26(1) of the ECT requires that the dispute concern 'an alleged breach of an obligation … under Part III' of the Treaty itself.[54] Part Three of the ECT, which includes Articles 10 to 17, is the part devoted to investment protection. Article 19, on the other hand, can be found in Part Four of the ECT, and therefore outside of the obligations which can be challenged in the context of a dispute if not observed.

The provisions contained in Part Three, instead, do not contain any reference to the environment, climate change mitigation, renewable energy, energy efficiency or conservation. None of the standards of protection integrate any of these considerations, and no specific provision exists to incorporate, for instance, the principle of non-regression or the right to regulate, which can be found in many other agreements concluded during the same decade. Similarly, the definition of 'protected investment', which determines the scope of application *ratione materiae* of the treaty, reflects a very outdated and static perception of the energy sector. To be protected, an investment has to be 'associated with an Economic Activity in the Energy Sector.'[55] The definition of 'Economic Activity in the Energy Sector', provided for by Article 1(5), refers to a closed list of activities – exploration, extraction, refining, production, storage, land transport, transmission, distribution, trade, and marketing or sale of energy materials – while Annex EM lists the 'Energy Materials and Products' to which those activities must refer. These lists seem to be associated with products and materials that are largely fossil fuels-related, clearly reflecting the energy sector as it existed when the ECT was being drafted. On the other hand, they do not seem entirely adequate to include recent trends and activities in the energy sector, mostly related to renewable energy and energy efficiency and conservation.[56]

IV. ECT 2.0: A Missed Opportunity for the Environment and the Climate?

While the ECT may have not been receptive to environmental considerations and concerns at the time of its drafting, the treaty is supposed to reflect new

[53] See eg Netherlands Model BIT (1997); Germany Model BIT (2005); United Kingdom Model BIT (2005/6); and France Model BIT (2006).

[54] Cima (n 1) 86.

[55] ECT, Article 1(6).

[56] S Maynard and A Ason, 'Is the Energy Charter Treaty ready to Embrace Energy Transition?' (2019) *TDM*.

developments and challenges in international energy markets, which explains why, in 2017, the Parties to the ECT launched a modernisation process aimed at updating, clarifying, and modernising a number of its provisions.[57] While there is hardly any doubt that climate change qualifies as a new challenge, and the efforts aimed at facilitating the transition to a low-carbon economy as new developments affecting international energy markets, the specific items open for discussion and reform which were announced in November 2018 did not mention climate change, clean energy, or any related concern. Instead, they simply included several investment protection issues, ranging from definitions to traditional investment protection standards, as well as some issues related to dispute settlement, such as frivolous claims, valuation of damages, and third-party funding.[58]

Nevertheless, several of the existing items referred to provisions that could have been re-written in a more environmentally-friendly way, as suggested by the Negotiating Directives for the Modernisation of the ECT, adopted by the European Council in July 2019, which identified the core objectives of this modernisation process as 'to facilitate investment in the energy sector in a sustainable way between the ECT Contracting Parties by creating a coherent and up-to-date legally binding framework that provides for legal certainty and ensures a high level of investment protection' and 'to lead to a new modernised treaty which should reflect climate change and clean energy transition goals and contribute to the achievement of the objectives of the Paris Agreement.'[59]

Unfortunately – at least from an environmental and climate perspective – the reform does not seem to have resulted in an instrument capable of promoting the renewable energy transition and contributing to the objectives of the Paris Agreement. New environmental language has been introduced in the ECT without, however, providing any concrete innovation in the overall landscape of international investment treaties; the additions and changes that have been made, in fact, simply reflect the treaty practice that has existed since the 1990s, when the ECT was first negotiated. This hardly makes it a 'modern' version of its predecessor.

A. Cornering the Environment into Narrow Exceptions

One element of the reform has been the re-drafting of Article 24 of the ECT, titled 'General Exceptions.' There is no doubt that the new text of the provision takes into account environmental considerations more than it did before. However, on closer inspection one can clearly notice that the reform has simply brought the

[57] Cima (n 1) 76.

[58] The complete list can be found on the ECT website at www.energychartertreaty.org/modernisation-of-the-treaty/.

[59] Council of the European Union, Note, Negotiating Directives for the Modernisation of the Energy Charter Treaty, Brussels, 2 July 2019, 3.

exception clause of the ECT in line with all other exception clauses, considering that the original text was especially narrowly drafted.

The original version of Article 24 presented two main shortcomings. First, in regards to 'environmental' exceptions, it only referred to measures 'necessary to protect human, animal, or plant life or health', which is the formulation that can be found for the first time in GATT Article XX(b). There is instead no reference to the second traditional 'environmental' exception – the one enshrined in GATT Article XX(g) – which concerns measures 'relating to the conservation of exhaustible natural resources.' This formulation clearly shows that, already in 1994, the ECT was not up to date in terms of environmental exceptions, as most FTAs have instead replicated the entirety of GATT Article XX, including paragraph (g). The second main shortcoming concerns the scope of application of the exception. In fact, the original version of Article 24 excluded three provisions of Part Three from its applications – including Article 13 on expropriation – and further excluded Part Three in its entirety from the application of subparagraph (i) – 'necessary to protect human, animal, or plant life or health.' It follows that the exception clause could not be used to justify a measure adopted for environmental reasons.

The reformed version of Article 24 would correct both shortcomings by adding a reference to measures 'relating to the conservation of exhaustible natural resources' and by eliminating the restriction of the application of the environmental exceptions to Part Three of the treaty. Article 13 is still excluded from the application of the whole of Article 24, but it has now been provided with a specific carve-out (see later Section IV(B)).

This new version of Article 24 can hardly be defined as 'modern' for at least two reasons. First, it simply serves to bring the ECT general exceptions clause in line with what has been treaty practice since the late 1990s and the early 2000s. The EU-Chile FTA, for instance, made reference, in 2002, to both environmental exceptions, and so did most FTAs signed by the European Union, and since then, by other countries.[60] Most importantly, the focus on exceptions significantly limits the space that is concretely devoted to environmental and climate considerations and maintains a clear hierarchy between economic and non-economic concerns. By adopting what I have called elsewhere an 'exception-based model',[61] the protection of foreign investments remains the rule while the possibility for the host state to pursue environmental or climate change-mitigation objectives is simply tolerated if the conditions of the exceptions are met. The consequences of such an approach are of both practical and symbolic nature. In practice, considering the applicable rules on interpretation and on the burden of proof, exceptions are difficult to be successfully relied upon by the respondent state.[62]

[60] See eg US-Chile FTA, Article 23 and CETA, Article 28.3.

[61] Cima (n 37).

[62] E Cima, 'Promoting Renewable Energy through FTAs? The Legal Implications of a New Generation of Trade Agreements' (2018) 52(4) *JWT* 663, 687–93; H Horn and PC Mavroidis, 'Burden

As to the symbolic consequence, relying on exceptions reiterates the message that non-economic interests are to be subordinate to economic ones, contrary to the message sent by the IPCC, the current COPs, and Agenda 2030. The risk is an abuse of this subordination by tribunals, like in in the recent decision in *Eco Oro v Colombia*, where the tribunal swept aside an environmental exception in the Colombia–Canada FTA 'declaring this provision to be effectively irrelevant in investment arbitration.'[63]

B. A Few Environmental Provisions : Nothing New under the Sun

In addition to re-drafting Article 24, and expanding the scope of environmental exceptions, the reform of the ECT has resulted in three new environmental provisions: the principle of non-regression, the recognition of the countries' right to regulate, and the environmental carve-out in the definition of indirect expropriation. However, looking at how it has been emphasised with regard to the general exceptions, the reform has done nothing more than carry the text of the ECT up to speed with current treaty practice.

The principle of non-regression, as already described above in Section III(B), has existed in investment agreements since NAFTA, which was adopted the very same year as the ECT. Article 1114(2) of NAFTA reads:

> The Parties recognise that it is inappropriate to encourage investment by relaxing domestic health, safety or environmental measures. Accordingly, a Party should not waive or otherwise derogate from, or offer to waive or otherwise derogate from, such measures as an encouragement for the establishment, acquisition, expansion or retention in its territory of an investment of an investor.

Revised Article 19 should incorporate the very same principle at paragraph 3. This is a provision that has been introduced in trade and investment agreements consistently since NAFTA. These provisions started off as mere exhortations ('it is inappropriate to encourage investment by relaxing domestic health, safety or environmental measures') and later started being phrased as binding obligations. However, the reformed ECT seems to be still lagging behind in two ways. First, it overlooks the fact that, recently, the practice seems to be going beyond asking countries not to reduce their environmental standards by encouraging

of Proof in Environmental Disputes in the WTO: Legal Aspects' 11 (Research Institute for Industrial Economics, IFN Working Paper No. 793, 2009); JE Viñuales, 'Seven Ways of Escaping a Rule: Of Exceptions and Their Avatars in International Law' in L Bartels and F Paddeu (eds), *Exceptions in International Law* (Oxford University Press, 2020) 65.

[63] J Benton Heath, 'Eco Oro and the Twilight of Policy Exceptionalism' (IISD Investment Treaty News, 20 December 2021). *Eco Oro Minerals Corp. v Republic of Colombia*, ICSID Case No. ARB/16/41, Decision on Jurisdiction, Liability, and Quantum (9 September 2021) at [826]–[837].

them to improve them.[64] Secondly, as Section IV(C) will explain in further detail, the revised ECT has incorporated the principle of non-regression in Article 19, which falls outside of the scope of the treaty's ISDS and is confined to its own separate dispute settlement system.

The second 'environmental' provision that has been newly introduced is the recognition of the Parties' 'right to regulate within their territories to achieve legitimate policy objectives, such as the protection of the environment, including climate change mitigation and adaptation, protection of public health, safety or public morals.' This is an important addition to Part Three of the ECT, but again, it is nothing new.[65]

Finally, Article 13 has been re-written with the addition of a carve-out to the definition of indirect expropriation. Article 13(4) now clarifies that 'non-discriminatory measures that are adopted to protect legitimate policy objectives, such as public health, safety and the environment (including with respect to climate change mitigation and adaptation), do not constitute indirect expropriation.' Once again, an important – yet old addition. For many years investment chapters in FTAs have increasingly started to define what does not constitute indirect expropriation. They have done so by providing guidance on what factors need to be taken into account to determine if there has been an indirect expropriation, and through the incorporation of '(a mitigated form of) the police powers doctrine.'[66] Often, they include a specific exemption – or carve out – excluding from the definition of indirect expropriation changes to a country's regulatory framework to protect the environment. A notable example is Article 8(12) of CETA which, read in combination with Annex 8-A, allows the Parties to adopt 'non-discriminatory measures … that are designed and applied to protect legitimate public welfare objectives, such as health, safety and the environment' as they 'do not constitute indirect expropriations.'[67]

C. Dispute Settlement: One Step Forward and Two Steps Back

Several new environmental provisions, including the one incorporating the principle of non-regression, will be contained in a new chapter on Sustainable Development. However, the Public Communication adopted in June 2022 clarifies

[64] See eg EU-South Korea FTA, Article 13.3; US-Jordan FTA, Article 5; US-Singapore FTA, Article 18.1.

[65] See eg CETA, Article 8.9.

[66] Titi (n 29) 9. Several tribunals have admitted the applicability of the police power doctrine to shield environmental regulation and, more recently, environmental measures. See eg *S.D. Myers v Canada*, Award at [281]; *Methanex v USA*, Award, part IV, ch. D at [7]; *Chemtura v Canada*, Award at [266].

[67] CETA, Annex 8-A. Other examples include COMESA Investment Agreement, Article 20(8); US-Chile FTA, Annex 10-D; US-Austl. FTA, Annex 11-B; China-N. Z. FTA, Annex 13; Turk.-Sing. FTA, Annex 12-A; US-CAFTA-DR, Annex 10-C; S. Kor.-Viet. FTA, Annex 9-B; Costa Rica-Colom. FTA, Annex 12-B.

that 'a dedicated dispute settlement mechanism will be applicable to disputes between the Contracting Parties regarding the interpretation and application of the new provisions on sustainable development' and that 'such dispute settlement mechanism will include a possibility to refer the matter to a conciliator.'[68] For many years, the sustainable development and environment chapters in FTAs have been structured in a similar way: they are provided with their own dispute settlement and enforcement mechanisms (usually conciliation or mediation). It is precisely for this reason that they have often been criticised as lacking any real strength. A separate dispute settlement mechanism means that the provisions contained in these chapters cannot be raised in a trade or an investment dispute. Certainly, they can still inform a tribunal's decision, as evidenced for instance by the *Al Tamimi v Oman* decision, where the tribunal relied on the environmental chapter of the applicable agreement (Chapter 17 of the US-Oman FTA) to interpret the minimum standard of treatment of foreign investors.[69] However, it is up to each tribunal to decide the role and importance given to the sustainable development chapter of the agreement in its interpretation of investment provisions, thus not providing states or investors with any real stability and predictability of future decisions. Moreover, a separate dispute settlement mechanism shows a lack of integration between investment and environmental provisions, maintaining a system where the hierarchical relationship between the two sets of provisions remains clear.

V. Conclusions

From an environmental or climate perspective, the text of the ECT has hardly been 'modernised'. The new or updated provisions certainly stand out when compared to the original text of the ECT. However, this is possible simply because the text of the ECT was almost entirely unreceptive to the environmental voices that were entering trade and investment negotiations during the 1990s. The new or updated provisions would have been modern 20 or 25 years ago, when NAFTA was being negotiated, or when the EU was negotiating 'a new generation' of trade and investment agreements with many of its trading partners. 'Old wine in new bottles' seems to be the clearest and simplest way to summarise in just one sentence the 'environmental' outcome of the modernisation process.

Concretely, the impact of this reform may not be so significant, when considering the difficulties that the Energy Charter Conference is facing, at the time of writing, to adopt the revised text of the treaty. Yet, after four years of negotiations,

[68] Decision of the Energy Charter Conference, Public Communication Explaining the Main Changes Contained in the Agreement in Principle, CCDEC 2022 (24 June 2022) 7.

[69] *Adel A Hamadi Al Tamimi v Sultanate of Oman*, ICSID Case No. ARB/11/33, Award (Nov. 3, 2015) at [387]–[389].

only a few small steps have been made to ensure that investments in a sector as key as the energy sector can actively contribute to climate change mitigation. The revised text continues to send a message – the supremacy of investment protection over environmental or climate protection – that seems to clash with current developments in international economic law and governance. This is not the message we find in many bilateral investment negotiations, nor is it the message we find in regional negotiations or in multilateral economic and climate conferences. It is not the message that should have been reached at the conclusion of a process aimed at 'modernising' the ECT.

3

The Energy Charter Treaty 2.0: Promoting and Protecting Energy Investments in an Era of Sustainable Development

YLLI DAUTAJ

I. Introduction

The energy sector, as well as the overall economy, must become greener. Such a statement can no longer be treated as a mere contemporary policy objective or political concern. It should manifest as an unequivocal fact rooted in the environmental crisis and climate change.

Thus, there is an imminent need for reforming the economy in a holistic, overreaching, and groundbreaking manner. Such sudden structural reform includes the energy architecture, ie facilitating the green transition in order to adapt to a sustainable development era. This is not a unique view, but rather a mainstream position nowadays. The Paris Agreement leaves little (if any) room for debate and clearly articulates that finance flows should be consistent with a pathway to low greenhouse gas emissions. The Paris Agreement makes it clear that we need a climate-resilient development in order to limit the rise in global average temperature to 1.5°C pre-industrial levels.[1] To achieve this, foreign direct investments (FDI) will be crucial and instrumental. Moreover, apart from the commitment of states to adaptation and mitigation, powerful global governance actors have made their voices emphatically loud and clear, too. For example, the G-20 concluded that the international energy architecture needs to better reflect the changing realities of the world energy landscape.[2] Along the same lines as this, the International Energy Agency (IEA) rightly noted that '[c]urrent global trends in energy supply

[1] Paris Agreement to the United Nations Framework Convention on Climate Change, 12 December 2015, T.I.A.S. No. 16-1104, II (17) available at: digitallibrary.un.org/record/831039.

[2] C Downie, 'Global Energy Governance in the G-20: States, Coalitions, and Crisis' (2015) 21(3) *Global Governance*.

and consumption are patently unsustainable' and that '[w]hat is needed is nothing short of an energy revolution'.[3] Undoubtedly, many aspects of energy architecture need to be achieved in order to get our sustainable ducks in row.

In this chapter, I focus on the area of my expertise, ie investment promotion and protection, in general, and in the energy sector, in particular. I focus on what international investment agreements (IIA) with investor-state dispute settlement (ISDS) clauses (jointly, investment treaty arbitration or ITA) can contribute as it currently stands (if at all), and what it may come to offer subsequent to sustainable development reforms. Some actors believe that ITA is working contrary to climate change. For example, the International Panel on Climate Change argues that IIAs stand in the way of climate change.[4] They are not alone;[5] however, I strongly disagree with such a thesis. My position is that ITA can indeed facilitate the green transition by promoting and protecting FDI in the renewable energy sector. I agree with the then President of the International Bar Association (IBA), David W Rivkin, namely, that 'international arbitration should play a critical role in developing the legal framework of the post [Paris Agreement] world' and that 'it is vital that a neutral, effective mechanism exist for resolving disputes between investors and states, particularly in order to incentivise foreign investment in renewable energy'.[6] However, this should not be understood as a blind endorsement for status quo. It is not. Rather, it is quite the opposite. I advocate in favour of a modernised IIA and ISDS landscape; one that is structurally designed to accommodate sustainable development.

However, in order to make the ITA regime compatible with the environmental crisis and climate change, while also redressing other legitimacy concerns of the regime, the current ITA landscape must be reformed – materially (IIA) and procedurally (ISDS).

To illustrate: (i) the balancing between energy needs, economic growth, and climate change mitigation and adaptation, (ii) the various positions for or against ITA, and (iii) possible solutions, this chapter focuses on how the modernised Energy Charter Treaty (ECT 2.0) – a multilateral IIA – can achieve the purported

[3] International Energy Agency (IEA), 'World Energy Outlook 2008' (2008) 37, iea.blob.core.windows.net/assets/89d1f68c-f4bf-4597-805f-901cfa6ce889/weo2008.pdf.

[4] Corporate Europe Observatory, 'Busting the myths around the Energy Charter Treaty – A guide for concerned citizens, activists, journalists and policymakers' (2020) 29-30, www.tni.org/files/publication-downloads/busting_the_myths_around_the_energy_charter_treaty-web.pdf.

[5] See eg OD Akinkugbe and A Majekolagbe, 'International investment law and climate justice: the search for just green investment order' (2023) 46(2) *Fordham International Law Journal* and M Dietrich Brauch, 'The Agreement in Principle on ECT "Modernization": A Botched Reform Attempt that Undermines Climate Action' (*Kluwer Arbitration Blog*, 17 October 2022) arbitrationblog.kluwerarbitration.com/2022/10/17/the-agreement-in-principle-on-ect-modernization-a-botched-reform-attempt-that-undermines-climate-action/.

[6] See now deleted speech D Rivkin, 'COP2 1: Climate Change Related Disputes: A Role for International Arbitration and ADR' (7 December 2015) (can no longer be found online) and 'David W. Rivkin Asserts Arbitration and ADR will Play a Critical Role in Climate Change and Sustainability at COP 21' (*Debevoise and Plimpton*, 7 December 2015) www.debevoise.com/news/2015/12/david-w-rivkin-asserts_sustainability-cop-21.

goals and strike the right balance. Put very simply, I agree with the European Union's initial consideration, ie that the objective of the modernised ECT should be to facilitate investment in the energy sector in a sustainable way, such that the ECT 2.0 should reflect climate change and clean energy transition goals and contribute to the achievement of the objectives of the Paris Agreement.[7] Meanwhile, I disagree with the decision to withdraw from the ECT. My position is that:

(1) ECT 2.0 would be an effective international legal instrument to govern energy investments and work as a global governance tool that facilitates a green economy transition, and
(2) ECT 2.0 coordinates and strikes a balance between the purposes and objectives articulated by various stakeholders, including states, corporations, international organisations, and international energy and climate change organisations.

II. The Competing Positions, why this Study Matters, and what this Chapter Sets Out to Do

A. Competing Positions

There are primarily three competing positions on the utility of the ECT and ECT 2.0. Conversely, it is the siding with either of the said positions that will affect positively or adversely the standing and currency of the ECT. The positions are:

(1) ECT facilitates a transition to renewable energy by promoting and protecting investors/investments in the energy sector. ECT 2.0 does so even more.
(2) ECT hinders a green transition by protecting fossil fuel investments. ECT 2.0 remedies major concerns and facilitates a transition to renewable energy.
(3) ECT hinders a green transition by protecting fossil fuels investments and ECT 2.0 does not remedy major concerns.

I would tend to agree with Position (1). I do not think that promoting and protecting fossil fuel investments is mutually exclusive with a green transition, especially where robust compliance mechanisms are put in place as well as environmental protocols. A coordinated and well-organised phase-out, while not undercutting the global south's ability to compete fairly, is crucial. If not, the unintended consequences may be that many states simply refuse to work towards climate change adaptation and mitigation. Moreover, we may harm those already suffering even further. I am afraid that too sudden a change may lead to less change.

[7] Decision of the Energy Charter Conference, 'Adoption by Correspondence – Policy Options for Modernisation of the ECT' (6 October 2019) 2–3, www.energycharter.org/fileadmin/DocumentsMedia/CCDECS/2019/CCDEC201908.pdf.

B. Why this Study Matters

The ECT is arguably the most important IIA in existence.[8] For any advocate of ITA, the faith of the ECT should be treated with the highest alertness. This is especially true given that much of the contemporary criticism is accurate. Some parts of the ECT are outdated. The ECT is a so-called 'old generation' IIA. Hence, this study matters for proponents of the ITA regime, on the one hand, and for those (like me) that advocate in favour of moderate reforms that do not undercut the fundamental elements of international arbitration and international investment law (IIL), on the other hand.

Global governance through various international instruments has propelled a green transition. This is evident through the SDG, the European Green Deal, the Paris Agreement, the United Nations Framework Convention on Climate Change (UNFCCC), etc. Scholars have rightly noted that too 'little attention has been given to the capacity of the existing institutional architecture to promote investment in clean energy technologies', in particular the ECT.[9] It is indeed important that IIAs – such as the ECT (which received heightened importance due to its multilateral character and subject-matter uniqueness) – and ISDS also play an important role in this scheme of global energy governance.[10]

Some influential European states (France, Italy, the Netherlands,[11] Poland, and Spain) have withdrawn from the ECT, making it impossible for the European Commission (EC) to do much else other than to propose a withdrawal for the entire EU.[12]

It is important that the fight for climate justice does not come at the expense of the Global South. One should be very mindful of environmental imperialism, as well as 'greenwashing'. Even if well-intended, the unintended consequences of

[8] C Verburg, 'Modernising the Energy Charter Treaty: An Opportunity to Enhance Legal Certainty in Investor-State Dispute Settlement' (2019) 20 *Journal of World Investment & Trade*.

[9] K Tienhaara and C Downie, 'Risky Business: The Energy Charter Treaty, Renewable Energy, and Investor-State Disputes' (2018) 24 *Global Governance* 451, 452.

[10] See V Korzun, 'Enforcing Soft Law in International Investment Arbitration' (2023) 56(1) *Vanderbilt Journal of Transitional Law* 64–65.

[11] Ironically it was the then Prime Minister of the Netherlands, Mr Ruud Lubbers, that took the initiative steps with respect to the signing of the ECT. See TW Wälde, 'Introductory Note by Thomas W. Wälde' (1995) *International Legal Materials* 362.

[12] European Commission, 'European Commission proposes a coordinated EU withdrawal from the Energy Charter Treaty' (Press Release, 7 July 2023) energy.ec.europa.eu/news/european-commission-proposes-coordinated-eu-withdrawal-energy-charter-treaty-2023-07-07_en and L Bohmer, 'European Commission submits formal proposals for the EU and Euratom to withdraw from the ECT; Commission opines that sunset clause never applied to intra-EU disputes, but it nevertheless proposes the adoption of a subsequent agreement on this issue' (*IAreporter*, 7 July 2023) www.iareporter.com/articles/european-commission-submits-formal-proposals-for-the-eu-and-euratom-to-withdraw-from-the-ect-commission-opines-that-sunset-clause-never-applied-to-intra-eu-disputes-but-it-nevertheless-proposes-the/. The European Commission had been handed the mandate to represent all EU Member States in the modernization negotiations. Council of the European Union, 'Negotiating Directives for the Modernisation of the Energy Charter Treaty' (2 July 2019) data.consilium.europa.eu/doc/document/ST-10745-2019-ADD-1/en/pdf.

disregarding economic development in the Global South would be a global harm of equal proportions.[13]

The bottom line is that this study matters because it elevates the discussion on how to best balance investment promotion and protection with broader environmental goals without undercutting the fundamental elements of international arbitration and IIL (including de-politicisation, neutrality, and economic development).

C. What this Chapter Sets Out to Do

I will argue that the ECT is the single most important piece in the existing institutional architecture on international energy investment promotion and protection. I will explain why I believe that the ECT 2.0 complements the Paris Agreement by providing adequate policy space to states, so that they can meet their broader obligations, whilst also protecting energy investments, including (mostly) green investments.

Furthermore, I will argue that ECT 2.0 with its ISDS mechanism manifests as a crucial architecture that assists in expediting the transition to clean energy by facilitating, promoting and protecting the flow of investment into the renewable energy sector. I will argue that this largely benefits small and medium-sized (SME) investors and external stakeholders. I will explain why a withdrawal from the ECT simply means that ECT 1.0 and/or IIA 1.0 will reign supreme for quite some time after which only SMEs will take the long-term hit. I will explain that a refusal to recognise the importance of ITA means more non-transparent, contractual ISDS (which could include various freezing clauses and so on).

Advocating against ECT 2.0 equals (unintentionally) arguing in favour of fossil fuel promotion and protection. Advocating against the moderate reform of IIAs equals arguing in favour of the old generation IIAs (at least for the foreseeable future). Advocating against ITA equals arguing in favour of contractual ISDS.

III. The Energy Charter Treaty: Facilitating, Promoting, and Protecting Energy Investments

A. ECT: An Introduction

The ECT was signed in 1994 and entered into force in 1998. It has 50 articles and 14 annexes. Adding to this patchwork, there are also several understandings,

[13] See Akinkugbe and Majekolagbe (n 5) and U Natarajan, 'Climate Justice' in M Valverde, K Clarke, E Darian-Smith and P Kotiswaran (eds), *The Routledge Handbook of Law and Society* (Routledge, 2021).

declarations and interpretations that have been made part of the overall ECT regime.

The treaty came into existence with the objective of establishing a legal framework in order to promote long-term cooperation in the energy field.[14] 'The ECT covers promotion and protection of investments, trade in energy, transit in the energy sector, environmental aspects as well as the settlement of disputes under the Treaty.'[15] In other words, the treaty was signed largely to serve as a post-Cold War bridge between the East and the West, following years of geopolitical and ideological divide.[16] The ECT achieved its purported objectives by supporting a transition in the East to market economy. Put simply, East was to provide energy security to West and in turn receive much needed capital (FDI) and technology transfer.[17]

ECT provides for a reliable legal framework for energy investments and transit. It facilitates energy cooperation by promoting and protecting energy investments. Put differently, the ECT makes possible and protects long-term energy investments by protecting against political risk.

The ECT has 52 Member States and the EU, including states as diverse as Afghanistan, Albania, Georgia, Kyrgyzstan, Mongolia, Turkey, Turkmenistan, Ukraine, and Uzbekistan. Additionally, the ECT has 38 observer Member States (signatories to the energy charter) and various organisations, cooperations, etc., including states as diverse as Pakistan, Syria, the US, China, Colombia, Iran, Iraq, Sierra Leone, Tanzania, UAE, etc. Even though the EU bloc is likely to withdraw, the impact of ECT as a global instrument for energy cooperation may live on.

B. Energy Investments and Typical Interfering State Measures

It is important to have some (albeit brief) knowledge about: (1) the nature of energy investments, (2) the category of energy investments, and (3) the measures that could interfere with such investments.

First, energy investments tend to be long-term; prone to political risk; capital intensive; and subject to quite substantial sunk costs in order to even get the operation going in the first place.[18] Second, energy investments are typically made in oil and gas; power generation, transmission, and supply; offshore renewables; onshore renewables; nuclear; hydrogen/storage; etc. Finally, typical

[14] Kaj Hobér, *The Energy Charter Treaty – A Commentary* (2020) 1.

[15] ibid.

[16] Energy Charter Secretariat, 'The Energy Charter Treaty, Trade Amendment and Related Documents' (24 April 1998) 8–9, investmentpolicy.unctad.org/international-investment-agreements/treaty-files/2427/download.

[17] Wälde (n 11) 361.

[18] See eg J Tropper and K Wagner, 'The European Union Proposal for the Modernisation of the Energy Charter Treaty – A Model for Climate-Friendly Investment Treaties?' (2022) *Journal of World Investment & Trade* 817–18.

measures that interfere with energy investments include denials or revocations of permits for exploration or extraction activities; phase-out of fossil fuel-based energy sources; and removal of incentives (eg feed-in-tariffs).

C. Promoting Energy Investments: Remembering the Past, Appreciating Today, and Improving the Future

We tend to forget that policy objectives and political concerns swing like a pendulum, that policy objectives and political concerns of the past are cyclically revisited with great newfound passion, but also that the better idea tends to prevail at the end. This lesson on human behaviour is not insignificant in the debate on the ECT. We must never forget the times in which the ECT was drafted and signed, what its aim was, and what it did indeed achieve. At the time of signing the ECT, Thomas W Wälde wrote:

> The major international oil companies seem to have considered – in the early stages – that they had sufficient leverage to do without the Charter. The industry was concerned over the 'sovereignty' references in the Treaty and the potential interventionist-oriented institutional arrangements implicit in some proposals. The possibility of a hard-law environmental article worried the industry as well as some governments (eg the UK concern over the use of EC environmental law to challenge national planning decisions). Several European countries – and energy industries – felt threatened by the liberal, competitive and anti-monopolistic approach of the Charter to controversial issues such as pipeline access and reciprocal free trade – which means access to European markets of cheap goods from the CIS.[19]

It was true then, and it is true now. Major oil and gas corporations will do just fine without the ECT. They would even do fine without IIAs. They have the necessary leverage, and if not in the North, they will have it in the South. If extracted in the East, it will be imported to the West. Moreover, back then – as now – the issue of adequate policy space for states, including for environmental purposes, was considered carefully. Multinational corporations wanted less, and states wanted more. That is what effectively led to old generation IIAs. We now have the opportunity to remedy that wrong by including environmental obligations and ensuring adequate policy space to states, including but not limited to ensuring compliance with the Paris Agreement and the UNFCCC.

Conversely, back then – as now – it is the states as well as SMEs that will take a big hit if IIAs are terminated, generally, and if the ECT is terminated, in particular. The most significant adverse impact will be had on energy investments made by SMEs in the renewable energy sector and underdeveloped states that will be forced to comply with the demands of multinational corporations (which may include freezing clauses, non-transparent ISDS, waivers of immunity from execution, etc.).

[19] Wälde (n 11) 361.

In light of Wälde's spot-on observation from 1995, I will briefly cover two important rationales for the ECT; that is, (1) the economic (sustainable development) rationale, and (2) the policy rationale.

i. Economic (Sustainable Development) Rationale

One of the main purposes of the ITA is economic development.[20] Surely the idea – ie that investment promotion and protection will lead to increased investment – has been challenged. I will not delve into this debate, but will rather treat the three pillars of ITA – (i) economic development, (ii) neutrality, and (iii) de-politicisation – as axioms. However, I just want to say briefly from a practical experience that when consulting clients in transborder bargains – whether commerce, trade, or investment – we do not necessarily mention 'you could benefit from fair and equitable treatment' or 'you may consider relying on an ISDS clause in another IIA through the most favoured nation standard'. Such is not the name of the game at the pre-establishment phase. However, significant due diligence goes into analysing and assessing legal stability and the overall investor landscape in the host state. If the state (directly or through representation) makes additional commitments or assurances, it's for the better. If the state has taken certain measures to promote investments in a particular sector, it's for the better. Thus, the theory that investment protection does not lead to economic development is utter nonsense to someone who actually deals with these matters. If the ITA system is undercut, this will be evident, but the price for the lesson will be too high.

The crux of the matter is quite straightforward and should be simple to digest, namely, we need FDI and energy, and therefore investor/investment protection for energy investments. IIA and ISDS facilitate and promote investment by protecting it. The regime manifests as a political risk insurance mechanism.

In addition, and to be utterly frank, we could not even meet our global challenges without sufficient investments in the energy sector. Let us start with an easy point: there is no way to ensure access to affordable, reliable, sustainable and modern energy for all (SDG 7) without sufficient FDI in the sector.[21] The fact of the matter is that 670 million individuals live without electricity; there has been

[20] C Schreuer, 'Investment Protection: Original Purpose and Features' in C Baltag and A Stanic (eds), *The Future of Investment Treaty Arbitration in the EU: Intra-EU BITs, the Energy Charter Treaty, and The Multilateral Investment Court* (Kluwer Law International, 2020) 5; Corporate Counsel International Arbitration Group, 'Investor-State Dispute Settlement (ISDS) Reform' Submission to UNCITRAL Working Group III 1-2 (18 December 2019), uncitral.un.org/sites/uncitral.un.org/files/cciag_isds_reform.pdf; and *Kingdom of Spain v Infrastructure Services Luxembourg S.á.r.l.* [2021] FCAFC 112 at [2] (stating that the ICSID Convention is an important international convention underpinning and supporting the flow of investment capital around the world). For a contrary position, see Corporate Europe Observatory (n 4) 10.

[21] United Nations Sustainable Development Goals, 'Goal 7 – Ensure access to affordable, reliable, sustainable and modern energy for all', sdgs.un.org/goals/goal7.

a sharp increase in energy prices; electrification has slowed; and investments in renewable energies have declined (eg, due to lack of incentives).[22] Even so, this is hardly the entire picture. How can we ensure decent work and economic growth (SDG 8) without access to affordable and reliable energy? How can we promote industry, innovation, and infrastructure (SDG 9) without affordable and reliable energy? How can we offer sustainable cities and communities (SDG 11) without sustainable and modern energy for all? How can we combat climate change (SDG 13) without investing in sustainable energy? I could go on, but the very bottom line is that not a single sustainable development goal can be achieved without investments in the energy sector.

Serious actors, such as leading financial institutions, understand this. It is an easy point to make, but equally one that may sound bold in present times, and especially in light of the nonsensical theses loudly 'presented' by various NGOs and 'interest groups'.[23] For example, the World Bank has rightly noted the need for FDI in the extractive industries, but also explained that its work in the extractive sector focuses on:

(1) Maximising benefits in a way that contributes to sustainable and inclusive development, including minimising negative impacts on people and the environment.
(2) Accelerating the energy transition and climate action by reducing emissions from the extractive sector.[24]

Serious actors are not 'dropping the ball' on adaptation and mitigation. Quite the opposite is true. We need to make sure that energy (and incidental mining) investments align as best as possible with sustainable development – ie contribute to economic development/growth while also protecting/enforcing global values (eg combating climate change and protecting human rights). To achieve such an aim, we must move beyond IIA and ISDS 1.0, including ECT 1.0. We need to be better; we need to be greener. The ECT 2.0, like other new generation IIAs, is a clear step towards a globally conscious direction. There is a strong economic development argument to make in favour of ECT, especially ECT 2.0. Over time, the concept of economic development has come to be part of sustainable development, which is an applaudable direction and trajectory. Sustainable development has three dimensions: social, economic and environmental.[25]

[22] ibid.

[23] See eg Corporate Europe Observatory (n 4) 29–30, IISDS, 'What Is the Energy Charter Treaty and What Does it Mean for Sustainable Development?' (*YouTube*, 26 April 2022), www.youtube.com/watch?v=Hbku_wACwfM, and Corporate Europe Observatory, 'The fossil fuel industry's secret weapon: the Energy Charter Treaty' (YouTube, 13 June 2018), www.youtube.com/watch?v=lLVvwOrk91Q&t=10s.

[24] The World Bank, 'Extractive Industries', www.worldbank.org/en/topic/extractiveindustries/overview#1.

[25] G.A. Res. 70/1, 2030 Agenda for Sustainable Development, at 3 (25 September 2015). Arguably, 'sustainability' has four pillars, adding also 'human'.

ii. Policy Rationale

Now to the often under-articulated policy rationale. The policy rationale in favour of, inter alia, Bretton Woods, international economic law broadly, IIAs, ISDS, and ECT was more fashionable post-World War II and the Cold War. Today, polarisation is growing and the idea of interdependence through transborder commerce, trade, and investment is spoken of with distaste. The global governance efforts of mutual intercourse between sovereign states seem to have halted with blocs of sovereigns emerging and competing with other blocs.

Historically, an investor could not sue a host-state for interfering with his investment, nor could he claim investor protection under customary international law against a state. Instead, the aggrieved investor had to turn to its home state for protection through the venue of diplomatic protection.[26] Sometimes, the home state went as far as to engage in so-called 'gunboat diplomacy'. The period of the end of the 1800s and until the end of World War II saw a regressive era with respect to the enforcement of private economic rights against states. In 1889, an Argentinian jurist and diplomat elaborated the infamous 'Calvo doctrine', which restricted the protections offered to foreign investors (both substantively and procedurally). The essence of the Calvo doctrine was that foreign investors should be strictly subjected to the exclusive jurisdiction of national courts and offered the same treatment as domestic investors.[27] This idea became unsustainable.

The move away from the Calvo era slowly picked-up pace with the Second International Peace Conference of the Hague in 1907. However, it was not until the beginning of the 1960s (ie post-World War II) that the de-politicisation of investment disputes started taking shape effectively.[28] It was then that the ICSID Convention came about. It was the attracting of FDI and the de-politicisation of investment disputes that was said to be the main purpose with – and consequently the greatest accomplishments of – investor-State arbitration.[29] The ECT has the same underlying objective and purpose.

Furthermore, globalisation led to the increased use and need for ITA. It is my position that in a global economy that transcends borders, domestic dispute resolution mechanisms cannot sufficiently facilitate the enforcement of a global rule of law. Furthermore, I believe that international arbitration 'made global business possible between Western parties and emerging States and countries that embrace different ideological and legal traditions'.[30] As a result, the ITA

[26] See N Blackaby et al, *Redfern and Hunter on International Arbitration* (Oxford University Press, 2015) 441.

[27] ibid.

[28] See eg *Eiser Infrastructure Ltd v Kingdom of Spain* [2020] FCA 157 at [69] ('By providing [for ICSID arbitration], the Centre aims to improve the international investment climate and stimulate a larger flow of private international investment.').

[29] See E Gaillard and I Mitrev Penusliski, 'State Compliance with Investment Awards' (2021) 52(2) *ICSID REV*.

[30] TE Carbonneau, *The Law and Practice of Arbitration*, 7th edn (JurisNet LLC, 2020) 108.

has helped facilitate an increasingly global, interconnected, and interdependent economy – including in the energy sector through the ECT.

Therefore, I wish to remind the reader that the ECT was signed in 1994 to promote, facilitate, and protect energy cooperation and energy security in a post-World War II and Cold War era and designed specifically to overcome political division. One of its main aims was to establish a common energy governance that promotes interdependence through a move to a market economy.[31]

Again, the idea of 'sovereignty' with capital S is not new; the idea of 'mixed economies' (eg, state capitalism) is not new; and the frequent (and often vicious) challenges to liberal capitalism (rules-based order, democracy, and human rights) is also not new. It is our duty as international lawyers to engage in the discourse attentive to systemic and structural attacks on the foundations that were set in an era of relative peace and prosperity.

When walls fall, instruments for mutual intercourse replace the division. Such interaction can lead to interdependence and interconnectivity, but only if facilitated, promoted and protected. The ECT is one such legacy instrument incidental to walls falling.

D. Protecting Energy Investments

There has been a drastic growth of promoting and attracting foreign investment by offering investors protection through IIAs since the 1980s.[32] The investment protection found in these documents contains the IIL. Thus, IIL applies to the substantive matter that is to be adjudicated through ISDS (together, the ITA regime). Redfern and Hunter summarised the typical protections found in these IIAs as follows:

(1) the protection against expropriation or measures equivalent to expropriation without compensation;
(2) the right to be treated fairly and equitably;
(3) the right to full protection and security;
(4) the protection against arbitrary or discriminatory treatment;
(5) the right to national and MFN treatment;
(6) the right to the free transfer of funds and assets; and
(7) the protection against a state's breaches of its investment obligations and undertakings.[33]

[31] See Wälde (n 11) 362.
[32] Blackaby et al (n 26) 444–45.
[33] Blackaby et al (n 26) 470. More generally on international investment law, see R Dolzer, U Kriebaum and C Schreuer, *Principles of International Investment Law* (Oxford University Press, 2022).

Such substantive protection standards protect against undue state measures. As mentioned, the ECT covers primarily five broad areas, one being investment protection.[34] It is indeed an integral part of the treaty. The ECT offers the substantive protections set out above.[35]

In order to avail itself of arbitration (ISDS) for hearing any investor/investment grievances, the arbitral tribunal must have jurisdiction. For this purpose, a potential investor claimant must show that: (i) they are an investor as defined in the treaty (*ratione personae*), (ii) they have made an investment in the host state as defined in the treaty (*ratione materiae*), (iii) the treaty applies from a temporal standpoint (*ratione temporis*), and (iv) the state has given its consent to arbitration (*ratione voluntantis*). Following the jurisdictional decision, we come to the merits phase (dealing with liability and the substantive protection standards), and third comes the quantum phase (damages). In addition, during the ISDS process, there are many procedural intricacies unique to ITA compared to international commercial arbitration (ICA).

The most frequently used ITA/ISDS regime is ICSID. Other frequently chosen alternatives include the International Chamber of Commerce (ICC), the Stockholm Chamber of Commerce (SCC), or ad hoc arbitration pursuant to the UNCITRAL Arbitration Rules.[36] Awards rendered pursuant to the ICSID regime are enforced under the ICSID Convention, while arbitral awards rendered pursuant to the other regimes are enforced pursuant to the New York Convention.[37] The ECT offers ISDS through:

(1) ICSID Arbitration rules (if the investor's home state and host state are members of the convention) or ICSID Additional Facility Rules (if the investor's home state or host state are not members to the ICSID convention);
(2) Ad Hoc Arbitration pursuant to the UNCITRAL Arbitration Rules; or
(3) SCC Arbitration rules.[38]

IV. The Energy Charter Treaty 2.0: Facilitating, Promoting, and Protecting Energy Investments in an Era of Sustainable Development

In order to assess whether the ECT 2.0 is positive or negative, or whether it goes far enough, we need to determine for ourselves whether we believe that: (a) we

[34] Hobér (n 14).
[35] Articles 10 (Promotion, Protection and Treatment of Investments), 13 (Expropriation), and 14 (Transfers Related to Investments) of the ECT.
[36] See eg K Hobér and J Dahlquist, *Investment Treaty Arbitration – Problems and Exercises* (Edward Elgar, 2018) 10.
[37] ibid 11.
[38] Article 26 (Settlement of Disputes between an Investor and a Contracting Party) of the ECT.

need IIAs. If the answer is 'yes' or 'maybe', do we need it in the current shape (IIA 1.0) or reformed (IIA 2.0)? Having made up our minds on that, (b) do we need the ECT? If the answer is 'yes' or 'maybe', do we need it in the current shape (ECT 1.0) or reformed (ECT 2.0)? Finally, even if we make up our minds on the IIL aspect of IIAs, generally, and the ECT, more particularly, (c) do we need ISDS/ITA? If the answer is 'yes' or 'maybe', do we need it in the current shape (ISDS 1.0) or reformed (ISDS 2.0)? I will cover (a) and (c) together under the first sub-heading below. (b) will be covered separately.

A. Legitimacy Concerns with ITA 1.0 and ITA 2.0

We need IIAs and ISDS, but not necessarily in the current way, shape and form (IIA and ISDS 1.0, ie ITA 1.0). The structural design needs to be reformed, while ensuring that the fundamental elements of the IIL or international arbitration (ITA 2.0) are not undercut.[39]

Serious challenges have been made against ITA. Both substantively, ie with respect to IIL as manifested in IIAs, and procedurally, ie with respect to ISDS. Moreover, a third area of more recent criticism is that the ITA regime fails to align with twenty-first century global concerns, eg environmental challenges, climate change, and human rights violations. As a result, several reform proposals have been made – ranging from more moderate reforms (eg increasing transparency, including a right to regulate clause, etc) to more transformational reforms (removing protection for legitimate expectations, establishing a multilateral investment court, etc).[40]

[39] Some argue that the ITA design should undergo fundamental shifts due to three main challenges; that is: (i) climate change, (ii) national security, and (iii) investor obligations. See A van Aaken, 'Investment Law in the Twenty-First Century: Things Will Have to Change in Order to Remain the Same' (2023) 26 *Journal of International Economic Law* 166, 166.

[40] For more on this, search and read more on the rather intensive discussion on the 'legitimacy crisis' of ITA/ISDS and the 'backlash' against the regime. For one major reform proposal, see in particular the European Union's proposal to elaborate a multilateral investment court (MIC). See eg Comprehensive Trade and Economic Agreement between Canada and the European Union, Can.-E.U. (signed 30 October 2016, not yet entered into force). For criticism of the EU proposal and its underpinnings, see eg European Federation for Investment Law and Arbitration (EFILA), A Response to the Criticism Against ISDS, 4-42 (2015) and Y Dautaj, 'Between Backlash and the Re-Emerging "Calvo Doctrine": Investor State Dispute Settlement in an Era of Socialism, Protectionism, and Nationalism' (2021) 41 *Northwestern Journal of International Law & Business*. For good discussions on legitimacy of ITA and the backlash movement, see eg JH Carter, 'The Culture of Arbitration and the Defense of Arbitral Legitimacy' in DD Caron et al (eds), *Practising Virtue: Inside International Arbitration* (Oxford University Press, 2016) 97–105; SW Schill, 'Conceptions of Legitimacy of International Arbitration' in Caron et al ibid; CN Brower and S Blanchard, 'From "Dealing in Virtue" to "Profiting from Injustice": The Case Against "ReStatification" of Investment Dispute Settlement' (2014) 55 *Harvard International Law Journal* 45; C Brown and K Miles, 'Introduction: Evolution in Investment Treaty Law and Arbitration' in C Brown and K Miles (eds), *Evolution in Investment Treaty Law and Arbitration* (Cambridge University Press, 2011) 3, 3–4; C Schreuer, 'Investment Protection: Original Purpose and Features' in Baltag and Stanic (n 20) 1, 5. For a strong assertion on 'regulatory chill' in the climate change context, see K Tienhaara, 'Regulatory Chill in a Warming World: The Threat to Climate Policy Posed by Investor-State Dispute Settlement' (2018) 7(2) *Transnational Environmental Law*.

Thus, even though IIL has been relatively well-received as an auspice of international economic law, and despite the fact that the interpretation and application by international arbitrators have generally been approved, the decision-making process and the content of IIAs have not gone unchallenged. Furthermore, given that 'the number of investment treaty arbitrations has grown, concerns over the investment treaty system have arisen.'[41]

The legitimacy crisis and backlash movement go to the core of criticising ITA; for example, claiming that the regime:

(1) is inconsistent;
(2) lacks in transparency;
(3) suffers in neutrality due to party-appointed arbitrators;
(4) suffers in neutrality and independence due to double-hatting;
(5) is investor-friendly;
(6) provides for investor rights but not obligations;
(7) downgrades the right to regulate;
(8) has too broad a fair and equitable treatment coverage;
(9) has too broad an investor and investment scope;
(10) includes umbrella clauses;
(11) does not align with 21st century global concerns;
(12) does not provide adequate policy space to regulate;
(13) lacks CSR obligations;
(14) fails to take into account other public international law regimes;
(15) does not allow for amici participation to the extent it should; and most importantly,
(16) leads to 'regulatory chill', ie that host states are afraid to regulate to combat global issues, such as environmental, climate change, and human rights.

ISDS and IIAs could be reformed to better respond to the criticism (much of which has great merit). For example, reforms could include:

(1) narrower definitions of investor and investment;
(2) investor obligations;
(3) outlining measures under the FET clause;
(4) clarifying the MFN clause;
(5) broader global policy objectives in the preambular language;
(6) an explicit right to regulate (tied to sustainable development and the Paris Agreement);
(7) pre-establishment assessments;
(8) increased transparency;
(9) increased amici participation;
(10) establishing an appeals mechanism;

[41] Hobér and Dahlquist (n 36) 9 ('During the last 15–20 years there has been a virtual explosion of investment arbitrations.').

(11) establishing an investment court system;
(12) allowing for regime interaction;
(13) allowing for counterclaims (including for environmental and human rights violations); and
(14) CSR obligations.

B. ECT Modernisation

The ECT was questioned when Russia withdrew in 2009. This goes to the very root of the ECT, which was to bridge East-West in the aftermath of the Cold War. The Energy Charter Conference had to adapt to the new reality and amend its practices quickly. From 2010 the Energy Charter Conference adopted the road map for modernisation and the 'geographical expansion'.[42] In 2015 the new International Energy Charter was adopted as a 'further political declaration aimed at updating the European Energy Charter'.[43] Kaj Hobér has rightly noted:

> The International Energy Charter reflects global modern energy challenges and identifies common principles as well as areas of international co-operation in the energy field for the twenty-first century. The growing interest in, and importance of, international energy issues is reflected in the fact that more than ninety States are now involved in the so-called Energy Charter Process.[44]

Some years later, in 2017, the decision to modernise the ECT was made.[45] In 2018 a list of topics (25) was approved for modernisation discussions.[46] In November 2019, the Energy Charter Conference established the Modernisation Group to negotiate the modernisation.[47]

In the Modernisation Group, 15 negotiation rounds took place between July 2020 and June 2022.[48] EC had the strongest call for reform and made it clear

[42] Decision of the Energy Charter Conference, 'Road Map for the Modernisation of the Energy Charter Process' (24 November 2017), www.energycharter.org/fileadmin/DocumentsMedia/News/20101124-Energy_Charter_Process_Modernisation_Road_Map.pdf.

[43] Hobér (n 14) 5.

[44] ibid.

[45] Decision of the Energy Charter Conference, 'Modernisation of the Energy Charter Treaty' (28 November 2017), www.energycharter.org/fileadmin/DocumentsMedia/CCDECS/2017/CCDEC201723.pdf. For a good overview of the ECT Modernization perspectives, see the Kluwer Arbitration Blog's 'ECT Modernisation Perspectives' work, at arbitrationblog.kluwerarbitration.com/category/ect-modernisation/. See eg E Shirlow and L Abrahams, 'ECT Modernisation Perspectives: An Introduction' (*Kluwer Arbitration Blog*, 20 July 2020) arbitrationblog.kluwerarbitration.com/2020/07/20/ect-modernisation-perspectives-an-introduction/.

[46] Energy Charter Secretariat, 'Approved Topics for the Modernisation of the Energy Charter Treaty' (29 November 2018), www.energycharter.org/media/news/article/approved-topics-for-the-modernisation-of-the-energy-charter-treaty/.

[47] Decision of the Energy Charter Conference, 'Modernisation of the Energy Charter Treaty' (6 November 2019), www.energycharter.org/fileadmin/DocumentsMedia/CCDECS/2019/CCDEC201910.pdf.

[48] Decision of the Energy Charter Conference, (24 June 2022) www.energycharter.org/fileadmin/DocumentsMedia/CCDECS/2022/CCDEC202210.pdf.

early on that '[o]ne of the objectives of this reform is to align the ECT with the Paris Agreement and the objectives of the Green Deal'.[49] An agreement in principle (AIP) was presented on 24 June 2022.[50] However, the voting was postponed.[51] At that time, the EC was in favour of the AIP.[52]

That being so, France, Germany, Poland, Italy and the Netherlands withdrew from the ECT despite EC advocating in favour of adopting the modernised ECT. One year later, on 7 July 2023, the EC announced its decision on proposing the withdrawal of the EU and Euratom from the ECT.[53] This was as a result of the withdrawing states blocking the vote in favour of ECT 2.0. During the withdrawal phase, the EC suggests entering into an inter se agreement between EU Member States on ISDS and with respect to the sunset clause.[54]

On 11 July 2023, the ECT Secretary-General, Guy Lentz, urged EU Member States to vote in favour of the ECT 2.0.[55] In a press release he stated, among other things:

> A solid and reliable legal environment is a prerequisite for mobilising much-needed private sector investments in clean energy sources. In this context, adopting the modernised ECT text could play a pivotal role in de-risking EU investments while allowing countries to reach their energy transition objectives. In particular, small and medium-sized enterprises in renewable electricity generation and the energy efficiency sector would have gained the most since they are key to achieving the energy transition and rely on the investment protection the ECT offers.[56]

[49] www.energycharter.org/fileadmin/DocumentsMedia/CCDECS/2019/CCDEC201908.pdf. See also www.europarl.europa.eu/doceo/document/P-9-2020-005555-ASW_EN.pdf.

[50] Energy Charter Secretariat, 'Agreement in Principle on the Modernisation of the Energy Charter Treaty' (24 June 2022), www.bilaterals.org/IMG/pdf/reformed_ect_text.pdf.

[51] See L Bohmer, 'European Commission to present concrete legal proposals for a coordinated withdrawal from the Energy Charter Treaty in the coming days' (*IAreporter*, 5 July 2023), www.iareporter.com/articles/european-commission-to-present-concrete-legal-proposals-for-a-coordinated-withdrawal-from-the-energy-charter-treaty-in-the-coming-days/.

[52] See L Bohmer, 'European Commission seeks Postponement of Tomorrow's Vote on Modernised ECT, as EU Member States Disagree on Proper Approach' (*IAreporter*, 21 November 2023), www.iareporter.com/articles/european-commission-seeks-postponement-of-tomorrows-vote-on-modernised-ect-as-eu-member-states-disagree-on-proper-approach/.

[53] European Commission, 'European Commission proposes a coordinated EU withdrawal from the Energy Charter Treaty' (n 12) and Bohmer (n 12).

[54] See J Tropper, 'Withdrawing from the Energy Charter Treaty: The End is (not) Near' (Kluwer Arbitration Blog, 4 November 2022), arbitrationblog.kluwerarbitration.com/2022/11/04/withdrawing-from-the-energy-charter-treaty-the-end-is-not-near/; Bohmer (n 12); J Tropper, 'An inter se Modification of the ECT to Exclude Intra-EU Arbitration – How Can It Work?' (*Kluwer Arbitration Blog*, 19 June 2023), arbitrationblog.kluwerarbitration.com/2023/06/19/an-inter-se-modification-of-the-ect-to-exclude-intra-eu-arbitration-how-can-it-work/; F Simon, 'Brussels calls for pause in ECT reform talks after losing key EU vote' (*euractiv.com*, 21 November 2022) www.euractiv.com/section/energy/news/brussels-calls-for-pause-in-ect-reform-talks-after-losing-key-eu-vote/.

[55] G Lentz, 'Statement by the Secretary General of the Energy Charter Secretariat on the draft Council Decision proposing the withdrawal of the European Union from the Energy Charter Treaty' (11 July 2023), www.energycharter.org/media/news/article/statement-by-the-secretary-general-of-the-energy-charter-secretariat-on-the-draft-council-decision-p/?tx_news_pi1%5Bcontroller%5D=News&tx_news_pi1%5Baction%5D=detail&cHash=44c59eb08571a57c64875f5eb94512d2.

[56] ibid.

I echo this statement loud and clear. It should be remembered that the EC has claimed that ECT 1.0 is incompatible with EU environmental objectives. Other old generation IIAs may have the same issues.

i. ECT Statistics

Before embarking on questions to consider in the reform work, and before outlining the reform proposals, it will be worthwhile for the readers to consider the actual empirical data. This is especially important considering the massive backlash, which is often rooted less in data and more in subjective feelings and mere speculations.

There are 158 known ISDS cases under the ECT regime (2023). We have often heard that 'ECT protects the fossil fuel industry' or that the ECT is 'incompatible with climate change'.[57] In that light, let us see the types of energy investments that are actually the most arbitrated:[58]

(1) 59 per cent renewable energy
(2) 34 per cent fossil fuels (with most investment disputes dealing with infrastructure, second comes exploitation, and thirdly comes exploration)
(3) 4 per cent N/A
(4) 3 per cent nuclear

Similarly, we have often heard that 'ECT protects multinational corporations'. In light of this, let us actually see what types of claimants mostly pursue ISDS under the ECT regime:[59]

(1) SME (387)
(2) Holdings (223)
(3) Individual investors (60)
(4) Investment funds (21)
(5) Large corporations (10)
(6) Banks (6)

Finally, we have often heard that investors win against states, ie that there is a form of 'investor bias'. In that light, let us see who is actually the most successful by looking at the statistics on the outcome:[60]

(1) In 40 out of 87 final awards the claimants were awarded damages (breach in 45)
(2) 11 out of 158 cases were settled

[57] IISDS (n 23) and Corporate Europe Observatory, 'The fossil fuel industry's secret weapon' (n 23).
[58] Statistics of ECT Cases (1 May 2023), www.energycharter.org/fileadmin/DocumentsMedia/Disputes/20230501_-_Statistics_-_Cases_under_the_Energy_Charter_Treaty.pdf.
[59] ibid.
[60] ibid.

(3) 8 out of 158 cases were discontinued
(4) 3 out of 158 cases were annulled

I think it is fair to say that neither ITA as a regime nor ECT as a part of that regime is rigged in anyone's favour, nor does it protect one type of investor over another. A more accurate description is that there is a level playing field between states and investors and that the biggest beneficiaries of the system are SMEs, particularly in the renewable energy sector. There is a virtue in facts and truth.

ii. Questions to Consider when Reforming the ECT

When discussing reforming the ECT, there are a handful of questions that need to be consulted. These questions are at the heart of any reform, ie whether it complies with the era of sustainable development. The questions to consider before I proceed to highlight the amendments in ECT 2.0 are:

(1) Does ECT 1.0 restrict a country's ability to regulate in order to speed up the green transition in the energy sector?
(2) Does ECT 1.0 privilege and protect the fossil fuel industry?
(3) Does ECT 2.0 restrict a country's ability to regulate in order to speed up the green transition in the energy sector?
(4) Does the ECT 2.0 privilege and protect the fossil fuel industry?

Essentially the questions ask whether the ECT 2.0 is apt for the task to facilitate a green transition. If it does deliver, by how much? Finally, should we go ahead with it? Why? Why not?

iii. ECT 2.0

The ECT 2.0 has led to four major reforms, ie: (1) jurisdictional amendments, (2) investment protection amendments, (3) sustainable development amendments, and (4) procedural amendments.[61]

First, the jurisdictional amendments have, inter alia, seen a narrowing of the definition of investor and investment. Most notably: (a) there is a requirement on the investor of 'substantial business activities' and 'physical presence, employment, turnover generation or payment of taxes' in the host state; (b) with respect to investment, the Salini test is endorsed and there is an explicit exclusion of judicial and administrative decisions; and (c) the 'economic activity in energy sector' now covers hydrogen, anhydrous ammonia, biomass, biogas, and synthetic fuels (in an attempt to incentivise a green transition through promoting and protecting investments in such areas).[62]

[61] See Energy Charter Secretariat (n 50). For a good take on the reforms, see MJ Alarcon, 'ECT Reform: The Final Countdown' (Kluwer Arbitration Blog, 3 August 2022), arbitrationblog.kluwerarbitration.com/2022/08/03/ect-reform-the-final-countdown/.

[62] Energy Charter Secretariat (n 50) 6–11.

Second, the investment protection standards have seen a narrowing, too, as well as some additions. Most notably: (a) an explicit right to regulate has been inserted; (b) the fair and equitable treatment standard now lists the measures and clarifies the concept of legitimate expectations (but does not remove it); (c) the most favoured nation treatment is clarified, ie it does not extend procedurally and does not work to include substantive treatment in comparator treaties; (d) the scope of indirect expropriation has been limited (focusing on measures being 'manifestly excessive'); and (e) the denial of the benefits clause has been amended so that it can be invoked after arbitration has been requested.[63]

Third, several sustainability amendments have been inserted explicitly to reflect the sustainable development era and a push towards new generation IIAs. Moreover, such language reaffirms the right to regulate in order to achieve legitimate policy objectives. Most notably: (a) the preambular language has been edited; (b) the right to regulate has been inserted explicitly; (c) a non-regression clause has been inserted (make sure investments are not induced by lowering environmental standards); (d) language imposing climate change obligations have been inserted explicitly (eg referring to states' obligations vis-à-vis the implementation of the Paris Agreement and UNFCCC); (e) language on corporate social responsibility (CSR) has been inserted explicitly (as an obligation of the state); (f) a requirement to implement domestic laws for environmental impact assessment (EIA) in the pre-establishment phase has been inserted; (g) several exceptions to the investment protection standards have been made clearer; (h) a flexibility mechanism has been inserted so that states can unilaterally exclude protection of fossil fuels from the scope of the treaty (with the treaty being applicable to current investments for a ten year phase-out period while excluding new investments); (i) language offering protection for investments also in the economic sector of hydrogen, anhydrous ammonia, biogas, and synthetic fuels (green or at least greener sources of energy); and (j) a public obligation to carry out impact assessments of new energy investments carried out (eg on the effects on population, human health, biodiversity, environment and climate, and cultural heritage).[64]

Finally, there have been several crucial procedural amendments. Most notably: (a) ECT 2.0 excludes ISDS between states in a regional economic integration organisation (REIO), ie excluding intra-EU disputes (albeit some tribunals may nevertheless refuse this for pre-existing investments); (b) language increasing transparency in ISDS; and (c) conciliation and diplomacy between states for their failure to adhere to and comply with the sustainable development aspects of the treaty. In fact, the initial proposal included state-to-state arbitration between states for their failure to comply with the sustainable development obligations. Unfortunately, this was eventually rejected.[65]

[63] Energy Charter Secretariat (n 50) 31–36 and 39–40.
[64] Energy Charter Secretariat (n 50) 3–4, 30, 31, 51–55, 122–24.
[65] Energy Charter Secretariat (n 50) 67–81.

The ultimate question is whether such amendments as mentioned above balance investment promotion and protection with broader environmental goals (most notably climate change). I am of the unequivocal view that it does, and that a treaty of this sort would not only be the greenest IIA, but indeed the greenest treaty world-wide given its practical utility.[66] Had the state-to-state arbitration been included, such development would have indeed been a ground-breaking achievement.

iv. ECT 2.0: if it Enters into Force versus if it does not

The ECT 1.0 does not necessarily restrict a country's ability to regulate in order to speed up the green transition in the energy sector. There are far more cases where the ECT has actually been brought against interferences with renewable energy investments than for the protection of fossil fuels – especially successful ones. That being the case, the ECT 1.0 does indeed protect the fossil fuel industry, by design.[67] It was one of its major aims. If the architects desire otherwise, they can agree to that respect – eg utilising the flexibility mechanism designed in the ECT 2.0.

The ECT 2.0 does not restrict a country's ability to regulate in order to speed up the green transition in the energy sector. Rather, it facilitates such transition, especially where the flexibility mechanism is adopted and due to increased policy space to regulate within, including by specific references to environmental obligations. Notwithstanding this, the ECT 2.0, again by design, does protect the fossil fuel industry in case the state in question has attracted such investment and offered it protection. There is nothing inherently wrong with this; it is a sovereign undertaking that can be sanctioned by a rules-based system.

All in all, the ECT 2.0 is indeed apt for the task to facilitate a green transition. It does deliver and may be considered not only the greenest IIA, but the greenest treaty there is.[68] My take is that we should not only be in favour of ECT 2.0 but that we should advocate loudly for it. It can achieve all the original goals of the ECT 1.0 with the additional benefit of adding sustainable development as its main objective. A remarkable achievement indeed!

In short, if ECT 2.0 comes into force, the treaty will: (i) provide for sufficient policy space for states to meet their environmental (and human rights) obligations;

[66] See J Kunstyr and O Svoboda, 'ECT Modernisation Perspectives: "Can the EU Make the ECT the Greenest Investment Treaty of them All?"' (*Kluwer Arbitration Blog*, 25 July 2020) arbitrationblog.kluwerarbitration.com/2020/07/25/ect-modernisation-perspectives-can-the-eu-make-the-ect-the-greenest-investment-treaty-of-them-all/.

[67] See eg U Rusnák, 'ECT Modernisation Perspectives Modernisation of the Energy Charter: The Long Story Told Short' (Kluwer Arbitration Blog, 21 July 2020) arbitrationblog.kluwerarbitration.com/2020/07/21/ect-modernisation-perspectives-modernisation-of-the-energy-charter-the-long-story-told-short/.

[68] See Kunstyr and Svoboda (n 66).

(ii) offer more robust jurisdictional requirements; (iii) tighten the substantive protection standards; (iv) offer no intra-EU ISDS; (v) making ISDS even more transparent (outside intra-EU context of course); and most importantly (vi) offer a flexibility regime potentially excluding fossil fuels after 10 years.

Meanwhile, if the ECT 2.0 does not enter into force, the treaty will: (i) protect fossil fuel investments for the duration of the sunset clause (20 years); (ii) offer protection under the provisions of the ECT 1.0 for the duration of the sunset; and (iii) see being entered into an inter se agreement between EU Member States to exclude both intra-EU Arbitration and the sunset clause (if at all possible, which itself will invite years of litigation and arbitration).[69]

Put simply, the alternative to ECT 2.0 is status quo, ie: (i) ECT 1.0, (ii) other old generation treaties, and (iii) contractual (often non-transparent) arbitration.[70] That can hardly be satisfactory in an era of sustainable development.

V. Concluding Remarks

There is major political risk in energy investments, including renewable energy investments (eg local opposition, regime changes, etc). ECT with ISDS promotes and protects energy investments (mostly green), and thereby facilitates a green transition. ECT manifests as an instrument that is crucial to actually meeting the SDGs by 2030.

Investments in extractive industries, such as oil and gas, but also mining of raw materials needed for renewable energy production, can lead to wealth creation and poverty reduction (economic development rationale). However, if not governed accurately, such investments can cause adverse effects on the environment and human rights. Aspects that are damaging to human, social, economic, and environmental life are global issues about which we should all be concerned.

In order to tackle our global issues we need to strike the right balance, implement the agreed amendments, and monitor its evolution. In order to tackle our global issues, we need effective global governance.

IIAs with ISDS clauses are good global governance tools. The ECT can be highly effective – especially in its modernised form – in order to tackle the challenges head-on in the energy sector.

Withdrawing from IIAs/ECT could hamper the actual ability to meet the SDGs by adversely affecting FDI streams directly and human, social, and environmental indirectly, ancillary, or incidentally (including the ability to meet the targets in the Paris Agreement).

[69] See Tropper (n 54).
[70] See van Aaken (n 39) 166, 171.

ECT 2.0 will facilitate a green transition by promoting, attracting, and protecting energy investments (mostly green) while working in tandem with sustainable development goals.[71] This is what a twenty-first century citizenry expects and demands in an era of sustainable development.[72]

As with any negotiation, give-and-take is key. As Vera Korzun rightly noted, '[t]here are two sides to every story'.[73] In ECT 2.0, the environmentally conscious (including me) arguably received what we bargained for. I agree with the former ECT Secretary-General, Urban Rusnák, in that: 'Undermining the ECT modernisation process through unrealistic requirements might be dangerous as such calls could easily become a self-fulfilling prophecy'.[74] The alternative to ECT and ISDS is not all that compelling; it would mean revisiting inadequate domestic legal frameworks and local courts.[75] Meanwhile, multinational corporations will simply proceed with contractual ISDS but with even more leverage at hand, including freezing clauses and waivers of all sorts (including from execution immunity). SMEs will take the hit for undercutting ITA. I agree with Charles H Brower (when discussing EU's investment court proposal) in that:

> Large multinational investors may not like the EU's vision, but seem unlikely to oppose it, in part because investment treaties do not rank high on their list of institutional concerns, and in part because multinational enterprises have other options in managing disputes with host states. Small- and medium-size investors might oppose the EU's proposal for an investment court, but lack the political capital to influence treaty negotiations.[76]

In addition, the sudden withdrawing from ECT can have unintended consequences for the Global South and developing world. They may be stuck with only large multinational investors with increased leverage.

As if that was not enough, the great paradox is that withdrawal from the ECT triggers the sunset clause (ie ECT 1.0) and status quo IIA 1.0 for an additional 21 years in total. There is approximately 2.15 trillion euros in fossil fuel assets that

[71] K Beckman, 'Interview: A new Energy Charter Treaty as a complement to the Paris Agreement' borderlex.net/2020/06/18/interview-a-new-energy-charter-treaty-as-a-complement-to-the-paris-agreement-on-climate-change/.

[72] See Y Dautaj and E Shirlow, 'ECT Modernisation Perspectives: An Update' (Kluwer Arbitration Blog, 9 August 2021) arbitrationblog.kluwerarbitration.com/2021/08/05/ect-modernisation-perspectives-an-update/. See also U Rusnák, 'Comment: Quo Vadis Energy Charter Treaty?' (12 April 2021), www.energycharter.org/media/news/article/comment-quo-vadis-energy-charter-treaty/?tx_news_pi1%5Bcontroller%5D=News&tx_news_pi1%255%E2%80%A6%201/3%20Comment:%20Quo%20Vadis%20Energy%20Charter%20Treaty? and Rusnák (n 67).

[73] Korzun (n 10).

[74] Rusnák (n 72).

[75] See eg J McGlaughlin, 'ECT Modernisation Perspectives: Big Shoes to Fill? Governing Foreign Energy Investments in an Energy Charter Treaty Lacuna' (*Kluwer Arbitration Blog*, 9 May 2023), arbitrationblog.kluwerarbitration.com/2023/05/09/ect-modernisation-perspectives-big-shoes-to-fill-governing-foreign-energy-investments-in-an-energy-charter-treaty-lacuna/.

[76] CH Brower, 'Politics, Reason, and the Trajectory of Investor-State Dispute Settlement' (2017) 49 *Loy U. Chi. L. J.* 271, 295.

can be stranded by 2050 if not phased-out properly and approximately 345 billion euros protected by the ECT.[77] Sure, there will likely be an inter se agreement to avoid the sunset clause between agreeing states, but it is not clear to what extent this will be effective (ie, how many participants it will have and whether ISDS tribunals would accept the agreement pursuant to Article 31 VCLT).[78]

Finally, since 2015 the ECT has seen a substantial interest in facing global modern energy challenges through cooperation in the energy field.[79] While EU Member States may leave, other states may join. Thus, '[w]ith countries from Africa and Asia joining, the ECT is turning into a global charter'.[80] Resultantly, the EU bloc may be an isolated and non-influential stakeholder in global energy diplomacy and governance. What a total and unintended disaster that would be.

[77] van Aaken (n 39) 166, 169 and B-J Verbeek, 'The Modernization of the Energy Charter Treaty: Fulfilled or Broken Promises?' (2023) 8(1) *Business and Human Rights Journal.*

[78] Tropper (n 54).

[79] Hobér (n 14) 5.

[80] Alarcon (n 61).

4

The Investment-Protection Status of Fossil Fuel-Related Investments in the Energy Charter Regime

MARTIN JARRETT

I. Introduction

A. Background: The Zombification of the Energy Charter Treaty

The substance of international investment law is made up of thousands of treaties. Most, however, have never and may never come to life, in the sense that an investor will take a claim under them. By contrast, two investment treaties have had vibrant lives throughout their existence: the Energy Charter Treaty (ECT)[1] and the North American Free Trade Agreement (NAFTA).[2] The vibrancy of the latter, however, is waning. In recent years, its provisions on investment-protection were neutered by a renegotiation that effectively makes claims, one, by Canadian investors and, two, against Canada near impossible,[3] and further limits the possibility for American investors and Mexican investors to sue Mexico and the United States, respectively.[4]

Until recently, the ECT looked to be going in the opposite direction. It was set to get a new lease on life through the 'ECT modernisation process'.[5] This was

[1] 1994 The Energy Charter Treaty, 2080 UNTS 100 (ECT 1.0).

[2] 1994 North American Free Trade Agreement, 32 ILM 296.

[3] In respect of investments made before NAFTA 2.0 took effect, claims can be taken, one, by Canadian investors and, two, against Canada for a three-year period (1 July 2023), see K Nasir Gore and E Shirlow, 'The USMCA/CUSMA/T-MEC's Entry into Force: Introducing a New Era in Regional ISDS with NAFTA 2.0' (*Kluwer Arbitration Blog*, 22 June 2020) arbitrationblog.kluwerarbitration.com/2020/06/22/the-usmca-cusma-t-mecs-entry-into-force-introducing-a-new-era-in-regional-isds-with-nafta-2-0/.

[4] C-E Côté and H Ali, 'The USMCA and Investment: A New North American Approach?' in G Gagné and M Rioux (eds), *NAFTA 2.0: From the first NAFTA to the United States-Mexico-Canada Agreement* (Springer, 2022) 90–92.

[5] For an overview of the modernisation process, see U Rusnák, 'ECT Modernisation Perspectives: Modernisation of the Energy Charter: The Long Story Told Short' (*Kluwer Arbitration Blog*, 21 July 2020) arbitrationblog.kluwerarbitration.com/2020/07/21/ect-modernisation-perspectives-modernisation-of-the-energy-charter-the-long-story-told-short/.

more than cosmetic surgery. The ECT was going to receive some new parts and have some old parts removed, all to make it ready to work in an era where addressing climate change is a top priority.[6] The negotiators worked on the details over many years. After all of their differences were resolved, an in-principle agreement emerged in June 2022.[7] A signing ceremony was set for November 2022.[8]

But in July 2022, the voices of the anti-ISDS camp began to chant that 'ECT 2.0'[9] was a failure.[10] Most particularly, they complained about the investment-protection benefits that fossil fuel-related investments would receive under it.[11] Governments listened: Austria,[12] Belgium,[13] France,[14] Germany,[15] Luxembourg,[16] the Netherlands,[17] Poland,[18] Slovenia,[19] and Spain[20] have indicated that they will

[6] See generally J Kunstyr and O Svoboda, 'ECT Modernisation Perspectives: "Can the EU Make the ECT the Greenest Investment Treaty of them All?"' (*Kluwer Arbitration Blog*, 25 July 2020) arbitrationblog.kluwerarbitration.com/2020/07/25/ect-modernisation-perspectives-can-the-eu-make-the-ect-the-greenest-investment-treaty-of-them-all/.

[7] See European Commission, 'Agreement in principle reached on Modernised Energy Charter Treaty' (*Trade – News*, 24 June 2022) policy.trade.ec.europa.eu/news/agreement-principle-reached-modernised-energy-charter-treaty-2022-06-24_en.

[8] International Energy Charter, 'Finalisation of the negotiations on the Modernisation of the Energy Charter Treaty' (*Modernisation of the Treaty*, 24 June 2022) www.energychartertreaty.org/modernisation-of-the-treaty/.

[9] 2022 Agreement in Principle on the Modernisation of the Energy Charter Treaty, www.bilaterals.org/IMG/pdf/reformed_ect_text.pdf (ECT 2.0).

[10] See eg T Kofler and N Jongerius, 'Greta Thunberg's arrest shows why we must abolish the Energy Charter Treaty' (*openDemocracy*, 23 Jan 2023) www.opendemocracy.net/en/oureconomy/greta-thunberg-energy-charter-treaty-lutzerath/; and E Beament, 'Abandon the Energy Charter Treaty' (*Ecologist*, 22 November 2022) theecologist.org/2022/nov/22/abandon-energy-charter-treaty.

[11] See generally L Parshley, 'The secretive legal weapon that fossil fuel interests use against climate-conscious countries' (*Grist*, 17 Jan 2023) grist.org/international/investor-state-dispute-settlements-keystone-pipeline/.

[12] N Kurmayer, 'Austria mulls withdrawing from Energy Charter Treaty' (*EURACTIV*, 21 November 2022) www.euractiv.com/section/politics/news/austria-mulls-withdrawing-from-energy-charter-treaty/.

[13] A-S Gayet, 'Belgian environment minister supports withdrawal from Energy Charter Treaty' (*EURACTIV*, 25 October 2022) www.euractiv.com/section/energy-environment/news/belgian-energy-minister-supports-withdraw-from-energy-charter-treaty/.

[14] D Basso and P Messad, 'France to withdraw from the Energy Charter Treaty' (*EURACTIV*, 21 October 2022) www.euractiv.com/section/energy-environment/news/la-france-va-se-retirer-du-traite-sur-la-charte-de-lenergie-annonce-emmanuel-macron/.

[15] R More, 'German cabinet approves exit from Energy Charter Treaty' (*Reuters*, 30 November 2022) www.reuters.com/business/energy/german-cabinet-approves-exit-energy-charter-treaty-2022-11-30/.

[16] F Simon, 'Another blow for Energy Charter Treaty as Luxembourg announces exit' (*EURACTIV*, 18 November 2022) www.euractiv.com/section/energy/news/another-blow-for-energy-charter-treaty-as-luxembourg-announces-exit/.

[17] K Mathiesen, 'The Netherlands to leave embattled Energy Charter Treaty' (*POLITICO PRO*, 18 October 2022) www.politico.eu/article/netherlands-leave-embattled-energy-charter-treaty-rob-jetten/.

[18] F Simon, 'Poland drafts law to "terminate" controversial Energy Charter Treaty' (*EURACTIV*, 2 September 2022) www.euractiv.com/section/energy/news/poland-drafts-law-to-terminate-controversial-energy-charter-treaty/.

[19] M Slana, 'Slovenia withdraws from Energy Charter Treaty' (*EURACTIV*, 17 November 2022) www.euractiv.com/section/politics/news/slovenia-withdraws-from-energy-charter-treaty.

[20] J Albisu, 'Spain confirms intention to withdraw from Energy Charter Treaty' (*EURACTIV*, 14 October 2022) www.euractiv.com/section/energy/news/spain-confirms-intention-to-withdraw-from-energy-charter-treaty/.

not sign ECT 2.0 and will also withdraw from 'ECT 1.0' (the current in-force version of the ECT). Indeed, at the time of writing, France, Germany, and Poland had acted on these statements of intent by submitting their instruments of withdrawal.[21] It should be expected that more states will follow. In February 2023, the European Commission indicated[22] in a non-paper that 'option 1 [was] the most adequate option' and it entailed that 'the EU, Euratom and Member States would engage in a parallel process of withdrawal from the ECT'.[23] For future reference, and the sake of simplicity, these states and other states that join them in withdrawing from ECT 1.0 are referred to as 'Withdrawing States'. Their withdrawals will not terminate ECT 1.0. Even if the European Union, Euratom,[24] and the Member States[25] withdraw, the ECT will still have 26 contracting parties.[26] These parties have an upcoming choice: either stay bound to ECT 1.0, withdraw from it, or sign up to ECT 2.0.

B. The Research Question

How should these parties exercise that choice if their goal is to reduce the investment-protection status of fossil fuel-related investments? This is the central research question of this contribution. The core finding is that Withdrawing States will likely offer a higher level of investment-protection status for fossil fuel-related investments compared to taking the option of signing up to ECT 2.0.

In coming to that finding, section II starts by explaining the legal situation that the Withdrawing States will find themselves in with respect to fossil fuel-related investments after they withdraw. As explained there, the Withstanding States cannot escape their investment-protection obligations towards fossil fuel-related

[21] 'Written notifications of withdrawal from the Energy Charter Treaty' (*International Energy Charter*, undated) www.energychartertreaty.org/details/article/written-notifications-of-withdrawal-from-the-energy-charter-treaty/.

[22] This course of action has not yet been endorsed as an official policy, see 'Non-paper from the European Commission: Next steps as regards the EU, Euratom and Member States' membership in the Energy Charter Treaty' (*EURACTIV*, 8 February 2023) www.euractiv.com/wp-content/uploads/sites/2/2023/02/Non-paper_ECT_nextsteps.pdf.

[23] ibid.

[24] Note that the European Union and Euratom are not one entity, but two separate international organisations, meaning that they are two separate contracting parties to ECT 1.0. This is reflected in the fact that they each submitted two separate instruments of accession to become contracting parties to ECT 1.0, see Council and Commission, 'Council and Commission Decision of 23 September 1997 on the conclusion, by the European Communities, of the Energy Charter Treaty and the Energy Charter Protocol on energy efficiency and related environmental aspects', Article 2.

[25] Not all Member States will withdraw because Italy has already withdrawn, see further 'Italy' (*International Energy Charter*, undated) www.energycharter.org/who-we-are/members-observers/countries/italy/.

[26] At the time of writing, the treaty had 54 contracting parties, see International Energy Charter, 'The Energy Charter Treaty' (*International Energy Charter*, 18 February 2019) www.energycharter.org/process/energy-charter-treaty-1994/energy-charter-treaty/. Considering that the European Union, Euratom, and the Member States (excluding Italy) make up 28 of those contracting parties, this explains the remaining figure of 26 contracting parties.

investments by simply withdrawing. On account of this, section II(A) then explores the legality of the option that Withdrawing States might pursue in order to escape their ongoing obligations under ECT 1.0, specifically concluding an inter se agreement among themselves. This analysis shows that this option would probably be legal, but through that thorough analysis, it is explained how this victory could become a pyrrhic one as regards the Withdrawing States' goal of eliminating their potential international responsibility towards fossil fuel-related investments under ECT 1.0 (section II(C)). Would the Withdrawing States be better served by signing up to ECT 2.0? Answering this question is the business of section III. It begins by examining the investment-protection status of fossil fuel-related investments under ECT 2.0. This examination reveals that in comparison to ECT 1.0, this status is much reduced under ECT 2.0. But if reducing the investment-protection status of fossil fuel-related investments is the goal, then ECT 2.0 contains some latent defects. In the last part of section III, these imperfections are highlighted and some suggestions are put forward on how they might be fixed. Section IV contains the conclusion.

II. Withdrawal from the Energy Charter Treaty

As previously noted, the Withdrawing States are dissatisfied with the investment-protection status that fossil fuel-related investments receive under ECT 1.0 and believe that ECT 2.0 does not go far enough in reducing this status.[27] Whether they are right is ultimately a political question, which will not be commented on, but it can be said that their legal point (that fossil fuel-related investments have investment-protection status under ECT 1.0) is correct. Legally speaking this means that fossil fuel-related investments are 'investments' under ECT 1.0. As such, they benefit from the investment-protection standards in ECT 1.0, including the obligations for contracting parties to treat such investments fairly and equitably[28] and not to expropriate them (unless compensation is paid).[29] As with most investment treaties, ECT 1.0 gives investors an option to sue a contracting party if that party has (allegedly) breached one of these investment-protection standards.[30] The theory is that with this possibility to sue contracting parties, which are mostly states, investors owning fossil fuel-related investments have the potential to stop governments taking actions targeted towards tackling climate change.[31]

[27] N Schmidt, 'Energy Charter Treaty begins to unravel as EU states exit – but risks remain' (*Investigate Europe*, 16 November 2022) www.investigate-europe.eu/en/2022/energy-charter-treaty-begins-to-unravel-as-eu-states-exit-but-risks-remain/.

[28] ECT 1.0 (n 1), Article 10(1).

[29] ibid Article 13.

[30] ibid Article 26.

[31] M Dietrich Brauch, 'The Agreement in Principle on ECT "Modernization": A Botched Reform Attempt that Undermines Climate Action' (*Kluwer Arbitration Blog*, 17 October 2022) arbitrationblog.

Given that that potential is real, as illustrated by (now-abandoned) claims that certain investors took against the Netherlands in respect of its coal phase-out plan,[32] what options are there to extinguish it? There are three: (i) amendment of the definition of 'investment' in ECT 1.0 to exclude fossil fuel–related investments from its scope; (ii) termination of ECT 1.0 (and not sign up to ECT 2.0); and (iii) withdrawing from ECT 1.0. As regards the first option, it is the one more or less adopted in ECT 2.0, as detailed in section III below. As regards the second option, it is currently off the table because there is a lack of political will for it,[33] although some voices have expressed the view that the latest withdrawals might have a domino effect that could trigger an eventual termination of ECT 1.0.[34] This brings us to the third option of withdrawing. Whereas a termination has the legal effect of essentially killing ECT 1.0 in its entirety, withdrawal has a more limited effect:

> ARTICLE 47 – WITHDRAWAL
>
> *(1)* At any time after five years from the date on which this Treaty has entered into force for a Contracting Party, that Contracting Party may give written notification to the Depository of its withdrawal from the Treaty.
>
> …
>
> *(3)* The provisions of this Treaty shall continue to apply to Investments made in the Area of a Contracting Party by Investors of other Contracting Parties or in the Area of other Contracting Parties by Investors of that Contracting Party as of the date when that Contracting Party's withdrawal from the Treaty takes effect for a period of 20 years from such date.

Accordingly, if a state withdraws from ECT 1.0, future investments will not have investment-protection status, whereas existing investments receive another 20 years of protection. Concretely, for existing fossil fuel-related investments, their owners can continue to sue Withdrawing States for another 20 years after they have withdrawn. If it were the case that there were few existing fossil fuel-related investments in the Withdrawing States and many were soon to be developed, then

kluwerarbitration.com/2022/10/17/the-agreement-in-principle-on-ect-modernization-a-botched-reform-attempt-that-undermines-climate-action/.

[32] For a summary of these claims, see S Putter, 'The Netherlands Coal Phase-Out and the Resulting (RWE and Uniper) ICSID Arbitrations' (*Kluwer Arbitration Blog*, 24 August 2021) arbitrationblog.kluwerarbitration.com/2021/08/24/the-netherlands-coal-phase-out-and-the-resulting-rwe-and-uniper-icsid-arbitrations/.

[33] At the time of writing, large economies that are contracting states to the ECT have indicated they will not terminate it, see D Carrington, 'UK must quit climate-harming energy charter treaty, experts say' *The Guardian* (10 February 2023) www.theguardian.com/environment/2023/feb/10/uk-must-quit-climate-harming-energy-charter-treaty-experts-say. Switzerland has been even clearer in saying that it will not withdraw, see J Lo, 'Switzerland says won't follow EU out of beleaguered Energy Charter Treaty' (*EURACTIV*, 10 February 2023) www.euractiv.com/section/energy/news/switzerland-says-wont-follow-eu-out-of-beleaguered-energy-charter-treaty/.

[34] E Beament, 'UK urged to quit treaty that "puts fossil fuel interests before climate action"' *The Standard* (21 November 2022) www.standard.co.uk/business/business-news/uk-urged-to-quit-treaty-that-puts-fossil-fuel-interests-before-climate-action-b1041425.html ('This proves that, on the mainland at least, political will is finally turning against one of the biggest obstructions to the energy transition that exists today.').

withdrawing would make good legal sense. But the opposite is true:[35] new fossil fuel-related investments are unlikely to be developed and the contribution of fossil fuel to the energy mix in future will probably decrease.[36]

This outcome has not been lost on the Withdrawing States. Accordingly, they have mooted that they could pursue an option to (partially) counter the effect of Article 47 of ECT 1.0, specifically by an inter se agreement between them.[37]

A. An Inter Se Agreement between the Withdrawing States

An inter se agreement is an agreement between a select number of treaty parties to a multilateral treaty to amend or terminate such treaty as between themselves, as opposed to all treaty parties.[38] The legal effect of this agreement would be that investors owning fossil fuel-related investments from a Withdrawing State would not have the protection of ECT 1.0 in other Withdrawing States.[39] The extent of this legal effect depends on the number of Withdrawing States: the higher the number, the greater its legal effect, and vice versa. In any case, this plan to conclude an inter se agreement gives rise to some interesting questions relating to its legality, which will be explored now.

Inter se agreements are regulated by the Vienna Convention on the Law of Treaties (VCLT).[40] The relevant provision stipulates:

> Article 41 – Agreements to modify multilateral treaties between certain of the parties only
>
> 1. Two or more of the parties to a multilateral treaty may conclude an agreement to modify the treaty as between themselves alone if:
>   (a) the possibility of such a modification is provided for by the treaty; or
>   (b) the modification in question is not prohibited by the treaty and:
>   (i) does not affect the enjoyment by the other parties of their rights under the treaty or the performance of their obligations;
>   (ii) does not relate to a provision, derogation from which is incompatible with the effective execution of the object and purpose of the treaty as a whole.

[35] According to research conducted by Investigate Europe, at least EUR 344.6 billion of fossil fuel-related investments have 'investment status' under ECT 1.0 in Europe, see N Schmidt, 'Energy Charter Treaty begins to unravel as EU states exit – but risks remain' (*Investigate Europe*, 16 November 2022) www.investigate-europe.eu/en/2022/energy-charter-treaty-begins-to-unravel-as-eu-states-exit-but-risks-remain/.

[36] See McKinsey & Company, 'Global Energy Perspective 2022' (*McKinsey & Company*, April 2022) www.mckinsey.com/industries/oil-and-gas/our-insights/global-energy-perspective-2022.

[37] See eg ClientEarth, 'EU rejection of reformed Energy Charter Treaty "historic moment" for climate action' (*ClientEarth*, 21 November 2022); and M Dietrich Brauch, 'Should the European Union Fix, Leave or Kill the Energy Charter Treaty?' (*Columbia Center on Sustainable Investment*, 9 February 2021) ccsi.columbia.edu/news/should-european-union-fix-leave-or-kill-energy-charter-treaty.

[38] J Mus, 'Conflicts between Treaties in International Law' (1998) 45 *Netherlands International Law Review* 208, 224–25.

[39] See ClientEarth (n 37); and J Tropper and K Wagner, 'Don't Pull the Plug on the Energy Charter Treaty' (*Völkerrechtsblog*, 16 May 2022) voelkerrechtsblog.org/dont-pull-the-plug-on-the-energy-charter-treaty/.

[40] 1969 Vienna Convention on the Law of Treaties, 1155 UNTS 331 (VCLT).

Because ECT 1.0 does not contain provisions that permit inter se agreements, the default rules in sub-section (b) are applicable. For sub-section (b) to apply, three requirements have to be met, the first of which is that inter se agreements are not prohibited under ECT 1.0. In this regard, Article 16 of ECT 1.0 is relevant,[41] and it reads as follows:

> ARTICLE 16 – RELATION TO OTHER AGREEMENTS
>
> Where two or more Contracting Parties have entered into a prior international agreement, or enter into a subsequent international agreement, whose terms in either case concern the subject matter of Part III or V of this Treaty,
>
> (1) nothing in Part III or V of this Treaty shall be construed to derogate from any provision of such terms of the other agreement or from any right to dispute resolution with respect thereto under that agreement; and
>
> (2) nothing in such terms of the other agreement shall be construed to derogate from any provision of Part III or V of this Treaty or from any right to dispute resolution with respect thereto under this Treaty,
>
> where any such provision is more favourable to the Investor or Investment.

These stipulations effectively prohibit inter se agreements that negatively impact on investors' treaty-advantages that are found in Part III or Part V.[42] As the provision being modified (Article 47) is found in Part VIII, this prohibition is not applicable. Considering that Article 47 seeks to preserve investors' treaty-advantages under Part III and Part V, this conclusion might appear overly formalistic.[43] But this objection can be met. Perhaps most importantly, an interpretation of Article 16 that would see it spread its wings to any provision in Part VIII would do violence to its wording: it is explicitly restricted to Part III and Part V. Second, Article 47 is functionally different from the provisions of Part III and Part V. While the latter define substantive and procedural treaty-advantages of investors, Article 47 defines the temporal scope of such rights in case of a party's withdrawal. For these reasons, the conclusion stands that the prohibition contained in Article 16 does not apply to Article 47.

The second requirement, which is found in Article 41(1)(b)(i) of the VCLT, prohibits inter se agreements that negatively affect the treaty rights or obligations of the remaining treaty parties. This requirement rarely causes problems[44] – and so it is here. The basic explanation for this conclusion is that this requirement only becomes problematic in respect of treaties that create obligations

[41] See M Burgstaller, 'European Law and Investment Treaties' (2009) 26 *Journal of International Arbitration* 181, 210.

[42] K Hobér, *The Energy Charter Treaty* (Oxford Universitiy Press, 2020) 318.

[43] See J Tropper, 'Withdrawing from the Energy Charter Treaty: The End is (not) Near' (*Kluwer Arbitration Blog*, 4 November 2022).

[44] A Rigaux et al, 'Art.41 1969 Vienna Convention' in O Corten and P Klein (eds), *The Vienna Conventions on the Law of Treaties: A Commentary* (Oxford University Press, 2011) para 31.

of an integral nature.[45] These obligations protect a collective interest of global concern. The paradigm case of a treaty with integral obligations is the Genocide Convention.[46] ECT 1.0 does not relate to a global concern in the nature of preventing genocide. Its obligations are more bilateral in nature, meaning that some parties can renounce their obligations without negatively affecting the obligations of the other remaining treaty parties.[47]

This brings us to the third requirement found in Article 41(1)(b)(ii) of the VCLT, which is that the modification of the relevant provision (Article 47) is compatible with the general purpose of ECT 1.0 considered as a whole. ECT 1.0 does not have a single purpose, but numerous purposes, one of which is the legal protection of investments.[48] As the proposed inter se agreement would reduce the temporal scope of this protection otherwise enjoyed by the investors of the Withdrawing States, it is apparently the case that such modification is incompatible with the purpose of offering legal protection to investments. But there is good reason to doubt this conclusion. The commentary on this provision is that any modification must be assessed with regard to the treaty 'considered as a whole', meaning that modifications of a limited scope are unlikely to be seen as 'incompatible'.[49] This is particularly the case when the treaty is of a reciprocal nature,[50] as ECT 1.0 is; in other words, the change will only negatively affect investors of the Withdrawing States.

B. A Chance for Investors

The conclusion is that an inter se agreement to modify Article 47 of ECT 1.0 between the Withdrawing States would be permissible under Article 41 under VCLT.[51] But, and this point has to be emphasised, this is an issue between the Withdrawing States, not between the Withdrawing States and the investors; in other words, this inter se agreement is effective between the Withdrawing States, but it cannot extend to their investors. The simple reason behind this conclusion is that Article 41 regulates inter se agreements between treaty parties.[52] Investors are not treaty parties. Investors are third parties. Accordingly, the question is whether

[45] K von der Decken, 'Article 41' in O Dörr and K Schmalenbach (eds), *Vienna Convention on the Law of Treaties: A Commentary* (Springer, 2018) 783.

[46] J Pauwelyn, 'A Typology of Multilateral Treaty Obligations: Are WTO Obligations Bilateral or Collective in Nature?' (2003) 14 *European Journal of International Law* 907, 911.

[47] ibid 929.

[48] T Wälde, 'International Investment Under the 1994 Energy Charter Treaty' in T Wälde (ed), *The Energy Charter Treaty: An East-West Gateway for Investment and Trade* (Kluwer, 1996) 252.

[49] Rigaux et al (n 44) para 32.

[50] ibid para 35.

[51] But see Tropper (n 43) and H Huremagić, 'Mission Impossible? Implementing Komstroy and Modifying the Energy Charter Treaty' (*Völkerrechtsblog*, 17 November 2021).

[52] VCLT (n 40) Article 1.

an inter se agreement concerning its parties' reciprocal obligations for the benefit of third parties may change the treaty-advantages deriving from these obligations?

i. Investor Treaty-Advantages in ECT 1.0: Treaty Rights or Derivative Benefits?

The answer to this question depends on the nature of those treaty-advantages, specifically whether they are direct treaty rights that investors hold themselves or derivative treaty-benefits that they enjoy at the discretion of the treaty parties.[53] In the case of the latter, all that would be needed to extinguish these benefits is an Article 41-compliant inter se agreement.[54]

This introduces a key theoretical question in international investment law:[55] do investors have 'direct rights' or 'derivative benefits' under investment treaties? Much scholarship has been produced on this question, but it has not settled on a final answer. The same is true of the arbitral jurisprudence on it.[56] Perhaps because of the deadlock, a third way has emerged.[57] It posits that there is no general rule on this question, but it is rather a matter of looking at the relevant treaty text and asking whether it creates a direct right or a derivative benefit.[58]

Much can be said in favour of this approach. It mimics the approach that is endorsed in the VCLT. That endorsement is found in Article 36. It specifies that the question whether a treaty creates a third-party right depends upon whether the treaty parties intended to create such a right, with any such intention being evidenced primarily in the treaty text, as confirmed in the commentary on this provision.[59] For the sake of strict legal correctness, it should be noted that the VCLT is not formally applicable to the question whether ECT 1.0 creates direct rights or derivative benefits for investors because it only applies to state-state treaty matters. The customary rules of the law of treaties are applicable,[60] but it is assumed that they correspond to the provisions of the VCLT,[61] with some obvious

[53] Note that the investor holds any treaty rights at the discretion of the treaty parties, as opposed to holding them at the discretion of the treaty party that has responsibility for respecting such treaty rights, namely the host state.

[54] See F Lavopa, L Barreiros, and V Bruno, 'How to Kill a BIT and not Die Trying: Legal and Political Challenges of Denouncing or Renegotiating Bilateral Investment Treaties' (2013) 16 *J Int'l Ec L* 869, 888.

[55] A Peters, *Beyond Human Rights: The Legal Status of the Individual in International Law* (Cambridge University Press, 2016) 303.

[56] See ibid 301–306.

[57] T Voon, A Mitchell, and J Munro, 'Parting Ways: The Impact of Mutual Termination of Investment Treaties on Investor Rights' (2014) 9 *ICSID Review* 451, 459 (and the references cited therein).

[58] Peters (n 55) 303.

[59] See P d'Argent, 'Art.36 1969 Vienna Convention' in Corten and Klein (n 44) para 7.

[60] VCLT (n 40) Preamble.

[61] M Fitzmaurice, 'Treaties' in A Peters and Rr Wolfrum (eds), *Max Planck Encyclopedia of Public International Law* (Oxford University Press, February 2021 (last update)) para 20. Although Fitzmaurice expresses some doubts about the customary status of Article 36, other authors have concluded that it has to have customary status, see d'Argent (n 59) para 4; and A Proelss, 'Article 36' in Dörr and Schmalenbach (n 46) 723.

modifications to take account of the fact that they are being applied between investors and states. Because of this similarity, and for the sake of simplicity, VCLT is referred to in the legal analysis below.

ii. Investor Treaty-Advantages as Treaty Rights?

Accordingly, the question is, have the parties to ECT 1.0 created a treaty right in favour of investors in Article 47? There is nothing in the wording of Article 47 that explicitly indicates that this treaty-advantage is properly viewed as a treaty right. Considering that the commentary on Article 36 of the VCLT indicates that third-party rights must be established 'in concreto',[62] this does not bode well for its status as a 'treaty right'. Having said this, the commentary does not insist that it must be explicitly stated that the particular treaty text creates a treaty right, but only that the intention must be clearly evidenced.[63] The difficulty is that what amounts to 'clear evidence' is not elaborated on, although one commentary mentions that if a putative third-party right has a corresponding procedural possibility to enforce it, then it is probably a treaty right.[64] The putative third-party right in Article 47 does not provide for this possibility. In this context it might be thought that via Article 26 of ECT 1.0, which is the provision on investor-state arbitration, investors might be able to enforce any right that they have under Article 47, but only treaty-advantages found in Part III of ECT 1.0 can be enforced with this provision.[65]

Considering that third-party rights should not be found too easily,[66] the conclusion is that Article 47 does not create a treaty right for investors. It is worth noting that even if it did, an investor must still fight another battle to gain the benefit of it, if the Withdrawing States conclude an inter se agreement to nullify Article 47. That battle is proving[67] that the treaty parties intended that this right could only be revoked with the consent of its beneficiaries.[68] If that battle is won, then the effectiveness of the inter se agreement becomes subject to the consent of investors,[69] which they presumably would not give. The main weapon that an investor would deploy to win this battle would be Article 16 of ECT 1.0. Article 16 was previously encountered in section II(A): it effectively prohibits inter se agreements that limit the substantive scope of investors' treaty-advantages found in Part III and Part V.[70] In that spirit, it might be argued that Article 47 is also irrevocable, but such an argument is open to attack on the ground that it extends by stealth the application of Article 16, which is explicitly limited to Part III and

[62] d'Argent (n 59) para 8.
[63] ibid para 7.
[64] Proelss (n 61) 718.
[65] ECT 1.0, Article 26(1).
[66] d'Argent (n 59) para 7.
[67] The burden of proof lies on the third party, see P d'Argent, 'Art. 37 1969 Vienna Convention' in Corten and Klein (n 44) para 11.
[68] VCLT (n 40) Article 37(2).
[69] VCLT (n 40) Article 37(2).
[70] Hobér (n 42) 318.

Part V.[71] Additionally, there is Article 42. It regulates amendments to ECT 1.0. It does not have any saving clause for investor rights under ECT 1.0, but rather indicates that the treaty parties may amend ECT 1.0 as they see fit.

C. A Pyrrhic Victory for Withdrawing States

On account of the analysis above, the Withdrawing States could probably conclude an inter se agreement that modifies Article 47 to eliminate the 20-year investment-protection period for investments existing at the time of their withdrawals. The key word in this conclusion is 'probable'. For practising lawyers who advise investors, what this word actually means is that there is a risk to the investment-protection status of investments that are effectively under their legal supervision. After identifying this risk, they will switch to risk-management mode. Fortunately from their perspective, there is a risk-management tool available to them: changing the ownership structure behind an investment.[72] What this means specifically is transferring the ownership of an investment to a company in a corporate group that has investor status, either under the ECT or another investment treaty.[73] This manoeuvre might look like a gaming of the system of an investment-treaty arbitration, but it is settled doctrine that it does not amount to an abuse of rights,[74] unless it is effected with a view to initiating an investment-treaty claim because of a brewing dispute with the host state.[75] In executing this manoeuvre, one point must be borne in mind: this transfer should be effected before the host state's withdrawal. If it is completed thereafter, there is a chance that an arbitral tribunal would view any transfer of ownership as the 'making of a new investment', thereby meaning that the investment will not have investment-protection status under ECT 1.0.[76]

This is not the only reason for the practical uselessness of withdrawing. Another factor is the small number of Withdrawing States,[77] at the time of writing. This situation could, however, change. If the European Union and its Member States withdraw, a cascading process could begin that leads to the eventual termination of ECT 1.0.[78] Whether that process is likely to eventuate is a political question that

[71] ibid.

[72] K Tienhaara et al, 'Investor-state disputes threaten the global green energy transition' (2022) 376 *Science* 701, 701.

[73] For a comparative analysis of ECT 1.0 against other investment treaties, see generally J Salacuse, 'The Energy Charter and Bilateral Investment Treaty Regimes' in Wälde (n 48) 321.

[74] U Kriebaum, C Schreuer, and R Dolzer, *Principles of International Investment Law*, 3rd edn (Oxford University Press, 2022) 71.

[75] A El Far, *Abuse of Rights in International Arbitration* (Oxford University Press, 2020) para 4.100 (summarising the jurisprudence on this point).

[76] ECT 1.0 (n 1) Article 47(3).

[77] Tropper (n 43).

[78] J Lo, 'European exodus from Energy Charter Treaty raises climate questions' (*Climate Home News*, 25 October 2022) www.climatechangenews.com/2022/10/25/european-exodus-from-energy-charter-treaty-raises-climate-questions/.

cannot be commented upon here. But suppose that ECT 1.0 is terminated. Does that mean that the investments, which currently enjoy investment-protection status under ECT 1.0, lose this status? Potentially not. Behind ECT 1.0 lies dozens of other investment treaties between the contracting parties.[79] As an example, consider Germany, one of the Withdrawing States.[80] It has 19 in-force investment treaties with other contracting parties.[81] If ECT 1.0 is terminated, then these other investment treaties might also be terminated, but noting that this is a separate political decision divorced from the political decision regarding a withdrawal from ECT 1.0, there is no necessary entailment here. The reason for this is that the risk-reward ratio is different when a contracting party compares ECT 1.0 to other bilateral investment treaties. As regards ECT 1.0, a contracting party has potential legal liability towards investors from many states, including capital-exporting states, thereby making the risk value relatively high. As the same state's investors, however, have concentrated their investment activities in a small number of the other contracting parties, that factor makes the reward (of staying in ECT 1.0) value relatively low. These values can change in respect of a particular bilateral investment treaty.[82]

D. The Futility of Withdrawing from ECT 1.0

Drawing together the various strands outlined above, the efforts of the Withdrawing States are unlikely to yield any fruit, in the sense that the current levels of legal protection for existing fossil fuel-related investments will be decreased.[83] Considering that the Withdrawing States could conclude an inter se agreement that prevents their own investors from bringing ECT 1.0-based claims against other Withdrawing States, and such an agreement would probably be legally effective, this conclusion might appear surprising. But the Withdrawing States cannot stop ECT 1.0-based claims from investors from non-Withdrawing States. With a simple manoeuvre of changing the ownership of a fossil fuel-related investment from a company in a Withdrawing State to a company in a

[79] Tienhaara (n 72) 701.

[80] See n 21 above.

[81] UNCTAD, 'Germany' (*Investment Policy Hub*, undated) investmentpolicy.unctad.org/international-investment-agreements/countries/78/germany.

[82] For an example of this kind of strategic thinking, see the comments of Jean-Christophe Füeg (Head of International Energy Affairs, Swiss Federal Office of Energy) on a Swiss withdrawal from ECT 1.0: 'Just as food for thought: Would you think that Swiss investors, who have billions of assets in the EU (much of it in renewables), would appreciate seeing their investors' protection rights waived by a Swiss exit?', see J Lo, 'Switzerland says won't follow EU out of beleaguered Energy Charter Treaty' (*EURACTIV*, 10 February 2023) www.euractiv.com/section/energy/news/switzerland-says-wont-follow-eu-out-of-beleaguered-energy-charter-treaty/.

[83] As explained in section II above, a withdrawal from ECT 1.0 does cancel investment-protection status for future fossil fuel-related investments, but as such investments are unlikely to be made in the future, the real question is the investment-protection status of existing fossil fuel-related investments.

non-Withdrawing State, investors can take advantage of this opening. They then would have the benefit of all of the investment-protection standards in ECT 1.0 for their investments for another 20 years on in the Withdrawing State.

But this does not have to be the case. As discussed in section I, ECT 2.0 has been agreed to in principle. It would replace ECT 1.0 in its entirety; in other words, there is chance for contracting parties to change the degree of legal protection currently offered to fossil fuel-related investments under ECT 1.0 by signing up to ECT 2.0. For those states who take this chance, what changes will they create to the current regime for fossil fuel-related investments? Alternatively, for the Withdrawing States, what are they missing out on?

III. A Comparison with Energy Charter Treaty 2.0

To answer this question, we need to delve into the details of ECT 2.0. The major destination is the definition of 'investment'. In Article 1(6) of ECT 2.0, this definition keeps the same form that it has in ECT 1.0, but its operation is drastically changed by a new annex, specifically Annex NI.

A. A New Definition of 'Investment'

The provisions of Annex NI are lengthy and (apparently) complex, but they ultimately have a simple operation. Essentially, the European Union,[84] the Member States of the European Union[85] (that are contracting parties),[86] Switzerland,[87] and the United Kingdom[88] (the 'New Definition Parties') create new definitions of 'investment'. Each new definition of 'investment' differs between the New Definition Parties,[89] but these differences are in the details. Fundamentally, the New Definition Parties exclude fossil fuel-related investments from 'investment' for the purposes of Part III of ECT 2.0,[90] which is the part containing the investment-protection standards.

To illustrate this point, consider the legal situation of the United Kingdom in respect of fossil fuel-related investments. If ECT 2.0 comes into force and the United Kingdom signs up to it, fossil fuel-related investments within its territory will not be 'investments' for the purposes of the investment-protection standards.

[84] ECT 2.0 (n 9) Annex NI, Section B(1).
[85] ibid.
[86] Includes all Member States, with the exception of Italy.
[87] ECT 2.0 (n 9) Annex NI, Section B(2).
[88] ECT 2.0 (n 9) Annex NI, Section B(3).
[89] Note that the new definition of 'investment' is the same between the European Union and its Member States that are contracting parties, meaning that there is a new definition of 'investment' for each of the European Union (plus the relevant Member States), Switzerland, and the United Kingdom.
[90] ECT (n 9) Annex NI, Section B (para 1).

This exclusion does not only apply in respect of investments from other New Definition Parties, but all contracting parties who sign up to ECT 2.0. This is the substantive scope of application of the new definitions of 'investment'.

Turning to the temporal application of the new definitions, for a fossil fuel-related investment made after 15 August 2023, this exclusion applies immediately – they do not have the benefit of investment-protection standards under ECT 2.0.[91] For a fossil fuel-related investment made before this date, it enjoys another 10 years of benefits under ECT 2.0 from the date that ECT 2.0 comes into force for the relevant New Definition Party (and, in any case, no later than 31 December 2040).[92] Importantly, for those existing fossil fuel-related investments, the legal protection offered by ECT 2.0 is substantively different from that offered under ECT 1.0.[93] Most particularly, the rules on expropriation and fair and equitable treatment, which investors most frequently allege have been breached in investment-treaty arbitrations,[94] are subject to new carve-outs,[95] which effectively offer states more room to regulate without breaching ECT 2.0.

A final point is that other contracting parties, which have not opted to create a new definition of 'investment', may limit the investment-protection status for existing[96] fossil fuel-related investments from New Definition Parties. To date only Japan,[97] Switzerland,[98] and Turkey[99] have taken up this possibility. Accordingly, and by way of example, investments from New Definition Parties in Japan are subject to the new definition of 'investment' that they apply to investments within their territories. For the sake of legal correctness, it is worth noting that Switzerland and Turkey have not excluded fossil fuel-related investments from New Definition Parties from 'investment' where it appears in Part Three, but have rather declined to give their unconditional consent to investor-state arbitrations involving such investments.[100] Practically speaking, this other form of exclusion has the same effect as excluding fossil fuel-related investments from the scope of Part Three in one important respect: they reduce the potential international responsibility that Switzerland and Turkey face under ECT 2.0 in respect of fossil fuel-related investments.

[91] ECT 2.0 (n 9) Annex NI, Section B(1) (European Union and Member States), Section B(2) (Switzerland), and Section B(3) (United Kingdom).

[92] ibid Annex NI, Section C(1), (European Union and Member States), Section C(2) (Switzerland),and Section C(3) (United Kingdom).

[93] See generally M José Alarcon, 'ECT Reform: The Final Countdown' (*Kluwer Arbitration Blog*, 3 August 2022) arbitrationblog.kluwerarbitration.com/2022/08/03/ect-reform-the-final-countdown/.

[94] Kriebaum, Schreuer, and Dolzer (n 74) 186.

[95] For expropriation, see ECT 2.0 (n 9) Article 13(3)–(5). For fair-and-equitable treatment, see ECT 2.0 (n 9) Article 10(2).

[96] Note that this option does not apply in respect of existing fossil fuel-related investments, see ibid Annex NI, Section B(i) & (ii).

[97] ECT 2.0 (n 9) Annex NPT.

[98] ibid Annex IA-NI.

[99] ibid.

[100] ibid Article 26(3)(d).

Let us take stock of all of these legalities. First, in 26 contracting parties,[101] there will be no legal protection for future fossil fuel-related investments and another 10 years' worth of protection for existing fossil fuel-related investments. Second, the substantive scope of the legal protection will be reduced for all investors compared to what is offered under ECT 1.0. Third, in Japan, Switzerland, and Turkey, legal protection for fossil fuel-related investments will be reduced for investors from New Definition Parties. How does all of this compare to the current situation where ECT 1.0 will stay in effect and certain contracting parties will withdraw? Quite badly, if reducing the legal protection for fossil fuel-related investments is the goal,[102] remembering that investors can manoeuvre to stay protected under ECT 1.0 by rearranging the ownership behind their fossil fuel-related investments.[103]

B. Energy Charter Treaty 2.0 and Other Investment Treaties

Another reason why withdrawing from ECT 1.0 is a largely ineffective option is because there are dozens of other investment treaties under which the affected investors can receive basically the same level of legal protection that they receive under ECT 1.0.[104] But is this not also the case in respect of ECT 2.0? Is it not the case that if an investor is negatively affected by changes in ECT 2.0, then it can fall back to other investment treaties and the legal protection offered under them? The short answer is 'no'. The explanation for this answer comprises a couple of planks, the first of which is that Article 16 has been deleted in ECT 2.0. As previously noted in section II(A) above, Article 16 operates to ensure that other investment treaties operate in parallel to ECT 1.0, meaning that an investor could claim under ECT 1.0 or another investment treaty, at its discretion. With Article 16 deleted in ECT 2.0, then comes the second plank that kills off these other investment treaties. It is Article 59 of VCLT and it reads as follows:

> Article 59 – Termination or suspension of the operation of a treaty implied by conclusion of a later treaty

[101] These contracting parties are: Austria, Belgium, Bulgaria, Croatia, Cyprus, Czechia, Denmark, Estonia, European Union, Finland, Greece, Hungary, Ireland, Latvia, Lithuania, Luxembourg, Malta, The Netherlands, Portugal, Romania, Slovakia, Slovenia, Spain, Sweden, Switzerland, and the United Kingdom. Note that France, Germany, and Poland have been excluded from this list because, although they were contracting parties that were New Definition Parties, they have since withdrawn from ECT 1.0, thereby giving rise to the assumption that they will not sign up to ECT 2.0.

[102] See eg a recent opinion piece from two prominent German politicians, Robert Habeck and Katharina Dröge: 'In allen Investitionsschutzabkommen sollte das Recht auf gemeinwohlorientierte Regulierung verstärkt und der Schutz für Investitionen in fossile Energieträger abgeschafft werden.' ('In all investment treaties, the right to regulate in the public interest should be strengthened and protection for fossil fuel-related investments should be reduced'), R Habeck and K Dröge, 'Neue europäische Handelsagenda' (*Die Tageszeitung*, 21 May 2022) taz.de/Internationale-Wirtschaftsverflechtungen/!5853918/.

[103] See section II(C) above.

[104] Salacuse (n 73) 348.

> 1. A treaty shall be considered as terminated if all the parties to it conclude a later treaty relating to the same subject-matter and:
>   (a) it appears from the later treaty or is otherwise established that the parties intended that the matter should be governed by that treaty; or
>   (b) the provisions of the later treaty are so far incompatible with those of the earlier one that the two treaties are not capable of being applied at the same time.

Regarding the first element of Article 59 that the subsequent treaty (ECT 2.0) must have the same subject-matter as the earlier treaty or treaties (the other investment treaties), this is clearly satisfied. Second, Article 59(1)(a) would apply because, by deleting Article 16, the contracting parties have indicated that they do not want the other investment treaties to apply in parallel to ECT 2.0. Accordingly, the outstanding issue of investors having multiple layers of investment-protection would be resolved, if ECT 2.0 became effective.

C. Correcting Some Imperfections with Energy Charter Treaty 2.0

Not only does ECT 2.0 significantly reduce the scope of investment-protection for fossil fuel-related investments compared to staying in or withdrawing from ECT 1.0, it also ensures that investors cannot escape this new regime by claiming investment-protection under other investment treaties.

But these changes do not go far enough for the critics of the ECT,[105] who have pushed for the withdrawals from ECT 1.0 and put ECT 2.0 on ice for the time being. Whether this claim that ECT 2.0 'does not go far enough' is right or wrong is a political matter, and, as such, it will not be commented on. But it is considered that some changes might be made to ECT 2.0. In putting forward these proposed changes, it is acknowledged that drafting a treaty is a negotiation, not a dictation of 'improvements' by one party to the others. For this reason, these proposed changes are focused on repairing some shortcomings in ECT 2.0 as regards the new system that it sets up for fossil fuel-related investments. Because of this orientation, that is, supporting a system that all contracting parties have agreed to in principle, these proposed changes are not born of a political agenda.

i. The Calculation of Compensation in Cases Involving Fossil Fuel-Related Investments

First, there is a problem on the horizon as regards the calculation of compensation in cases involving fossil fuel-related investments for which investment-protection

[105] See eg C Eckes, L Main-Klingst and L Schaugg, 'Why a coordinated withdrawal from the Energy Charter Treaty is inevitable' (*EURACTIV*, 24 January 2023) www.euractiv.com/section/energy/opinion/why-a-coordinated-withdrawal-from-the-energy-charter-treaty-is-inevitable/.

will end. As an example, imagine that the investment in question is a coal-fired power station. It is located in a state that has limited the scope of the definition of 'investment'. In 2033, it will no longer fall within this definition.[106] The relevant breach occurs in 2030. When it comes time to calculate the compensation for this breach, the investor seeks an amount based on the cash-flow value of the investment, noting that its operating life runs until 2050. The state retorts that any compensation based on cash-flow value must be capped at 2033. It reasons that after 2033, the investment is not protected under ECT 2.0, meaning that, if the breach had occurred in this period, the state would not have to pay compensation. Considering this, it is irrational that the state should pay compensation with reference to a date beyond 2033.

This argument of the state makes for good logic, but it is doubtful whether it is doctrinally correct. The applicable customary rules stipulate that full reparation must follow an international wrongful act,[107] which a breach of ECT 2.0 would be.[108] To eliminate this doubt, a clause such as the following might be inserted into ECT 2.0:

> Article X – Calculating Compensation in Cases Involving Certain Fossil Fuel–Related Investments[109]
>
> (1) In this article:
>
> (a) 'Certain Fossil Fuel–Related Investment' means any Investment for which the temporal scope of its status as an Investment has been limited under Annex NI (Section C).
>
> (b) 'Expiration Date' means the date on which a Certain Fossil Fuel–Related Investment loses its status as an Investment for the purposes of Part III.
>
> (2) Article X(3) applies in any adjudicative proceeding initiated by the Investor under Article 26(2) that involves a Certain Fossil Fuel-Related Investment.
>
> (3) If the adjudicative body decides to award cash-flow value-based compensation[110] in adjudicative proceedings where a Contracting Party has breached an obligation under Part III in respect of a Certain Fossil Fuel–Related Investment, then its operating life is capped at its Expiration Date.

These proposed provisions are not treaty-ready text, but rather some foundational text to work from. One point that needs to be discussed is the discretion given to arbitral tribunals regarding the calculation. In keeping with the settled doctrine of international investment law,[111] they can decide whether to use a cash-flow value-based calculation or another method, such as book value. As, however, book value

[106] ECT 2.0 (n 9), Annex NI, Section C(1), (European Union and Member States), Section C(2) (Switzerland),and Section C(3) (United Kingdom).

[107] 2001 Responsibility of States for Internationally Wrongful Acts, Article 31(1).

[108] See ibid Article 2.

[109] This article would be best placed in Part V of ECT 2.0 (n 9).

[110] B Sabahi, *Compensation and Restitution in Investor-State Arbitration: Principles and Practice* (Oxford University Press, 2011) 107–108.

[111] I Marboe, *Calculation of Compensation and Damages in International Investment Law*, 2nd edn (Oxford University Press, 2017) para 7.14.

might far exceed the cash-flow value of a fossil fuel-related investment, contracting parties might seek to limit arbitral tribunals' discretion and exclude book value-based compensation.

ii. Exception for Continued Use of Fossil Fuel-Related Investments

Another proposed change is one for an exception for continued use of a fossil fuel-related investment after an expropriation. The situation in sight here is one where the state waits until a fossil fuel-related investment is no longer protected under ECT 2.0, expropriates it, and then continues to use it, with the result that the investment continues to emit carbon emissions. As an example, again imagine that the investment in question is a coal-fired power station. Its investment-protection status expires in 2033. The day after the expiration date, the state shifts ownership of this investment to a state-owned enterprise and continues to operate it. This continued operation of the investment defeats the purpose of redefining the meaning of 'investment', which was to give the contracting parties the chance to take high carbon-emitting energy sources out of their energy mix,[112] all without the prospect of having to pay compensation under ECT 2.0 (or any other investment treaty that it should replace).[113]

How might an exception be carved out to still give investors protection, with the result that contracting parties will be inclined to behave in the manner described above? The mechanics would not be difficult. The relevant treaty text might read as follows:

Section D[114]

(1) In this section:

(i) 'Certain Fossil Fuel–Related Investment' means any Investment for which the temporal scope of its status as an Investment has been limited under Annex NI (Section C).

(ii) 'Continued Usage' means a situation where a Certain Fossil Fuel–Related Investment is used in a manner that generates carbon emissions that are equal or similar to the carbon emissions that such investment produced before the breach mentioned in Section D(2).

(iii) 'Expiration Date' means the date on which a Certain Fossil Fuel–Related Investment loses its status as an Investment for the purposes of Part III.

(2) The provisions of Section C do not apply if a Contracting Party:

(i) breaches Article 13(1) in respect of a Certain Fossil Fuel–Related Investment; and

(ii) permits the Continued Usage, either itself or through another person, of such investment after its Expiration Date.

[112] 'Public Communication Explaining the Main Changes Contained in the Agreement in Principle' (*International Energy Conference*, 24 June 2022) www.energycharter.org/fileadmin/DocumentsMedia/CCDECS/2022/CCDEC202210.pdf.

[113] See section II(C) above for a discussion of these other treaties.

[114] These provisions would be best placed in ECT 2.0 (n 9) Annex NI.

IV. Conclusion

As with the other suggested amendment to ECT 2.0 outlined in section III(B), this amendment is not treaty-ready text, but it is offered as a foundation to work from. In making that offer, however, a dose of reality needs to be swallowed: these amendments are likely to never to come under consideration. The reason for this likely outcome is that ECT 2.0 will probably never come into force.[115] Those contracting parties that pushed hardest for the significant changes seen in ECT 2.0 (compared to ECT 1.0) are the Withdrawing States. If they withdraw from ECT 1.0, then it is unlikely that other contracting parties will sign up to ECT 2.0. ECT 2.0 is likely to go down as a 'what if' in the history of international investment law.

This contribution has investigated whether this fate is deserved. In undertaking that investigation, the basic question was not whether ECT 2.0 was perfect, but whether 'signing up to it' was a better option compared to the others, which are 'staying in ECT 1.0' or 'withdrawing from ECT 1.0'. Considering that the scopes of application of certain investment-protection standards have been reduced and, in many contracting parties, future fossil fuel-related investments have no protection and existing fossil fuel-related investments have time-limited protection, ECT 2.0 represents a better deal compared to ECT 1.0, if reducing the investment-protection status of these investments is the goal. But how does ECT 2.0 compare to a withdrawal from ECT 1.0?

For any Withdrawing State, it will have no obligations towards future investments, but ECT 2.0 offers the same in respect of fossil fuel-related investments, so this is not a unique benefit. Additionally, this 'benefit' also applies to future clean-energy investments, which is something that cannot help promote the building of such investments. But this is not the major drawback of withdrawing. This major drawback is well known: ECT 1.0 remains effective for another 20 years in respect of existing investments. Practically speaking, this means that existing fossil fuel-related investments in Withdrawing States have the benefit of generous investment-protection standards (compared to ECT 2.0) for another 20 years. The way out of this predicament is through an inter se agreement. Under this agreement, Withdrawing States would agree to eliminate this prolongation of ECT 1.0. It is considered that this agreement would probably be legally valid, but practically ineffective.

Considering all of the above, the conclusion is that if contracting parties wish to reduce the investment-protection status of fossil fuel-related investments, they should sign up to ECT 2.0. What has to be emphasised is that this preference is one that can be made without hesitation. That being the case, the question arises: why are many contracting parties to ECT 1.0 ready to withdraw from it? A comprehensive answer to this question cannot be offered here, but it is suspected

[115] See P Bekker and R Wilson, 'Will Coordinated European Withdrawal be the Death Knell of the Energy Charter Treaty?' (*CMS Law-Now*, 16 February 2023) cms-lawnow.com/en/ealerts/2023/02/will-coordinated-european-withdrawal-be-the-death-knell-of-the-energy-charter-treaty.

that these withdrawals are part of a strategy that would lead to the termination of ECT 1.0. This outcome would eliminate the investment-protection status for fossil fuel-related investments under ECT 1.0, but it might be difficult to realise: all contracting parties have to agree to it.[116]

Apparently, the Withdrawing States are playing roulette: they are betting that their withdrawals will lead to the termination of ECT 1.0. Like any bet, if they lose, there will be a price to pay, specifically the opportunity to reduce the investment-protection status of fossil fuel-related investments via ECT 2.0. Time will tell whether this bet pays out.

[116] VCLT (n 40) Article 54(b). Note that this default rule applies because ECT 1.0 does not contain any provisions for its termination. In this regard, the provisions on amendment of ECT 1.0 do not qualify because the law of treaties draws a distinction between amendment and termination, see P Sands, 'Art.39 1969 Vienna Convention' in Corten and Klein (n 44) para 29.

PART 2

Change Through Investor-State Dispute Settlement

5

Turkey's Energy Charter Treaty Investment Arbitration Map: An Analysis of Arbitral Tribunal Positions on Unmeritorious Applications[1]

CAN EKEN AND VOLKER ROEBEN

I. Introduction

Investment arbitration under the ECT has raised concerns for many state parties, including European Union Member States. As a result, the European Commission has recently called for a coordinated withdrawal by the EU and its Member States from the ECT.[2] Despite this discomfort among some, the Treaty is still widely accepted by states and remains as binding international law. While the Treaty has sometimes been blamed as the reason for states' unsuccessful energy transition towards low-carbon energy, the cases analysed in this chapter show otherwise. There are six cases against Turkey.[3] The arbitrations instituted by investors under the ECT against Turkey provide a case study to test whether the ECT in its current form is providing enough security to states. The chapter finds that the Turkish cases prove a success for the host state since the investors lost all six cases at the jurisdiction or admissibility stage.[4]

[1] Can Eken thanks Nicolas Di Miele, a great undergraduate second-year student in our law school, for his contribution to researching the cases and summarising them for him.

[2] V Djanic, '[UPDATED] EUROPEAN COMMISSION RECOMMENDS COORDINATED EU WITHDRAWAL FROM ENERGY CHARTER TREATY' (*iareporter.com*, 8 February 2023).

[3] The six cases are *Libananco Holdings Co. Limited v Republic of Turkey*, ICSID Case No. ARB/06/8; *Cementownia 'Nowa Huta' S.A. v Republic of Turkey*, ICSID Case No. ARB(AF)/06/2; *Europe Cement Investment & Trade S.A. v Republic of Turkey*, ICSID Case No. ARB(AF)/07/2; *Alapli Elektrik B.V. v Republic of Turkey*, ICSID Case No. ARB/08/13; *Cem Cengiz Uzan v Republic of Turkey*, SCC Case No. V 2014/023; *Nabucco Gas Pipeline International GmbH in Liqu. v Republic of Turkey*, ICSID Case No. ARB/15/26.

[4] In one case, the investor discontinued the proceedings.

Before we delve into the relevant ECT articles and arbitrations, it is important to note why the ECT was created in the first place. Eastern European states were eager to be granted access to Western markets and Western European countries were seeking ways to improve their energy security which led to the December 1990 Dublin Summit of the European Council.[5] These first negotiations in 1990 later led to the ECT.[6] Due to this reciprocal energy need between Eastern and Western European countries, ECT 'was specifically conceived to regulate economic activity (trade and investment) in the energy sector'.[7] Later, the ECT extended outside of Europe. It has currently 53 members.[8] As per the explanation of the ECT's official website, the ECT 'provides a multilateral framework for energy cooperation that is unique under international law'.[9] It 'offers a specialised regime for the regulation of the energy sector'.[10] As these definitions show, the ECT aims to give protection to investors in the energy sector. With this security for investors, energy investments and the energy transition flourish with the network of ECT signatories. Naturally, there have been disputes between states and investors, and the key question is how these are resolved in practice, in particular whether host states have been able to defend arbitrations that do circumvent proper procedural safeguards.

Turkey has defended a large number of arbitrations. This chapter will analyse those six disputes which all arose out of the ECT against Turkey as case studies. These cases present a unique lens through which the approaches that arbitral tribunals have used to distinguish between legitimate and illegitimate arbitrations can be seen. This chapter has four further sections. Section II provides the context in which the critique of the ECT system of investment protection ought to be seen. In Section III the relevant provisions discussed in these six cases are set out. In the Section IV, the arbitral tribunals' position on these provisions in the Turkey cases is analysed. In Section V, Turkey's energy policy is considered in light of the impact, if any, that these arbitrations could have had. Since the disputed ECT provisions are relevant to all disputes arising out of the ECT, the conclusions in this article on how tribunals can deal with unmeritorious applications will potentially apply to all future ECT cases.

[5] E Cima, 'Retooling the Energy Charter Treaty for climate change mitigation: lessons from investment law and arbitration' (2021) 14(2) *Journal of World Energy Law & Business* 75–87, 75.

[6] ibid.

[7] AA Marhold, *Energy in International Trade Law: Concepts, Regulation and Changing Markets* (Cambridge University Press, 2021) 111.

[8] See www.energycharter.org/who-we-are/members-observers/. This is the current number as of 21 July 2023. The Energy Charter Treaty has raised concerns regarding many countries, including European countries, as a result – recently the European Commission (EC) has called for a coordinated withdrawal by the EU and its member states from the Energy Charter Treaty (ECT).

[9] See www.energycharter.org/process/energy-charter-treaty-1994/energy-charter-treaty/.

[10] Marhold (n 7) 154.

II. The Context: The ECT, its Functions, and the Controversies Surrounding it

The ECT 'Process has arguably become the only multilateral initiative in energy that has offered over-reaching legally binding guarantees for states and market players'.[11] The ECT protects all investors in the energy sector without differentiating between whether they are fossil fuel investors or renewable energy investors. Since the ECT does not have a preference as to whether it is renewable or fossil fuel energy, it potentially creates an inconsistency for the states' new goals under the Paris Agreement. Therefore, the ECT has come to be seen as 'an obstacle to addressing climate change'.[12] State parties have undertaken commitments to protect the environment and reduce carbon emissions to tackle global warming.[13] The Paris Agreement is the most important international agreement identified with regards to the fight against global warming, and the promotion and encouragement of renewable energy.[14] States agreed to the goal 'of holding average global warming well below 2 degrees C and pursuing efforts to hold it below 1.5 degrees C'.[15] To achieve this goal, states need to reduce the use of fossil fuels and increase renewable energies.

'The drive towards modernising the ECT started within a decade of its entry into force. It primarily resulted from the Russian Federation's advocacy to change the ECT, and ultimately contributed to the establishment of the political declaration, the International Energy Charter'.[16] Former ECT Secretary General Urban Rusnak has pointed out that 'If the modernisation process fails, I don't see a future for the Treaty'.[17] He further states that it 'would seriously hamper the ability of the world to meet the Paris climate targets. The Paris Agreement does not protect investment. The ECT does. It's a complement to the Paris agreement'.[18]

[11] I Kustova, 'A treaty a la carte? Some reflections on the modernization of the Energy Charter Process' (2016) 9(5) *Journal of World Energy Law & Business* 367.

[12] See www.reuters.com/sustainability/climate-energy/eu-propose-exit-energy-charter-treaty-over-climate-concerns-2023-06-29/.

[13] For an analysis of how environmental concerns should be considered in ISDS, see C Eken, 'Should Environmental Concerns be Considered in Investment Arbitration Rulings?' (*aria.law*, 2021) aria.law.columbia.edu/should-environmental-concerns-be-considered-in-investment-arbitration-rulings/.

[14] For the explanations about the Paris Agreement and relevant documents see unfccc.int/process-and-meetings/the-paris-agreement?gclid=CjwKCAjw8ZKmBhArEiwAspcJ7uHhOWr6eI65rfqTgy2MYTpxpvBAu7rfpqQJyfRxWxzBhLB8_z55jhoCrtkQAvD_BwE; for the Paris Agreement, see unfccc.int/sites/default/files/english_paris_agreement.pdf.

[15] See unfccc.int/topics/adaptation-and-resilience/the-big-picture/new-elements-and-dimensions-of-adaptation-under-the-paris-agreement-article-7.

[16] K Roiger-Simek, 'The Modernization of the Energy Charter Treaty: Dead in the Water?' (2024) 26(1) *Austrian Review of International and European Law* 122.

[17] Secretary General, Energy Charter Secretariat, Karel Beckman, 'Interview: A New Energy Charter Treaty as a Complement to the Paris Agreement' (*Borderlex*, 2020) borderlex.net/2020/06/18/interview-a-new-energy-charter-treaty-as-a-complement-to-the-paris-agreement-on-climate-change/.

[18] ibid.

This summarises the function of the ECT in the energy transition as well as its modernisation process.

The modernisation discussion recently gained more attention with the increasing obligations of states to protect the environment. Importantly, the European Union (EU) submitted a proposal with a focus on aligning the ECT with the Paris Agreement.[19] The process has also attracted much attention in academic literature.[20] During this process, an agreement in principle was reached on 24 June 2022.[21] According to this agreement in principle, a modernised ECT will bring states more flexibility. Under pillar 2, a novel mechanism 'allows Contracting Parties, based on a Conference decision, to exclude investment protection for fossil fuels in their territories, considering their individual energy security and climate goals'.[22] It further continues with examples: 'the EU and the UK have opted to carve-out fossil fuel related investments from investment protection under the ECT, including for existing investments after 10 years from the entry into force of the relevant provisions and for new investments made after 15 August 2023 as of that date with limited exceptions'.[23] This will give states an explicit right to exclude fossil fuel investments, even though a 10-year period provides existing investors protection. Compared to the 20-year sunset clause, this 10-year period is surely in favour of states. Apart from some flexibility and clarity in the definition of investor and investment, a modernised ECT will not remove the protection that investors have in the energy sector. It is observed that 'despite the modernisation efforts, the updated ECT still brings considerable risks for governments in their environmental, climate and energy policies'.[24]

Even though the ECT is seen as an obstacle to tackling global warming, this is a part of the overall dissatisfaction of some states with investment arbitration, especially European Union Member States. Thus, states have started withdrawing from the ECT. Withdrawals and preparations for withdrawals from the ECT

[19] J Tropper and K Wagner, 'The European Union Proposal for the Modernisation of the Energy Charter Treaty – A Model for Climate-Friendly Investment Treaties?' (2022) 23(5–6) *The Journal of World Investment & Trade* 813. For the EU proposal, see European Union, 'Text Proposal for the Modernisation of the Energy Charter Treaty' and 'European Union's Additional Submission to its Text Proposal for the Modernization of the Energy Charter Treaty' (May 2020) ccsi.columbia.edu/sites/default/files/content/docs/tradoc_158754%20(1)_0.pdf energy.ec.europa.eu/system/files/2021-02/eu_submission_revised_definition_of_economic_activity_in_the_energy_sector_0.pdf.

[20] See T Theofanopoulos, 'Modernisation of the Energy Charter Treaty – Evolution and Challenges [ProQuest Dissertations Publishing]' (2022) doi.org/10.26267/unipi_dione/1780; N Ismayilova, 'Talks over Energy Charter Treaty's modernization to start soon' (*Trend News Agency*, 2020); O Vaaranmaa, 'The Energy Charter Treaty, Frivolous Claims and the Looming Threat of Investor-state Dispute Settlement: Any Hope from the EU's Modernisation Proposal?' (2021) 8(2) *Groningen Journal of International Law* 270–87; PV Thiessen, 'Reforming the Energy Charter Treaty for sustainability?' (2022) 40(4) *Journal of Energy & Natural Resources Law* 465–89 and so on.

[21] See www.energycharter.org/fileadmin/DocumentsMedia/CCDECS/2022/CCDEC202210.pdf.

[22] ibid. Pillar 2: Flexibility at p 3.

[23] ibid.

[24] B-J Verbeek, 'The Modernization of the Energy Charter Treaty: Fulfilled or Broken Promises?' (2023) 8(1) *Business and Human Rights Journal* 97–102.

have become a recent trend. Most recently, the European Commission proposed a coordinated EU withdrawal from the ECT over climate concerns.[25] In the last year, three EU members, France, Germany, and Poland, have submitted written notifications of withdrawal from the ECT.[26] This is notwithstanding the fact that many users of the ECT against states are actually renewable energy companies. Spain, for example, has faced over 8 billion USD claims in total.[27]

Concerns about complying with state environmental goals are not the only reason why states withdraw from the ECT. Previously, Russia and Italy also withdrew from ECT in 2009 and 2014 respectively.[28] According to Global Arbitration News, Italy has such concerns about 1,000 planned lawsuits.[29] In addition, the largest arbitration award in history is related to the ECT.[30] However, leaving the ECT does not make states completely safe. Investors are still protected by many bilateral and multilateral investment treaties that states have also signed. Furthermore, even after withdrawing from the ECT, states are bound by its provisions for a further 20 years.[31] This type of clause is known as the 'sunset clause', and it is rather a long sunset clause. Therefore, even though states are withdrawing or considering withdrawing, it will not take immediate effect and it will also not leave investors without a right to bring claims against states under other investment treaties. Finally, the ECT is not the only institution that is under criticism. Investment arbitration in general is under criticism. Again, the European Union is a big supporter of multilateral investment courts rather than arbitration tribunals.[32] Thus, one needs to see the reaction towards the ECT alongside all the developments happening in the world. Investment arbitration is seen as a risk by states, potentially making them liable to pay millions or even billions to investors. Thus, it is understandable that states seek to limit or decrease the scope of this tool.

Considering the current ECT and the decisions in the six cases against Turkey, one can easily conclude that the modernised ECT would not change the decisions in these six cases. As discussed in this chapter, the existing ECT already gives authority to arbitration tribunals to interpret the definition of investor/investment as suggested in the modernised ECT. Therefore, a modernised ECT would not change the decisions in the cases analysed in this chapter.

[25] European Commission, Directorate-General for Energy, News Announcement (7 July 2023) energy.ec.europa.eu/news/european-commission-proposes-coordinated-eu-withdrawal-energy-charter-treaty-2023-07-07_en#:~:text=Therefore%2C%20the%20Commission%20is%20proposing,across%20the%20EU%20and%20beyond.

[26] Treaty: www.energycharter.org/media/news/article/written-notifications-of-withdrawal-from-the-energy-charter-treaty/.

[27] Solar-boom accessed 30 July 2023: www.euronews.com/my-europe/2022/12/27/spain-faces-8-billion-in-renewable-legal-claims-over-past-solar-boom.

[28] See www.energychartertreaty.org/treaty/contracting-parties-and-signatories/.

[29] GI Fiorelli, 'Italy Withdraws from Energy Charter Treaty' (*Baker McKenzie*, 6 May 2015) www.globalarbitrationnews.com/2015/05/06/italy-withdraws-from-energy-charter-treaty-20150507/.

[30] *Yukos Universal Limited (Isle of Man) v The Russian Federation* [2014] PCA AA 227 (UNCITRAL).

[31] ECT, Article 45.

[32] 'Multilateral Investment Court Project' (*European Commission*) policy.trade.ec.europa.eu/enforcement-and-protection/multilateral-investment-court-project_en.

III. Key ECT Provisions Raised in the Six Cases against Turkey

In the six cases, the ECT provision in question related to the definition of investment;[33] the definition of the investor;[34] promotion, protection and treatment of investments;[35] expropriation;[36] non-application of investment promotion and protection (ECT Part Three) in certain circumstances;[37] exceptions to the observance by sub-national authorities;[38] and the dispute settlement.[39] Regarding the definition of the investment, the jurisdiction of the Tribunal under the ICSID convention is also discussed in these cases.[40]

Article one of the ECT provides the definition of relevant terms in the ECT. According to Article 1/7 Investor means:

> (a) with respect to a Contracting Party:
>
> > (i) a natural person having the citizenship or nationality of or who is permanently residing in that Contracting Party in accordance with its applicable law;
> >
> > (ii) a company or other organisation organised in accordance with the law applicable in that Contracting Party;
>
> (b) with respect to a 'third state', a natural person, company or other organisation which fulfils, mutatis mutandis, the conditions specified in subparagraph (a) for a Contracting Party.[41]

Under this definition, both natural persons and legal persons can be an investor. The important factor here is that the investor must come from a Contracting Party. Thus, a natural and legal person from any signatory to ECT can be an investor. Also, an investor must be from a third state which means that the investor must come from a country that did not make the investment originally. Under this explanation, any natural or legal persons coming from a third-party signatory to the ECT can be an investor in another state signatory to the ECT.

[33] ECT, Article 1(6) and Article 1(7).

[34] 'Multilateral Investment Court Project' (n 32).

[35] ECT, Article 10(1).

[36] ibid Article 13.

[37] ibid Article 17.

[38] ibid Article 24, especially para (3)(c).

[39] ibid Article 26(1) and especially paras 1, 7 and (3)(b)(i); ICSID Convention, Article 25; www.globalarbitrationnews.com/2015/05/06/italy-withdraws-from-energy-charter-treaty-20150507/#:~:text=Officially%2C%20the%20Italian%20government%20justifies,Italy%20 around%20%E2%82%A C%20370.000%20annually; *Yukos Capital SARL v The Russian Federation*, PCA Case No. 2013-31. See policy.trade.ec.europa.eu/enforcement-and-protection/multilateral-investment-court-project_en.

[40] International Centre for Settlement of Investment Disputes, *ICSID Convention, Regulations, and Rules* (ICSID, 2006), Article 25.

[41] ibid Article 1(7).

Article 10 is about the promotion and protection of investment. According to Article 10/1:

> Each Contracting Party shall, in accordance with the provisions of this Treaty, encourage and create stable, equitable, favourable and transparent conditions for Investors of other Contracting Parties to make Investments in its Area. Such conditions shall include a commitment to accord at all times to Investments of Investors of other Contracting Parties fair and equitable treatment. Such Investments shall also enjoy the most constant protection and security and no Contracting Party shall in any way impair by unreasonable or discriminatory measures their management, maintenance, use, enjoyment or disposal. In no case shall such Investments be accorded treatment less favourable than that required by international law, including treaty obligations. Each Contracting Party shall observe any obligations it has entered into with an Investor or an Investment of an Investor of any other Contracting Party.[42]

Article 10 provides security to investors. Under this Article, investors are guaranteed that they will not be treated in a discriminatory manner. Investors will have the same security and transparency as their domestic counterparties. Investors will be treated fairly and equitably. The terms used in this Article are subject to interpretation. Therefore, arbitration tribunals will decide in each case whether the treatment breached the protection and security provided by Article 10 of the ECT.

According to Article 24/3:

> The provisions of this Treaty other than those referred to in paragraph (1) shall not be construed to prevent any Contracting Party from taking any measure which it considers necessary:
>
> (a) for the protection of its essential security interests including those
>
> (i) relating to the supply of Energy Materials and Products to a military establishment; or
>
> (ii) taken in time of war, armed conflict or other emergency in international relations;
>
> (b) relating to the implementation of national policies respecting the non-proliferation of nuclear weapons or other nuclear explosive devices or needed to fulfil its obligations under the Treaty on the Non-Proliferation of Nuclear Weapons, the Nuclear Suppliers Guidelines, and other international nuclear non-proliferation obligations or understandings; or
>
> (c) for the maintenance of public order.
>
> (d) Such measure shall not constitute a disguised restriction on Transit.[43]

Article 24/3 provides states with the autonomy to change their legislation or make any necessary arrangements when they deem necessary. However, paragraph one of this Article excludes the application of this Article to Articles 12 (compensation for losses), 13 (expropriation) and 29 (interim provisions on trade-related

[42] ibid Article 10(1).
[43] ibid Article 24/3.

matters). Thus, in the case of these three instances, this Article would not be applicable. Therefore, when states introduce new legislation or make changes to their legislation, they will still need to compensate ECT investors for their losses. This Article has become an important reason for states to bring change to their territories. Yet, states do not have this authority without any limit. Therefore, investors are still protected while states have a certain limited amount flexibility.

Article 13 is about expropriation. Article 17 is about the non-application of Part Three under certain circumstances. Moreover, ICSID's Article 25 was also discussed. According to this article:

> The jurisdiction of the Centre shall extend to any legal dispute arising directly out of an investment, between a Contracting State (or any constituent subdivision or agency of a Contracting State designated to the Centre by that state) and a national of another Contracting State, which the parties to the dispute consent in writing to submit to the Centre. When the parties have given their consent, no party may withdraw its consent unilaterally.[44]

Importantly, there is no definition of investment in the ICSID Convention.

IV. The Position of the Tribunals on Unmeritorious Cases

Having set out the contested ECT provision above, this section examines the positions that the tribunals have taken on these Articles. In particular, these positions focus on what investment is and what owning or controlling the investment is. In all six cases, the issue turns on the definition of investor.

It is important to highlight that in all six cases, Turkey prevailed. Investors lost all cases and covered the legal costs Turkey incurred during the arbitrations. In *Libananco*, the Tribunal considered whether the Claimant was the investor at the time of the events that had given rise to the present dispute occurred.[45] As a result, the Tribunal decided that they have no jurisdiction over the case because the Claimant had 'not proved that it owned shares in ÇEAŞ and Kepez before 12 June 2003' which is the date of the events giving rise to the present dispute occurred.[46] In another case, regarding the same events that occurred on 12 June 2003, Tribunal decided that 'the claim to jurisdiction is based on an assertion of ownership which the evidence suggests was fraudulent, an award to the Respondent of full costs will go some way towards compensating the Respondent for having to defend a claim that had no jurisdictional basis and discourage others from pursuing such unmeritorious claims'.[47] The previous opinion was reiterated in a later case

[44] ICSID Convention, Article 25/1.

[45] *Libananco Holdings Co. Limited v Republic of Turkey*, ICSID Case No. ARB/06/8, Award, 2 September 2011 at [130].

[46] ibid at [570.1].

[47] *Europe Cement Investment & Trade S.A. v Republic of Turkey*, ICSID Case No. ARB(AF)/07/2 at [185].

as well.[48] In *Cementownia v Turkey*, the Tribunal held that 'The Claimant has filed a fraudulent claim'.[49] In 2014, a Turkish citizen residing in Paris, Cem Uzan, initiated a case personally against Turkey.[50] This case failed as well.[51] In another case, the Tribunal also decided with Majority that 'the Tribunal dismisses with prejudice all claims for lack of jurisdiction under the Netherlands-Turkey BIT and the ECT'.[52] Another case that was initiated by Nabucco Pipeline against Turkey was discontinued upon the request of the Claimant, Nabucco Pipeline.[53]

In summary, throughout all of these cases, the Tribunals did not entertain unmeritorious claims at the merits stage. The applications were dismissed at the procedural stage.[54] This also provides an argument in favour of the ECT, despite all the criticism against it recapitulated in the previous section. The argument in favour of ECT also in the energy transition is that while ECT provides security for investors, states do also have protection against unmeritorious cases. The wording of ECT as it is, without any modernisation, is already providing security to states. Now, in the next section, with the new proposed Articles, it will be discussed whether the decision in these six cases would change or contribute to the security of states in comparison to the existing wording of ECT without any modernisation. There are also pending cases from Turkish investors against various states including Azerbaijan, Kazakhstan, Uzbekistan, Turkmenistan and Romania.[55] Whether the same balance would apply can be examined in the future.

V. Limits: Turkey's Energy Policy under Scrutiny

Turkey won all the cases on a jurisdictional basis. Certain important aspects of the six cases here analysed were the timing of the investment, and whether an investor is a foreign investor as required under the ECT. These are the requirements for tribunals to have jurisdiction over the case. ECT investors have strong protection. However, the lesson that can be taken from the six cases against Turkey is that investors should not bring unmeritorious cases. Turkey prevailed in all six cases

[48] *Cementownia 'Nowa Huta' S.A. v Republic of Turkey*, ICSID Case No. ARB(AF)/06/2 (September 2009).

[49] ibid at [177].

[50] *Cem Cengiz Uzan v Republic of Turkey*, SCC Case No. V 2014/023.

[51] ibid at [206].

[52] *Alapli Elektrik B.V. v Republic of Turkey*, ICSID Case No. ARB/08/13 at [425].

[53] *Nabucco Gas Pipeline International GmbH in Liqu. v Republic of Turkey*, ICSID Case No. ARB/15/26 (2015), Order Of The Secretary-General Taking Note Of The Discontinuance Of The Proceeding, 2 November 2015 at [7]–[11].

[54] Only in the *Nabucco* case, the investor discontinued the proceedings as stated above.

[55] The full list of cases: *Barmek Holding A.S. v Azerbaijan*, ICSID Case No. ARB/06/16; *Turkey Petrolleri Anonim Ortakligi v Kazakhstan*, ICSID Case No. ARB/11/2; *Federal Elektrik Yatırım ve Ticaret A.Ş. and others v Uzbekistan*, ICSID Case No. ARB/13/9; *Aktau Petrol Ticaret A.Ş. v Kazakhstan*, ICSID Case No. ARB/15/8; *Lotus Holding Anonim Şirketi v Turkmenistan*, ICSID Case No. ARB/17/30; *Fin. Doc S.r.l. and others v Romania*, ICSID Case No. ARB/20/35. See www.energychartertreaty.org/cases/list-of-cases/.

that occurred as a result of the ECT. The Turkey case study in this article shows that ECT is not always a successful tool for investors. States can prevail in these cases. Therefore, we can initially conclude that the ECT is a success story for states because it attracted energy investment and when those foreign investors launched arbitral proceedings, they could not successfully secure compensation.

However, we can also conclude as to the limits of this line of cases. After this first hurdle, the real discussion would turn on the merits of the case such as whether the action taken by Turkey was considered as expropriation under the ECT. The results might have changed if the jurisdiction hurdle was overcome by the investors in those cases. Turkey did not change its legislation in a way that could disturb foreign investors and affect their investments, which is a common reason for investors to sue a state. If no legislative changes are made by a state, there will be no change in the operation of investors, and no reason for investors to bring a claim. Therefore, further research should be conducted on how Turkey is successfully meeting Paris Agreement goals and environment-friendly regulations. Of course, states should keep up with achieving environmental goals as agreed by the Paris Agreement and other international conventions. However, while doing so, they should give due notice to investors, negotiate if necessary and allow them to comply with environmental regulations that states must follow under the Paris Agreement and other international conventions. If states announce all their climate goals and are transparent regarding the necessary changes, Tribunals must consider the need for the environmental regulation that will impact energy investments. If such regulations are adopted in a non-discriminatory way without targeting any specific companies, states of course have the right to regulate in their territory. Depending on the specific facts of each regulatory change, tribunals will make their decision by balancing the legitimate expectations of investors and applying reasonableness and proportionality tests as commonly applied in investment arbitration cases.

VI. Conclusion

The ECT has recently been seen to 'overprotect investors' which 'creates a regulatory chill'.[56] This chapter does not agree with this opinion. As explained, the function of the ECT was to protect investors in the energy sector and increase the energy transition between states. As regards this purpose, the ECT is a successful treaty. However, states also have enough protection. As all the cases analysed in this chapter prove, states have opportunities to dismiss unmeritorious cases, just as Turkey did when successfully prevailing in all six cases. Turkey, in these cases, emerges as a successful example of ECT tribunals balancing the interests

[56] O Quirico, *Investment Governance Between the Energy Charter Treaty and the European Union: Resolving Regulatory Conflicts*, Vol 19 (Brill, 2021) 26.

of investors and host states in having only meritorious cases brought against it. Turkey prevailed in all cases against herself under the ECT and was awarded the costs of arbitration, except with regards to the *SCC* case.

These six cases show at least three things: (i) ECT arbitration does not always work in favour of investors since Turkey won all the investment arbitration cases; (ii) ECT can be a tool for investors to bring unmeritorious cases (frivolous cases); and (iii) such cases fail without reaching the merits at the procedural stage through tribunals adopting restrictive interpretations of key provisions that control access to the merits stage. The Turkish cases indicate that the existing ECT without modernisation has enough safeguards to protect host states from unmeritorious cases. Tribunals adopted a narrow definition of investment and investor in these cases. Even if the modernised ECT was in force, the tribunals would still reach the same conclusion and Turkey would prevail in the same way. Therefore, while the modernisation of the ECT is ongoing, tribunals are provided with enough room for their interpretation to dismiss cases from investors without a legitimate basis. This is true for investment in fossil fuel as well as in renewable energy projects. In that sense, these cases have a positive influence on ECT investment law during the energy transition.

6

International Dispute Resolution and the Energy Transition Rollercoaster*

PETER D CAMERON**

I. Introduction

By several measures, disputes about energy resources and their use make up the largest group of disputes to reach international arbitration from a single sector of the global economy.[1] The sector seems likely to retain this status in the future or even enhance it due to the phenomenon commonly described as 'the Energy Transition'. This non-linear, policy-driven process aims to rebalance energy consumption around the globe away from fossil fuel dependence towards a significantly less carbon-intensive mix, with the aim of alleviating the adverse impacts of climate change. In the past, sweeping policy realignments have impacted on the energy sector, but the global scope and ambition of the Energy Transition seems likely to trigger an enduring or 'permanent' disruption that deeply impacts not only the energy segment of the global economy but socio-economic behaviour generally. This chapter will focus on an area where impacts have already become evident and are expected to be significant – investment – and poses the

* Parts of this chapter were based on papers delivered at the ITA-IEL-ICC Annual Conference on Energy Arbitration, at Houston, USA, in January 2022; the Biennial ICCA Conference at Edinburgh, UK, in September 2022, from discussion with participants at each event, and from comments by John Bowman and Pieter Bekker. Responsibility for the final version of this work and the opinions expressed therein lies entirely with the author.

** Peter D Cameron is Director of the Centre for Energy, Petroleum and Mineral Law and Policy at the University of Dundee, UK, and Professor of International Energy Law and Policy. He is a qualified barrister (England & Wales) (Middle Temple) and sits regularly as an arbitrator in international investment disputes.

[1] Statistics that regularly appear from ICSID, the ICC and other distinguished bodies confirm the relatively high proportion of cases that originate from this sector of the international economy: among the investor-state cases before ICSID from 1966 to 2022, those concerning energy amounted to 42% of the total, without including energy-related cases in areas such as construction, transportation, and finance: ICSID Caseload – Statistics (2023-1) 12.

question: is arbitration as the established mode of resolving energy disputes between states and investors suitable to tackle the kind of disputes about investment that arise from this dynamic context of Energy Transition? If it is not, its lack of suitability would seem to be a disincentive to the providers of the capital necessary for this major socio-economic change. Yet such investment has been deemed by the International Energy Agency (IEA) as essential to its success: 'around 70% of clean energy investment over the next decade will need to be carried out by private developers, consumers and financiers'.[2] Moreover, incentive schemes designed by states are particularly important to mobilise investment in clean energy and new technologies, so a failure to offer sufficient guarantees of legal protection to investors in the event of disputes could well have implications for the speed and even the feasibility of an Energy Transition.

To examine the above question, Section II of this Chapter sets out a characterisation of the new, still evolving context of Energy Transition from which disputes will arise and require resolution. It then identifies and examines three features that are key to an understanding and engagement with the question: first, it considers the new policy uncertainties created by the expanded role of the state vis-à-vis investments and commerce arising from the Energy Transition, an expansion notable in a sector where the state has long been present as a resource owner, regulator and contracting party (often through an entity with delegated authority) in energy activities, and where, as a result, policy uncertainties have long been a common risk for investors; second, it examines the impact of this new context on the guarantees that have typically been offered to investors for large-scale, long-term investments, and the challenges presented by the ongoing modifications of the investment treaty regime, especially the declining role of the protections offered to investors under the Energy Charter Treaty (ECT); and third, it examines briefly how the resolution of disputes arising from commercial agreements may be affected by the Energy Transition even when a state or its agency is not a party to them. Building on this initial analysis of three key features of the Energy Transition that impact on the use of arbitration in investment disputes, Section III considers several of the first international energy disputes that can be linked to Energy Transition policies, such as those arising from the withdrawal of legal incentives to invest in cleaner forms of energy or in energy-related activities, and legal measures taken to phase out fossil fuels including the early closure of power plants that rely on fossil fuels. Subsequently, Section IV considers the potential for disputes in the one part of the global economy that the Energy Transition is by definition striving to move away from, the production and consumption of fossil fuels. Irrespective of whether fossil fuels remain dominant in the global economy or decline in the years up to 2050, commercial and state entities will adapt their

[2] 'The Cost of Capital in Clean Energy Transitions' (*IEA*, 17 December 2021) www.iea.org/articles/the-cost-of-capital-in-clean-energy-transitions.

operations and plans according to their assessments of the risks that the Energy Transition gives rise to in the production, transport, sale, and purchase of such fossil fuels. This seems likely to provide a fertile source of disputes in the medium- to long-term, with arbitration usually the preferred choice for dispute resolution under such contracts. Finally, Section V draws together some conclusions from the above analysis in relation to the question asked at the outset, noting however that the evolving character of the Energy Transition means that any conclusions must have a provisional character only.

II. Multiplying Sources of Uncertainty and their Effects

A. Disputes about Energy Projects

Energy disputes exhibit several features, even if not present in every case.[3] Among them, we may note the long-term character of many energy projects and transactions which is subject to disruption by the volatility of inter-related energy markets. Other features of note are the international character of many energy investments and indeed the investors themselves, the concentrated character of capital in large entities, the pervasive role of the state, the strategic sensitivity for most countries of its energy sector (irrespective of the mix of energies), and the complexity of most energy activities. Whether the parties to a dispute are commercial entities, a state regulatory agency or ministry, a state enterprise, or the state itself as owner of resources, an energy dispute often arises from a breach of the expectations of one party about the operation of such long-term relationships and the legal mechanisms that are designed to ensure performance. The rights in energy disputes can arise from a wide range of instruments such as contracts, concessions, or licences. The preferred mode of settling these disputes is typically by means of international arbitration, arising from a contract, an investment treaty or, in some cases, a national investment law. The spectrum encompasses investor-state disputes, construction/industrial plant disputes, commercial disputes involving performance and price revisions, and insurance disputes. Litigation and the use of courts for enforcement purposes play an important secondary role.[4] Yet, mediation plays no significant role in the resolution of disputes in this sector.

[3] I have examined these features in some detail in 'International Arbitration and Energy Disputes' (2022) 3 *Global Energy Law and Sustainability* 1–17. For a more extended treatment of these issues, see PD Cameron, *International Energy Investment Law: The Pursuit of Stability*, 2nd edn (Oxford University Press, 2021).

[4] Some litigation has targeted states and international energy companies in national courts. See eg *Urgenda Foundation v State of The Netherlands* ECLI:NL:HR:2019:2007 (Supreme Court, 20 December 2019) (English translation in (2020) 59 I.L.M. 811); *Milieudefensie et al v Royal Dutch Shell* ECLI:NL:RBDHA:2021:5337 (District Court of The Hague, 26 May 2021).

Nor is this propensity to generate disputes peculiar to one form of energy; in recent years, traditional sources of energy have been overshadowed by renewable energy as a source of abundant disputes registered at the International Centre for Settlement of Investment Disputes (ICSID).[5] Notably, these are mostly based on a breach or breaches of the only single sector investment treaty, the ECT.[6]

B. The Energy Transition

A more dynamic view of energy disputes is now required, taking into consideration the actual and potential disruptive effects on the energy landscape of the Energy Transition. This is a non-linear, policy-driven process that aims to rebalance energy consumption around the globe away from fossil fuel dependence towards a significantly less carbon-intensive mix, with the overall goal of achieving Net Zero carbon emissions by a specific date, usually 2050.[7] Most governments have signed up to taking actions to achieve the overall objective within the framework of the legally binding international treaty on climate change, the Paris Agreement (with no less than 193 signatory states in 2015, when the Paris Agreement was concluded). A key assumption behind this process is that markets themselves will be unable to address the problem of global warming. Therefore, action by states is essential for any significant reversal of CO_2 emission trends to occur, with the result that the Energy Transition is a creation of a multiplicity of policy choices, not the play of market forces. Further, it differs from the wide-ranging processes that have affected the energy sector in the past, such as privatisation, liberalisation, or deregulation, in the sense that it is not about how to make the market work better. Its justification is supremely ambitious, and almost apocalyptic in tone: to save the future of the human species on the planet. However, no consensus prevails among the nearly 200 governments on the appropriate pathway for an

[5] Moreover, the dispute may well not arise from a feature of the resource itself, but more likely from the activity or structure put in place to develop and monetise it: the grant or termination of a licence or permit, the rights and obligations at issue in energy disputes can arise from a wide range of instruments, such as production sharing contracts, concessions, licences, joint operating agreements, gas and LNG sales contracts, transportation agreements, and power purchase agreements.

[6] The ECT provides a useful definition of the subject matter of an energy dispute. It may concern energy materials and products, energy related assets such as hydrocarbon exploration and production rights, power generation facilities, processing structures such as LNG terminals, transport or distribution facilities, or an economic activity such as exploration, generation, extraction, production, refining, storage, transportation by land or sea, transmission, distribution, trade, marketing or sale of energy materials or products: ECT, Article 1(4), (5).

[7] The International Renewable Energy Agency (IRENA) describes it in these terms: 'The energy transition is a pathway toward transformation of the global energy sector from fossil-based to zero-carbon by the second half of this century. At its heart is the need to reduce energy-related CO2 emissions to limit climate change' www.irena.org/energytransition. For a diverse selection of views on the Energy Transition, see PD Cameron, X Mu and V Roeben (eds), *The Global Energy Transition: Law, Policy and Economics for Energy in the 21st Century* (Hart Publishing, 2020) (Global Energy Law and Policy Series, vol 2).

Energy Transition or the choice of instruments that would be most appropriate to achieving emissions reductions as set out in the Paris Agreement by 2050. Indeed, apart from the fixing of two dates, the starting point for measuring emissions and the point at which Net Zero is to be reached, a high level of uncertainty characterises the pace, path, and parameters of the Energy Transition.[8] Much is left for the many individual governments to decide. The novelty of this process inevitably creates significant risks of policy incoherence and indeed reversals in the light of experience and lessons learnt, creating in turn doubts about the long-term stability of the regulatory structures put in place. This is a fertile ground for disputes along the value chain, especially between investors and host governments.

C. A Paradox

The significance of this lies in the fact that an expanded role for regulation by the state brings with it an acknowledged need to rely on the private sector as a source of investment capital to make the Energy Transition possible. The scale of this investment is very large indeed. On one recent estimate, global investment in the Energy Transition reached US$1.8 trillion in 2023, an increase of 17 per cent on the previous year.[9] Yet, the conclusions of that year's Conference of the Parties (COP) were that a trebling of renewable energy investment is still required.[10] More than any other kind of energy investment, experience demonstrates that this cleaner form of energy relies heavily on the provision of incentive schemes by governments to gain momentum. It is in this context that the IEA's statement about the proportion of investment required from the private sector becomes very significant.[11] So, the paradox of the Energy Transition is that the expansion of state regulation and other interventionist roles will simultaneously require efforts by the same states to secure very large-scale funding from the private sector: more State involvement and more reliance on private capital to achieve the goals of climate and energy policy.

For lawyers and policymakers, the challenge is how to adapt existing protections for investors, especially foreign investors, so that investment on this scale can flow. However, although the time frame of a transition is largely future-oriented, among its present or short-term impacts is to cast doubts upon the long-term future of hydrocarbons and coal and invite or force a reassessment of investments already made or which are a part of a process that has already started. To the extent that parties differ in their assessments of its effects on their business operations,

[8] For a review of the many diverse meanings given to Net Zero, see JF Green and R Salas Reyes, 'The History of Net Zero: can we move from concepts to practice' (2023) 23 *Climate Policy* 901–15.

[9] Bloomberg NEF, Energy Transition Investment Trends 2024, 30 January 2024.

[10] 'COP28 Agreement Signals "Beginning of the End" of the Fossil Fuel Era' (*UNFCCC*, 13 December 2023) unfccc.int/news/cop28-agreement-signals-beginning-of-the-end-of-the-fossil-fuel-era.

[11] See n 2 above.

a potential for disputes may well emerge among them, and with state partners. For existing investments, the Energy Transition has the potential to be highly disruptive.

D. Indirect Impacts

The disruptiveness for energy investments is also embedded in the wider state policy towards the energy sector. The 'sustainability' goal co-exists with other important policy objectives for states such as security of energy supply and affordability of or access to energy, but this entails a risk that environmental, or climate goals are put to one side if the other two goals of this 'policy trilemma' acquire a sudden urgency. In fact, this has happened in Europe after the conflict in Ukraine from early 2022, when shortages of gas drove prices up to unprecedented levels, with a knock-on effect on electricity prices for consumers, such that affordability became a major and pressing issue for many citizens and industrial users. It was a reminder that a crisis can readily and suddenly arise from the other two corners of the 'energy trilemma' in public policy. Indeed, following this 'energy crisis', governments have sought alternative fossil fuel sources to restore disruptions to their energy supply or have opted to heavily subsidise fossil fuels to shield consumers from price increases.[12] Moreover, it has triggered a considerable increase in investment in all forms of energy, including fossil fuels, whether through the licensing of new projects or the conclusion of long-term supply contracts from established producers. Thus, the general question arises, how much weight is to be given to each of these three policy objectives at this time of Energy Transition? A failure to design an energy security policy in ways that are compatible with an Energy Transition would likely mean that the long-term sustainability aspect of that Transition is undermined. With many governments taking their own decisions in response to this 'energy crisis', the approach to balancing each priority in the trilemma will vary, perhaps widely, given the very diverse circumstances that shape their national policies. Clearly, such policy deviations can generate an abundance of additional disputes to the ones that have already been identified. This is in addition to the important subset of disputes, discussed below: ones that are triggered by investors inter se as they differ in their assessments of policy risk and its impacts.

Policy realignments are also arising from impacts in the supply chain, creating a further, emerging category of energy disputes. Achieving a shift from carbon intensive forms of energy at scale requires a significant expansion of the production of minerals, such as lithium, cobalt, and copper, with a key role in battery

[12] European Commission, 'Diversification of Gas Supply Sources and Routes': energy.ec.europa.eu/topics/energy-security/diversification-gas-supply-sources-and-routes_en.

production, and the development of renewable energies.[13] Energy security considerations also dictate a review of new sources of these 'critical' minerals, threatening disputes with affected communities and indigenous peoples. So great is this shift that it is already giving rise to a new form of 'resource nationalism' among states, taking legal measures to ensure their ownership of these increasingly valuable resources, and to responding to familiar actions by local communities to prevent new mining projects from commencing.[14]

E. Three Impacts of the Energy Transition on Energy Disputes

In the following sections, three impacts of the Energy Transition are examined in connection with their propensity to generate investment disputes. First, given the crucial role of states in driving forward such a transition – and as examples, see the US Inflation Reduction Act and the EU's Green Energy Package – the dynamics in the relationship of the state vis-à-vis investments and commerce are already changing. Second, given the uncertainties about the pace of any national transition, the reliability of guarantees offered to investors for large-scale, long-term investments are threatened. Such guarantees in international law are already precarious with respect to the investment treaty regime, especially the sector specific ECT. Third, the Energy Transition is already impacting the kind of players that are active in energy markets: typically, new entrants with distinct business models are taking a place alongside the traditional corporate entities, bringing different understandings and expertise to the activities in which they engage.

i. The Roles of the State vis-à-vis Investments – The Arrival of the Transition State

Under the Paris Agreement, states have agreed to certain goals to hold the increase in the global average temperature to well below 2°C above pre-industrial levels and pursue efforts to limit the temperature increase to 1.5°C, above pre-industrial levels.[15] National climate action plans are to be communicated by the states that are party to the Agreement,[16] and recorded by the UN Secretariat.

[13] IEA, 'The Role of Critical Minerals in Clean Energy Transitions' (*windows.net*) iea.blob.core.windows.net/assets/ffd2a83b-8c30-4e9d-980a-52b6d9a86fdc/TheRoleofCriticalMineralsinCleanEnergyTransitions.pdf.

[14] A recent example from Europe is the Jadar mine project in Western Serbia, which is thought capable of supplying about 90% of European demand for lithium but which has had its licences revoked following popular opposition to it: Reuters, 'Serbian PM sees no chance for reviving Rio Tinto lithium project' (*reuters.com*, 13 December 2022) www.reuters.com/world/europe/serbian-pm-sees-no-chance-reviving-rio-tinto-lithium-project-2022-12-13/.

[15] Paris Agreement, Article 2.1(a).

[16] Paris Agreement, Article 4.

These Nationally Determined Contributions (NDCs) to achieving the global reduction targets will vary from one state to the next, but in general they imply varying multiple large-scale interventions by governments to achieve very significant emissions reductions by certain dates. Although the ultimate date for 'net zero', understood as 'the equilibrium between the number of anthropogenic greenhouse gases released into the atmosphere and the amount removed and stored by carbon sinks',[17] has usually been set by states at 2050 and in a few cases 2045, earlier dates matter since they yield evidence of progress or a lack thereof: by 2025 or earlier, emissions are expected to have peaked,[18] and by 2030, they are to be reduced by 43 per cent. In many cases, these climate policy interventions will have implications for commercial operations in the energy sector, often in ways that are hard to predict, with costs being impossible to calculate in advance. These implementing interventions are likely to be as diverse as the energy priorities and endowments of the many signatories to the Paris Agreement. Some are likely to be introduced post facto, in response to sudden, unexpected weather events – whether these are droughts, floods, storms, wildfires or extreme temperatures – or from local shortages of energy supply, such as those arising from the conflict in Ukraine in 2022 and after. As a result, the singular form of 'Energy Transition' is likely to prove less accurate in practice than the plural, Energy Transitions. Moreover, in this context a linear transition path is likely to be evident in only a handful of cases. Future investments in any form of energy must take this broad context of policy-induced uncertainty into account and shareholders of investing entities need to be alerted to its existence. Already there is plenty of evidence of such alerts in the annual world energy reports of energy agencies and in the filings of companies before the Securities and Exchange Commission (SEC) and other supervisory agencies around the world. Therefore, manifold, very significant uncertainties of possible outcomes for energy companies are evident in this transition.[19]

The Energy Transition also greatly promotes a distinct class of state interventions. For investment in renewable energy, specific incentives are typically required, often directed at foreign investors. These include investment incentives in the form of tax credits in the US Inflation Reduction Act,[20] the Canada Clean Technology Investment Tax Credit 2023,[21] non-tax incentives in the EU such as grants and

[17] Equinor (2022) 'Energy Perspectives' 10.

[18] Article 4 of the Paris Agreement uses the words 'as soon as possible'.

[19] To some extent, they are anticipated in publications by industry associations: see eg various publications at www.ipieca.org/resources.

[20] Environmental Protection Agency, 'Summary of IRA Provisions related to Renewable Energy' www.epa.gov/green-power-markets/summary-inflation-reduction-act-provisions-related-renewable-energy.

[21] www.congress.gov/117/bills/hr5376/BILLS-117hr5376enr.pdf (congress.gov); A Made-in-Canada Plan: Affordable Energy, Good Jobs, and a Growing Clean Economy' (*Canada.ca*, 28 March 2023) www.canada.ca/en/department-finance/news/2023/03/a-made-in-canada-plan-affordable-energy-good-jobs-and-a-growing-clean-economy.html.

loans to companies that are committed to innovation in this area, as well as to industrialisation and decarbonization,[22] or in India and China, a combination of feed-in tariffs, subsidies, and tax incentives.[23] In some cases, the use of incentives is a part of a wider industrial policy by the state concerned. Usually, governments will have broad discretionary powers to modify policies that offer such incentives in the event of a change of circumstances, potentially removing or significantly redesigning them in the aftermath of policy adjustments. There is then a heightened degree of regulatory and political risk related to these investments. As many disputes based on the ECT can attest, this is a fertile area for claims by investors against host states over the financial consequences of the exercise of their 'right to regulate' in the renewable energy sector.

The first generation of arbitral disputes over renewable energy had its roots in subsidy regimes which appeared in retrospect to many governments as overly generous to incoming investors, and in need of change or outright replacement. As dependence on subsidies has diminished, the next generation of disputes about renewable energy seems more likely to arise from changes in the market and transmission interconnection rules. Further, the heavy reliance of large solar and wind projects on finance that would be based on complex commercial relationships between sponsor, lenders and other parties in complex contracts makes commercial disputes more likely as such projects multiply.

Further, this context of heightened political risk is exacerbated by the impact of new clean energy technologies. Policy shifts are likely as governments take measures to promote low carbon technologies or facilitative technologies such as hydrogen or carbon capture, at a point in time when they are still at an early stage of development, little is known about their potential application, and regulatory frameworks are still evolving.

It is important to recall that this impact – an expanded range of state interventions – is occurring in a sector that has always had a high degree of involvement from the state as a regulator, participant and grantor of licences or permits as a natural resources owner. The extremely high (and volatile) degree of public interest in most or all phases of energy activity means that the state's presence – directly, or through one or more of its agencies or enterprises – has been ubiquitous. Moreover, the public interest it strives to promote may in many countries be concentrated on a single investment since a single hydrocarbons field, a nuclear power plant or a mine may have overwhelming importance for the national economy. Therefore, a policy or legal measure may be discriminatory in effect, even if it is cast in general terms, since it is relevant only to one investment or to very few investments. This is

[22] The umbrella initiative is the REPowerEU: commission.europa.eu/strategy-and-policy/priorities-2019-2024/european-green-deal/repowereu-affordable-secure-and-sustainable-energy-europe_en.

[23] Government of India, Ministry of New and Renewable Energy, 'National Green Hydrogen Mission' (January 2023) mnre.gov.in/national-green-hydrogen-mission/; for China's 14th Five Year Plan and its projects for renewable energy capacity additions, see IEA, 'Fossil Fuel Consumption Subsidies 2022' (February 2023) www.iea.org/reports/fossil-fuels-consumption-subsidies-2022, note 1.

exacerbated by the fact that an energy project is often legally based on a long-term contract linked to a physical location, making the production or generation facilities hard to move, and therefore vulnerable to discriminatory action. Historically, this pervasive role of the state in energy activities is given recognition in multilateral treaty instruments such as the ECT provision on sovereignty over energy resources (Article 18) and the Chapter on Energy in the Treaty for the Functioning of the European Union (TFEU), setting out provisions that guarantee a wide range of rights over energy resources and their use. For the international investor, then, even prior to the Energy Transition, the wide discretion typically reserved to states on energy matters creates a high level of political risk and a need for a variety of legal mechanisms to mitigate that risk and safeguard investments.[24]

The impacts on energy investment discussed above relate to policymaking, the 'creative' side of the state's response to the Energy Transition. However, impacts are evident in two other, different aspects of state activity. First, the 'Transition State' has to respond to an unprecedented demand for large-scale investment in expanded infrastructure, whether this is grids, pipelines, storage capacity or cross-border interconnectors. The scale of this demand is new, partly driven by the need to upgrade or modify infrastructure to cope with the additional renewable energy capacity and partly due to an unrelated development, a digital transformation in the global economy. For most states, this involves a recalibration of existing legal and regulatory frameworks applicable to the environment and planning that have their roots in law-making many decades ago, predating current thinking about the climate and energy. Further, there is a brokering role for the state, whether federal or unitary in character, in needing to manage community responses to investors' plans for such infrastructure expansion and related activity; securing a social licence to operate is key to mitigating delays in making such new investments. Indeed, there is not necessarily an alignment of interest between the government of the host state and the relevant or affected community. Opposition to a project by local communities may lead to the state being required by its constitutional framework and its courts to take regulatory measures that undermine an investor's interest. As new projects multiply to expand the supply of renewable forms of energy and to meet the demand for critical minerals, the risk of such actions – not originating in the executive part of the state – seems likely to increase.

Second, the Transition State must respond to the decisions of national courts or international legal entities in a context in which litigation initiated by civil society is rapidly expanding. At present, such actions are overwhelmingly directed to national courts rather than arbitral institutions. These judicial decisions are

[24] Apart from protections based on treaty, contract and domestic investment law, an investor may also choose to take out political risk insurance. The US Government's Overseas Private Investment Corporation (OPIC) defines 'political risk' as 'the possibility that political decisions or political or social events in a country will affect the business climate in such a way that investors lose a portion of their investment or expected return' (M Kantor, M Nolan and K Sauvant, *Reports of Overseas Private Investment Corporations Determinations* (2011)).

already impacting on state climate policy and have the potential to exert a greater impact.[25] In terms of risk, they have the potential to disrupt existing investments and agreements already finalised between investors and states.

ii. The Reliability of Guarantees Offered to Investors

Given the variety of legal instruments available to give effect to a climate policy – permits, licences, and the element of discretion in their oversight, as well as tax credits – and the inevitability of changing policies and priorities, it is unsurprising that a second impact of the Energy Transition is likely to be on the adequacy of legal security typically offered by governments for large-scale energy investments. The change in context is quantitative as well as qualitative. On one estimate, recent investment in lower-carbon technologies was the largest ever, at US$1.8 trillion, equivalent roughly to the amount being invested in fossil fuels.[26] However, if global investment is to follow a trajectory that will reach Net Zero CO_2 emissions by 2050, that amount would need to be almost tripled immediately and the higher amount sustained for the rest of the present decade.[27]

Investment on this scale is unlikely unless the guarantees or assurances available to investors through national laws, treaty commitments, and/or contractual arrangements are perceived as credible for sufficiently long periods to allow for recovery of investment costs and a pre-calculated expected gain. Based on arbitral jurisprudence to date,[28] the kind of measures that would typically be sought by investors are assurances from the state that are specific in character, making it clear that the assurance is given by the host state to the investor and not to investors in general. Such specific assurances of stability could be included in the form of a commercial contract with a stabilisation clause, or a separate stabilisation agreement as is common in the minerals sector, or in a separate investment law. Both the contract design and the investment itself could be structured to ensure that the investor receives fair and equitable treatment under any relevant investment treaty. The effect would be to give investors – and those willing to lend funds to them – a reasonable expectation that their calculations of financial viability will prove robust in the long-term. An additional requirement is a dispute settlement mechanism

[25] See the references in n 4 above, and the ruling of the European Court of Human Rights in *Verein KlimaSeniorinnen Schweiz and Others v Switzerland* (9 April 2024) www.echr.coe.int/w/grand-chamber-rulings-in-the-climate-change-cases. However, it may be noted that of three climate change cases ruled on by the ECHR, two of three were unsuccessful.

[26] 'Energy Transition Investment Trends 2024' (*BloombergNEF*, 30 January 2024) about.bnef.com/blog/global-clean-energy-investment-jumps-17-hits-1-8-trillion-in-2023-according-to-bloomberg-nef-report/. This includes investments in electrified transport, renewable energies, hydrogen, and carbon capture made in 2023.

[27] ibid.

[28] Many of the arbitral awards involving Spain and Italy before ICSID in recent years provide instances of discussions of this point. For example, see *ACF Renewable Energy Limited v Bulgaria*, ICSID Case No. ARB/18/1, Award, 5 January 2024 at [1333]–[1368].

that allows differences to be addressed away from the national courts of the host country. Without this, the above assurances would be hollow. National courts – in any country or region on the globe – or indeed sub-federal courts, do not usually foster among investors a sense of security about the process and outcome of a dispute that is sufficient for them to commit to a large-scale investment. In this respect, international arbitration will usually be preferred.

In one sense, the legal framework for international investment in new energy projects is both available and tried and tested. International energy contracts providing long-term stability to investors have been common for many years in the international energy industry, especially for hydrocarbons investments. The Energy Transition context provides some impetus for including new clauses or wording in standard contracts to take climate change mitigation into account. However, less sound is the framework of international investment treaties that offers investors various safeguards when investing in a foreign state and recourse to international arbitration if they consider a breach has occurred. This is widely acknowledged to be under strain, although opinions differ greatly about its scope and intensity. In particular, the ECT has suffered from a series of European countries declaring an intention to withdraw entirely from it. The reasons lie in part in the jurisdictional claims of the EU over investment treaty making,[29] and in the argument made that its provisions undermine state actions to address environmental problems and especially climate change by creating a chilling effect so that states are discouraged from exercising their right to regulate for fear of being drawn into costly and reputation-damaging arbitrations.[30] It is not necessary here to examine the merits of the arguments offered for withdrawal from the ECT's scope, other than to note that evidence to support the constraining effect on state intervention attributed to the ECT is sparse, especially with respect to fossil fuels.[31] At a time when unprecedented capital commitments are needed for the energy

[29] The Court of Justice of the EU held in the *Achmea* case that an arbitration clause in an intra-EU bilateral investment treaty was inconsistent with EU law, and in *Komstroy v Moldova*, it held that intra-EU investor-state arbitration under the ECT was also incompatible with EU law. Subsequently, in *PL Holdings v Poland*, it held that an equivalent ad hoc arbitration agreement was also incompatible with EU law. These views and the reasoning behind them have been overwhelmingly rejected by non-EU courts and arbitral tribunals. However, the legal context is one that contributes to uncertainty among investors.

[30] This is a view that has acquired much media coverage: for example, *the Guardian* (21 June 2022) which refers to a letter to the EU and signed by 76 climate scientists that links the ECT investor protections to obstacles to plant closures and prospective large compensation payments: www.theguardian.com/environment/2022/jun/21/young-people-go-to-european-court-to-stop-treaty-that-aids-fossil-fuel-investors. For a wider critique, see IIED/Columbia Center on Sustainable Investment, Briefing: Investor-State Dispute Settlements: A Hidden Handbrake on Climate Action (November 2023) and K Tienaara, 'Regulatory Chill in a Warming World: The Threat to Climate Policy posed by Investor-State Dispute Settlement' (2018) 7(2) *Transnational Environmental Law* 229–50.

[31] It has a limited membership geographically, lacks among its ratifying states all the major hydrocarbons producing states and includes only four states as members that are the 'home-states' of internationally operating oil and gas companies (France, Italy, The Netherlands, and the UK). Most of the claims leading to arbitration under the ECT have in fact concerned renewable forms of energy, not fossil fuels.

sector in pursuit of climate change goals, the ECT ought to have been a source of assurance to investors in the European context. Now, this is less likely to be the case.[32]

Otherwise, the protection given to investments by the investment treaty framework remains arguably both extensive and robust, irrespective of the various controversies surrounding the treaty regime.[33] An initial tendency in arbitral jurisprudence to favour investors rather than states under investment treaties, perhaps evident as long as two decades ago, appears to have been re-balanced with various clarifications and protections for states becoming more prevalent in recent treaties. It would seem to give both parties a greater chance of success in making and responding to claims.

To the extent that uncertainty develops about the assurances available to investors under the international treaty regime, contract provisions seem increasingly likely to respond by developing strengthened stabilisation clauses, or discrete instruments that have a stabilisation effect. Some may argue that legal incentives that constrain the sovereign powers of states in certain defined respects (the economic core) are not required but it is hard to see how investment on the scale required by the Energy Transition and within its timetable can proceed without specific guarantees given to investors about the long-term stability of core economic provisions.

Of course, it is possible to foresee changes in the design and operation of long-term investment contracts as the Energy Transition takes effect. For example, in the choice of law clause, investors, especially in the hydrocarbons sector, have sought in their negotiations to expand the choice of the host government's law to include international law. Since international law now includes the UN Framework Convention on Climate Change and the Paris Agreement, and the UN Sustainable Development Goals,[34] one of which includes access to energy, the question may arise whether a host government will be able to defend itself against claims that could arise out of mandatory phase outs by invoking the parties' choice of international law in their contracts. Similarly, there are many international petroleum contracts that include terminology such as 'good international petroleum industry practice'. Increasingly, this commonly used term might be understood as evolving with the Energy Transition to require acceptance from international oil companies of greater regulatory change by the host state to fulfil its international commitments with respect to climate change.

[32] However, see Section IV below for the operation of Article 47(3) ECT.

[33] Evident in for example the UNCITRAL proceedings in Working Group III on investor-State dispute settlement.

[34] At the UN Conference on Environment and Development at Rio de Janeiro in 1992, the 176 states confirmed the legal principles regarding sustainable development presented by the Brundtland Commission and formally adopted the concept of sustainable development as the new paradigm for international environmental law: see P Sands in V Lowe and D McGoldrick (eds), *Principles of International Environmental Law I: Frameworks, Standards, and Implementation* (Manchester University Press, 1995) 54.

A further issue might be noted that arises out of energy contracts concerning hydrocarbon projects. Among the wide-ranging obligations imposed on the contractor, there is often a requirement to carry out operations 'expeditiously'. In the drive to reach Net Zero, internationally operating energy companies are occasionally subject to pressures with respect to hydrocarbon drilling. Yet for some states the link between resource development and national well-being remains strong. It is therefore possible to envisage a dispute arising from host state frustration at a foreign contractor's hesitation to proceed with appraisal or production drilling. Such language is common in thousands of existing production sharing contracts around the world.

iii. The Commercial Profile of Company Claimants

For many years, the paradigm case of an international energy investor was the internationally operating hydrocarbons company, driven by high returns, able to manage a high cost of capital and to tackle a high degree of price volatility. They have often figured as claimants in seminal international arbitral awards.[35] Now, the energy sector is more diverse with many new players, differing in size, composition, and objectives. The renewable energy sector has tended to attract a variety of new investors, attracted by the prevalence of subsidies and incentives in that burgeoning sector. There has been a notable growth in the more capital-intensive power industry which has had lower profitability, but also lower cost of capital and less market volatility, as is common among regulated assets. Even among the large upstream oil companies, their operations in certain geographical regions have sometimes been transferred to smaller independent players with more focused portfolios and a range of financial models. New investors have also appeared that own assets with the sole purpose of financial gain, lacking any involvement in a company's internal decision-making. These 'portfolio' investors may appear in an arbitral claim alongside the direct investor as an affiliated indirect investor, such as a parent or holding company. However, a strong geopolitical dimension remains. Energy investment retains a familiar north-south aspect, even if more nuanced by south-south capital flows in the twenty-first century than was evident two or three decades ago.[36] Among the newer forms of energy, investment in renewable

[35] For example, *Libyan American Oil Co v Libya*, 20 ILM (1981), 1; *Kuwait v American Independent Oil Co*, 21 ILM (1982) 976.

[36] There has been a growth of investment by entities based in China, India, Russia, and the Middle East which challenges the north (and largely Western) flows of investment to the global south. However, statistics show that where such flows can be described as 'south-south', they remain significantly less than those from the north to the south. Indeed, UNCTAD data reveals that a significant part of the FDI between developing countries is ultimately owned by developed country multinational enterprises. When measured on the basis of ultimate ownership, the share of south-south investment in the total investment (2018 data) falls from 47% to 28%: United Nations (2019) World Investment Report 2019, Geneva. Whatever its scale, the south-south axis of investment has impacts on energy disputes: for example, India's Oil and Natural Gas Corporation (ONGC) registered a claim against Sudan in 2018 to

sources has begun to follow a similar pattern, with capital and expertise exported from a limited number of countries and regions in response to welcoming signals from governments keen to broaden their energy mix. Indeed, the extraterritorial necessity might lack geological roots, but the market-oriented ones are just as compelling to drive cross-border investment. Similarly, with nuclear energy, the international aspect of the industry is less related to the uneven geographical distribution of its raw material, uranium, than it is to the limited distribution of the necessary technical and commercial expertise, especially in processing and enrichment, and requiring multi-national consortia to be assembled for bids to construct and operate a new plant.

Like the investors themselves, the destination of capital commitments in the energy sector has become more diverse than ever before, with investments in renewable power and fuels reaching unprecedented levels in 2023; with linkages to non-energy sectors such as mining and infrastructure being reshaped;[37] and with the regulatory role of states in this reshaping of the energy mix likely to prove fundamental and pervasive. At the same time, if the terms of the Paris Agreement were to be fully implemented, this would leave 29 per cent of oil reserves stranded and by one estimate would destroy US$360 billion from the value of the largest IOCs measured by reserves, over one sixth of their total enterprise value.[38] The threat posed by a shift in investment priorities is evident when it is recalled that in a single year, banks provided about US$669 billion in financing to fossil fuel companies.[39] In this respect, the Energy Transition factor has two important impacts on future investment flows: it creates a perception of reduced risk associated with investment in lower carbon technologies and subsidised public programmes in order to promote the shift to lower carbon usage, which would allow a shift in capital allocation to these areas; at the same time, it creates a perception that traditional sectors such as fossil fuels, especially investment in coal assets, have become riskier, since a long-term project of around 25 years encounters scenarios of peaking markets for these energy resources.

Yet, one of the above features has a continuing, special significance for a potential investor in calculating the risk profile of an investment. The state will nearly

recover funds lost from an oil project when part of Sudan seceded in 2011, the first arbitration claim ever filed by ONGC against a government: GAR, 'Indian state energy company brings claim against Sudan' (17 April 2018).

[37] Bloomberg (n 26). Further, energy related claims can also extend to the various minerals such as lithium and cobalt that are essential to modern batteries to run electric vehicles. Mining disputes no longer seem to fall neatly into a different, largely unrelated category, and are more obviously, part of an energy supply chain.

[38] *Financial Times* (2 March 2020) Energy's stranded assets are a cause of financial stability concern (P Jenkins based on FT data).

[39] The year was 2022: www.thebanker.com/Cover-story-Why-are-banks-still-financing-fossil-fuels-1696231243#:~:text=The%20Royal%20Bank%20of%20Canada,financed%20%2420.0bn%20in%20Europe. If traditional private capital investors such as banks and large asset funds withdraw from the sector, 'non-banks' (less regulated and less accountable) may fill the gap if the cash flow is attractive. The capital flow need not simply cease altogether.

always have an extensive set of roles in the life of a project, as natural resources owner, regulator, and participant (that is, as contracting party through an entity acting with delegated authority), either directly or through one or more of its agencies or enterprises or through local components as are common in devolved or federal systems. For foreign investors, this often-overlapping series of roles implies a higher than usual degree of vulnerability to policy reorientations and indeed to policy inconsistency among governments and regulators from one region and country to the next. The risks of such policy reorientations are, I have argued in this Section, significantly increased by the impacts of the Energy Transition on the modern 'Transition State'. Another quite different aspect of the new diversity among energy investors is the decline in shared knowledge and experience among investors themselves. For decades, the typical contracts reached by international oil companies and host states included references to 'good international oil industry practice'. To the extent that the players share a similar approach to industry practice, the standard this refers to can be filled with meaningful content. For private equity firms that evaluate their energy assets in terms of a capacity to deliver a return in a few years, the perspective they bring to a joint venture, for example, will be very different. This opens the door to increasing commercial differences and investor-to-investor disputes among joint venture partners, and indeed between them and their supplier partners or sub-contractors.

In the above context, it is hardly surprising that energy arbitrations continue to be multi-jurisdictional, with parties from different countries joining to spread the risk and structuring their investments to take advantage of legal and fiscal benefits in a third country. Increasingly, enforcement and asset seizure for non-compliance with an award has also taken on a more international character.[40]

III. Transition Disputes, an Initial Assessment

There is a broad group of recent disputes that can be linked to Energy Transition phenomena, such as the search for new, cleaner kinds of energy or developing energy technologies or minerals important to the Energy Transition, and a phasing out of fossil fuels and mandatory closures of plants. In this Section, these initial experiences and their legal effects will be assessed, including the notion of 'legitimate expectations' in the context of the increased presence of the Transition State. As a baseline for this review, it takes the Paris Agreement of 2015, and so does not consider the many cases arising out of the measures taken by Spain, Italy,

[40] We may also note the emergence of arbitral award default coverage in political risk insurance policies offered by private and public insurers, including the World Bank's Multilateral Investment Guarantee Agency (MIGA). For a discussion of this, see P Bekker and A Ogawa, 'The Impact of Bilateral Investment Treaty (BIT) Proliferation on Demand for Investment Insurance: Reassessing Political Risk Insurance After the "BIT Bang" '(2013) 28 *ICSID Review* 314–50, at 346.

and the Czech Republic, around 2010–12 which have indeed led to many awards. Consideration of such awards would require at least one chapter to itself. The review draws heavily upon published awards, decisions, and reliable data from international institutions such as the ICC, ICSID, the PCA or the LCIA. Some of the arbitrations are still pending, giving the conclusions a provisional character. The sample of cases might be described as Energy Transition Disputes 1.0.

A. New Energies and Disputes

When the search for new forms of energy takes place, it is likely that familiar legal mechanisms for granting access such as permitting or licensing will be central to any arbitral disputes that emerge. If there is a dispute between the foreign investor and the host state, the conditions included in the grant of access may have been breached by subsequent state action. Specific measures that offer investors an incentive to commit capital are also likely to figure in the legal framework. An example is the production of biofuels in Panama, where an Italian company registered in the British Virgin Islands (BVI) brought an ICSID claim against the Panama government in 2020 for an alleged series of measures that made it impossible for the investor to proceed with a plan to manufacture bioethanol through locally sourced material.[41] Bioethanol is a renewable energy source made by fermenting the sugar and starch components of plant by-products, such a sugarcane, corn, or wheat. Initially, the government had passed a law envisaging the creation of a national biofuel industry, and an implementing measure subsequently required oil companies to mix gasoline with a certain percentage of bioethanol, resulting in a cleaner form of gasoline. This regulation set the price for the sale of bioethanol, taking care that the price covered the production costs, so that the local product was not undercut by any cheaper international version of the product. As the national plan took shape and these incentives were introduced, the investor obtained a ten-year renewable permit for the construction and operation of a biofuel plant and committed capital to purchase land and plant, concluding several long-term contracts with parties interested in buying its bioethanol. The investor claimed to have received assurances that this law was stable. When a new government took office, it set a new price formula for locally produced bioethanol. It also revoked the decree that required a proportion of bioethanol to be mixed with gasoline, in effect destroying the nascent industry in the country. In its claim seeking around US$100 million in damages,[42] the investor claimed that the government's assurances over the stability of the legal framework had created a legitimate expectation that was not met. Among the claims made by the claimant,

[41] *Campos de Pese S.A. v Republic of Panamá*, ICSID Case No. ARB/20/19: 1 March 2024.

[42] 'Greenberg Traurig Secures Victory for The Republic of Panama in ICSID Arbitration' (*gtlaw.com*, 4 March 2024) www.gtlaw.com/en/news/2024/03/press-releases/greenberg-traurig-secures-victory-for-the-republic-of-panama-in-icsid-arbitration.

Campos, under the Italy-Panama Bilateral Investment Treaty (BIT) were expropriation and denial of justice, and others based on the MFN clause. Despite the novelty of the energy element, the regulatory measures taken by the government to remove essential incentives and the claim made that they caused the claimant to cease operations are familiar ones in energy disputes between foreign investors and host states. In international investment law, a change of government does not affect obligations entered into by or on behalf of the state, which remains liable. However, in this case the tribunal found that it lacked jurisdiction, applying three tests of control over the investment, and finding insufficient evidence of legal or de facto control. Any specific features arising from this new energy source or the linkage of local legislative measures to an Energy Transition policy were therefore not examined by the tribunal.

A different kind of energy, yet rarely known to be in commercial use, is geothermal energy, a thermal form of energy extracted from beneath the surface of the earth, capable of providing a low carbon, renewable heat independent of weather conditions. It has already figured in several investor-state arbitrations.[43] For example, in an investment in Kenya,[44] a US-Canadian investor secured a 30-year licence to exploit geothermal resources in southwest Kenya, but the licence was revoked by the government after five years. The government alleged a lack of performance of the licence duties and a lack of capacity to carry out the work. In their assessment of the claim, the tribunal found that the forfeiture did not violate either local or international law. The claimant did not, in its view, have a legitimate expectation that it would not be required to commence drilling before a Power Purchase Agreement was in place.[45] There was no evidence of a representation by Kenya that could have induced such an expectation. A review of the reasoning adopted by the tribunal does not reveal the influence of any features arising specifically from or associated with the character of the energy source. The claim for US$340 million was dismissed.[46]

Disputes of a different kind arise from so-called critical minerals. An indirect effect of the Energy Transition is the recognition that many states will come to depend on imports of a limited range of minerals in quantities that are significantly higher than at present. Many of these (often 'battery') minerals are disproportionately located in a few, not necessarily investor-friendly states, highlighting the kind of vulnerability familiar to investors in traditional oil and gas producing states. To reduce this dependence and identify new sources, some states have sought to encourage investment in their territories. Two early examples of disputes arising from such efforts at investment promotion may be noted.

[43] In Indonesia there were disputes leading to arbitration involving CalEnergy in the 1990s, and in the Philippines in 2016.

[44] *WalAm Energy LLC v Republic of Kenya*, ICSID Case No. ARB/15/7. The request for arbitration was filed in January 2015.

[45] Award, 10 July 2020, para 527.

[46] ibid para 579. An application for annulment failed.

First, a dispute arose in Mexico concerning rights to mine phosphate sand deposits in waters offshore. With innovative technologies these may be extracted commercially in the foreseeable future, and their location in waters offshore hints at the notion of a 'blue economy' that may emerge in future years. A US company, Odyssey Marine Exploration, brought a claim under the North American Free Trade Agreement (NAFTA) on behalf of its Mexican subsidiary, ExO, arising out of a refusal by the Mexican authorities to grant an environmental permit.[47] In relation to NAFTA's successor, the United States Mexico Canada Agreement (USMCA), this is a 'pending claim' within the terms of Annex 14-C, paragraphs one and four, for which Mexico has promised to maintain its consent after the expiry of NAFTA.[48] The investor had been granted a mining concession for the deposit with a 50-year duration, covering about 3,000 square kilometers, and sought to extract the mineral using dredging techniques which, in contrast to terrestrial mining, had both cost advantages and a smaller environmental footprint, they alleged. An environmental impact assessment and development plan involving four years of preparation was rejected by the authorities, although in the same period, Mexican companies and state agencies were alleged to have secured permission to carry out activities in areas that were more ecologically sensitive than this one. The argument was that Mexico was in breach of Article 1105 NAFTA which requires Fair and Equitable Treatment (FET) and full protection and security; Article 1110(1) which prohibits indirect expropriations and Article 1102 that requires treatment no less favourable than that which the host state accords to its own investors.[49] The claim sought full compensation reflecting the fair market value of the concession and the claimant's investment in Mexico (US$2.36 billion, plus interest).[50] Once again, the legal issues are familiar ones, as is the treaty protection sought, even though the way that the natural resource was going to be extracted relied upon recently developed and innovative technology.

A second example concerns rare earths and uranium mining. An Energy Transition will require a very significant increase in the supply of certain minerals, such as cobalt, lithium, manganese, and rare earth elements that are required to produce permanent magnets for many of the new technologies. For some, the potential of nuclear power offers benefits in an Energy Transition, and hence there is a renewed interest in uranium deposits, for such applications. The grant of rights to search and exploit such minerals became a source of dispute in *Greenland Minerals v Greenland & Denmark* when the claimant's plans to start exploiting resources that it discovered were cast into doubt by a prohibition on uranium mining by the Greenland Government.[51] The resources

[47] *Odyssey Marine Exploration Inc v United Mexican States*, ICSID Case No UNCT/20/1; Claimant's Memorial, 4 September 2020.

[48] Claimant's Memorial at [207].

[49] Odyssey Marine Exploration at [217]–[352].

[50] Ibid at [433].

[51] *Greenland Minerals A/S v Government of Greenland and Government of the Kingdom of Denmark*: see Greenland Minerals Limited Press Release (26 July 2022) Draft Exploitation Licence Decision and

comprised rare earth elements with uranium as a by-product. In late 2021 there was a statutory prohibition on uranium exploitation that led to the claimant's application for a licence to exploit being rejected. In this instance, the investor was a foreign (Chinese-based) company, and the claim was being funded by a third party. The case has several interesting features in relation to the Energy Transition. First, the right to exploit is typically in most extractive industries closely linked to the right to explore since the risk allocation set at the exploration stage. Failure to identify commercially exploitable resources means that the loss falls on to the investor. Success means that a sharing arrangement agreed at the outset will not be revised in the light of the reduced risk after discovery. Without the guarantee of near automaticity of the transition from exploration to exploitation rights, most reputable investors would not proceed. In this case, the Mineral Resources Act sets out a scheme that allows such a transition from the exploration to the exploitation stage, subject to conditions that are largely procedural (a declaration of commerciality, feasibility study and delineation of the area). The Government's legislative intervention occurred after a successful exploration and stopped a further investment decision. Arguably, this is just the kind of regulatory act that the granting system set out in the basic resources law was designed to prevent (and thus to secure investment). Second, the decision by the aggrieved investor to initiate arbitration under Section 20 of the Exploration Licence resulted in a press release from the Government in which it asserted that the arbitration would 'take the case out of Greenland and outside Greenlandic law.' Further, it stated, '(a)rbitration is a form of private litigation where disputes can be settled outside the ordinary public courts'.[52] The right to take a dispute to arbitration was in fact one of the Standard Terms of the Exploration Licences issued under the Mineral Resources Act. Finally, the compensation that the claimant seeks has a maximum of US$11.5 billion,[53] which is around four times the annual Gross Domestic Product of Greenland.[54] This raises an important question for a tribunal about the proper scope of expected profits (as distinct from actual losses). The arbitration is ongoing, although its jurisdiction has been challenged. For our purposes, it may be noted that once again the legal issues appear familiar, and the strength of public policy objections to a project are also clear. In this case, however, the objection appears to be aimed at the extraction of uranium rather than rare earth elements, with the latter being incontrovertibly associated with an Energy Transition, and the former (uranium) less so.

White Paper Review. The prohibition applied to ores that exceeded a specific threshold set out in an Act of Parliament of December 2021.

[52] Statement of Claim (SoC), para 830.

[53] SoC, para 1517.

[54] J Hartmann, AE Bastida, AM Daza-Clark, 'Transition Minerals: A Cautionary Tale from Greenland' (*ejiltalk.org*, 29 January 2024) www.ejiltalk.org/transition-minerals-a-cautionary-tale-from-greenland/.

B. Disputes Arising from a Mandatory Closure and Phase-Outs

A growing number of energy disputes arise from measures that respond to evolving emission reduction policies. In Europe, these co-exist with the many ECT cases in which feed-in tariffs for renewable energy were revised, sometimes in ways that triggered international arbitrations. Notable arbitrations involved the Czech Republic, Italy, and Spain, but have also included Bulgaria, Latvia and Romania. Such claims are prima facie concerned with adaptations by governments to an existing policy and implementing regulatory framework in the face of costs that are deemed unsustainable by the governments concerned, often successor governments to those responsible for the original regulatory schemes. These measures differ from the policies that require closure, phasing-out or impose prohibitions on the use of fossil fuels. The latter sort of measure falls into a different category and is closely linked to an evolution of energy priorities that is more aligned with a state's climate policy. It can also arise from the decisions of national courts.

Below are several examples of states pursuing apparent climate change mitigation policies that investors have claimed negatively affect existing investments, with the initiation of arbitral proceedings as a result. Several cases arise from measures that have clear roots in a policy that fits the notion of an Energy Transition: for example, measures to accelerate a phase-out of coal in the generation of electricity. Others arise from measures less clearly related to an Energy Transition and possibly rooted in a national policy choice on the energy mix that has another basis: for example, Germany's measures to phase-out nuclear power.

The Netherlands faced potential ECT claims because of its decision to phase out coal in electricity generation from 2030. Following a decision of the Supreme Court to censor a lack of action by the Government in addressing climate change issues and the adoption of a Prohibition of Coal in Electricity Generation Act in 2019, a phased ban was introduced on the use of coal to generate electricity. The Act prohibits the use of coal as a fuel in the plants that generate electricity and does not affect other uses of the generating plants (for example, those that use biomass instead of coal to generate electricity). A transition period is offered until the end of 2029. Subject to certain conditions, compensation is available. This idea of a coal phase-out is not new and has also been adopted by both Germany and the UK with dates set for the closure of certain plants. However, in this case the compensation payments were deemed inadequate by RWE, and Uniper, both German-based utilities that owned coal-fired power plants in the country. In January 2021, a claim was submitted by RWE AG and RWE Eemshaven Holding II BV against the Netherlands under the ECT.[55] This was the first ever claim against the Netherlands

[55] *RWE AG and RWE Eemshaven Holding II BV v Kingdom of the Netherlands*, ICSID Case No ARB/21/4.

before ICSID. In April 2021, a claim was submitted by Uniper under the ECT.[56] Uniper had agreed to build a coal-fired power plant in 2007, following discussions with the Dutch Government. The plant opened in 2016 and cost a reputed €1.6 billion with an expected life of 40 years.[57] Both claims were discontinued.

Some features of this episode are worthy of note. At least one of the companies concerned expressly stated that it supported Dutch climate goals and the Energy Transition generally.[58] Not all companies affected chose to submit a claim.[59] A request by the Netherlands to the German courts led to a decision by the Supreme Court (Bundesgerichtshof) that the arbitration was inadmissible due to its intra-EU character. RWE subsequently requested the discontinuance of the proceedings under the applicable ICSID Arbitration Rule 44. Uniper's justification for discontinuance was different. As if to demonstrate that volatility is a characteristic of energy markets and not just government policy, Uniper was obliged to withdraw its claims following a bail-out package that was agreed upon with the German Government in mid-2022, due to a deterioration in its circumstances following gas shortages in 2022 (which required it to make expensive purchases on the spot market).

In Germany, a similar coal phase-out decision was taken in 2020, requiring the closure of the country's coal-fired power stations by 2038.[60] The rules differed according to whether the coal was domestic, 'brown coal', or lignite, on the one hand, or imported 'hard' coal on the other. The approach to phasing out brown coal is interesting since it appears to have been influenced by the earlier German experience with a phase-out of nuclear power, discussed below, which led to arbitration claims against it from Vattenfall. With brown coal, the approach was to offer relatively high levels of compensation to the coal operators, called 'voluntary' payments, and to implement the phase-out by means of a contract negotiated between the coal companies and the relevant federal ministries, aimed – it appears – at removing the potential exposure of the government to arbitral claims under, for example, the ECT. Article 24 of the contract requires the companies to expressly waive their right to international arbitration.[61] A negotiated contractual approach

[56] Uniper SE, *Uniper Benelux Holding B.V. and Uniper Benelux N.V. v Kingdom of the Netherlands*, ICSID Case No ARB/21/22.

[57] Uniper SE, *Uniper Benelux Holding BV and Uniper Benelux NV v Kingdom of the Netherlands*, ICSID Case No. ARB/21/22. See Claimant's Memorial, 20 May 2022: www.italaw.com.

[58] Press Release (16 April 2021) www.uniper.energy/news/uniper-seeks-judgement-for-the-future-of-maasvlakte.

[59] The Dutch company, NUON, owned by Vattenfall, apparently did not object to the closure as long as the plant's dismantling was funded and the workforce compensated: 'The Netherlands is facing its first ICSID arbitration, as German energy giant RWE makes good in earlier threats' (*iareporter*, 3 February 2021).

[60] Gesetzentwurf der Bundesregierung für ein 'Kohleaustiegsgesetz (3 July 2020).

[61] Article 24(2) states that the obligation to waive the right to seek legal remedies under international investment law 'extends in particular to arbitration proceedings arising from or relating to rights under the Energy Charter Treaty, to the rights of the companies and the enterprises they control under Art. 26 of the Energy Charter Treaty, and to any potential rights under other bilateral or multilateral investment agreements': from English translation in ClientEarth (September 2020) www.clientearth.org/media/vu5amwng/the-german-lignite-phase-out-contract-and-investment-arbitration-isds-ce-en.pdf.

has therefore been designed as an alternative to a more conventional regulatory approach to achieving its Energy Transition policy and avoiding arbitral claims from investors. Initial experience suggests it has had mixed success.[62]

An earlier phase-out policy was applied to the use of nuclear power, in the aftermath of the Fukushima accident in Japan. The German legislature adopted Nuclear Amendment No 13, a measure which imposed specific decommissioning dates for each nuclear plant. This triggered an ECT claim in 2012 by a Swedish investor, Vattenfall, for compensation to an amount of €4.7 billion.[63] In parallel domestic proceedings,[64] initiated by Vattenfall, the German Constitutional Court (Bundesverfassungsgericht) held that Nuclear Amendment No 13 was unconstitutional, affecting Vattenfall's right to distribute their residual energy, and affecting its right to property, guaranteed under the Basic Law.[65] Following negotiations, the parties entered into a Settlement Agreement in 2021, providing for €1.4 billion in compensation.[66] The ICSID arbitration was discontinued.

Germany faced other claims in respect of its renewable energy legislation. It amended its Renewable Energy Sources Act in 2016 so that the right to receive fixed feed-in tariffs from the State was replaced by a market-based pricing mechanism for renewable energy producers. In addition, a new Offshore Wind Energy Act required investors in offshore wind projects to participate in tariff auctions managed by the Federal Grid Agency, which would award bidders according to those offering the cheapest rate to the consumer. In response to the changed regulatory framework, a claim was brought against Germany by Strabag, a large construction firm, and by others under the ECT on the ground that the regulatory changes, combined with the exclusion of their projects from the public auction process, meant that they had no alternative but to abandon the investments, which had been made in reliance on the legal regime for offshore wind producers.[67]

[62] A claim was registered on 20 October 2023 by a Swiss investor in relation to its investment in a coal power plant in Lünen, Germany, based on the ECT: *Azienda Elettrica Ticinese (AET) v Federal Republic of Germany*, ICSID Case No. ARB/23/47.

[63] *Vattenfall AB and others v Federal Republic of Germany*, ICSID Case No. ARB/12/12. The arbitration was discontinued on 9 November 2021, following the entry into force of a Settlement Agreement. Germany agreed to pay compensation of around EUR 1.4 billion. This is not to be confused with an earlier case with the same parties about a power plant construction project, which was concluded with an award embodying the parties' settlement agreement in 2011: Vattenfall AB, Vattenfall Europe AG, *Vattenfall Europe Generation AG v Federal Republic of Germany*, ICSID Case No. ARB/09/6. The case concerned environmental restrictions imposed on a €2.6 billion coal-fired power plant under construction on the Elbe River. The final construction permit appears to have been granted by the City of Hamburg authority only subject to certain additional restrictions on the plant's impact on the river.

[64] Interestingly, claims pursued by nuclear utilities in German state courts succeeded on their merits, survived appellate review, and entered into the damages phase, all in a very few years.

[65] Press Release No 98/2020 of 12 November 2020; Order of 29 September 2020, 1 BvR 1550/19, 'The Sixteenth Amendment of 10 July 2018 to the Atomic Energy Act has not entered into force; the legislator remains obligated to enact new provisions.'

[66] 'Vattenfall asks for discontinuance of ICSID Arbitration against Germany after Settlement enters into force' (*iareporter*, 2 November 2021).

[67] Strabag SE, *Erste Nordsee-Offshore Holding GmbH and Zweite Nordsee-Offshore Holding GmbH v Germany*, ICSID Case No. ARB/19/29. The other known case is *Mainstream Renewable Power et al v Germany*, ICSID Case No. ARB/21/26 (claims brought by six Irish and German companies under

A different approach to phasing out fossil fuels has been evident in France and Italy. In France, a new law – known as the Hulot Act, after its promoter – prohibited the production of oil and gas after 2040, and the grant of new hydrocarbons exploration licences with immediate effect in France and its overseas territories. It thereby sought to implement the country's commitments under the Paris Agreement on climate change. However, the original intent was to prohibit production when the current 62 concessions reached the end of their terms. This was revised following an opinion delivered by the Conseil d'État on 1 September 2017.[68] The latter based its reasoning on the French Mining Code, and noted that Section L. 142-7 provides that:

> the duration of a concession may be successively extended for periods less than or equal to twenty-five years, with no limit placed on the number of possible extensions, [and so] must be construed, in light of the spirit and purpose of the mining regulations, not as making the granting of an extension optional but as allowing for the total duration of a concession to be adapted to the duration corresponding to the full exploitation of a deposit, which is not necessarily known at the time of the initial grant. This logic would, moreover, explain the fact that no limit is place on the number of possible extensions that may be granted. Thus, an extension may, if the concession holder demonstrates that a deposit has enough potential to justify continuing to be exploited, be regarded as a right, or at least as a legitimately expected effect. The public interest analysed in point eight above can therefore be said to be insufficient to justify the immediate cessation of all ongoing mining operations.

There is some controversy about the relationship between the above opinion, clearly based on the French Mining Law, and a memorandum commissioned by a Canadian oil company called Vermilion, which was published following circulation of an early version of the Hulot Act.[69] Reports on its content suggest it argued that a failure to allow extension of its permits and concessions after 2018 would disproportionately affect and diminish its property rights and its freedom to carry on a business. In the context of this chapter, however, it is the copious references it contained to the ECT that are relevant. It argued that France's commitments under the ECT prevent it from 'acting against the legitimate expectations of an investor as regards the key conditions for its investment and the stability of the legal and commercial environment'. Did this published opinion commissioned from a French law firm by the oil company have an influence on the thinking of the distinguished French judges in the Conseil d'État? There is no evidence of any influence upon the Conseil d'État's thinking or its Opinion. It is reasonable

the ECT concerning their treatment of investments in three offshore wind projects in the German North Sea).

[68] For this and the quotation below see M Vaudano, 'How the lobbies used the threat of ISDS to neuter the Hulot Act' *Le Monde* (4 September 2018) www.bilaterals.org/spip.php?page=print-art&id_article=37790.

[69] Vermilion was responsible at the time for around 75 percent of the production of hydrocarbons on French soil: Vermilion vs France' (*10isdsstories.org*) 10isdsstories.org/cases/case5/.

however to assume that they were aware of the memorandum and its arguments. What weight they gave to them, if any, is unknown.[70]

In Italy, similar legislative actions against hydrocarbons exploration and production went from the proposal stage to law in the form of Act No.11/2019. Article 11-ter of this Act suspended all exploration permits as well as new applications for production concessions for a period of 18 months,[71] subsequently extended twice. In effect, the moratorium was to allow the Government time to determine which areas, if any, were suitable for hydrocarbons activities, whilst considering environmental, social and economic sustainability factors in the framework of a Plan.[72] Administrative fees were also to be increased by 25 times because of the Act, and in the subsequent amending legislation it was expressly allowed for renewable energy generators to be installed on areas that were no longer designated for oil and gas exploration and production under the Plan. A modified version of this prohibition was subsequently introduced in 2022, excluding natural gas from its scope.[73] In this context of legislative acts constraining hydrocarbons activities in Italy, it is not surprising that there has already been a notable example of an investor claim with respect to a hydrocarbons investment. In the *Rockhopper v Italy* arbitration before ICSID, the investor claimed compensation of €275 million from Italy for a breach of its obligations under the ECT, including legitimate expectations.[74] The claimants, various companies in the Rockhopper group, had acquired companies with applications pending in Italy to obtain exploitation concessions from the relevant Ministry. In 2015 the Ministry found that the relevant environmental requirements had been complied with in its Environmental Impact Assessment (EIA), but a subsequent application by Rockhopper for a final exploitation concession was rejected. In its final award, the tribunal found that an Italian law of December 2015 which strengthened an

[70] The Law was adopted on 30 December 2017, and was not retroactive: LOI n° 2017-1839 du 30 décembre 2017 mettant fin à la recherche ainsi qu'à l'exploitation des hydrocarbures et portant diverses dispositions relatives à l'énergie et à l'environnement (Law no. 2017-1839 on the end of exploration and exploitation of hydrocarbons and diverse dispositions related to energy and the environment – Climate Change Laws of the World (*climate-laws.org*) climate-laws.org/documents/law-no-2017-1839-on-the-end-of-exploration-and-exploitation-of-hydrocarbons-and-diverse-dispositions-related-to-energy-and-the-environment-e69e?id=law-no-2017-1839-on-the-end-of-exploration-and-exploitation-of-hydrocarbons-and-diverse-dispositions-related-to-energy-and-the-environment_c16d).

[71] D Ruggero Di Bella and J Galvez, 'Oil & Gas: Is Italy Doing it Wrong All Over Again?' (13 March 2019) arbitrationblog.kluwerarbitration.com/2019/03/13/oil-gas-is-italy-doing-it-wrong-all-over-again/. This moratorium was extended twice to September 2021, after which a Plan for the Sustainable Energy Transition of Eligible Areas (PiTESAI) was approved in 2022, reintroducing the prohibition on oil exploration in areas expressly described as unsuitable, but also introducing a goal of boosting the production of natural gas.

[72] Of course, a tribunal can introduce a similar measure by adopting interim protective measures that include a ban on new drilling pending the outcome of the arbitral proceedings. For example, a three-year moratorium on new drilling was imposed by the tribunal in the UNCLOS Annex VII arbitration between Ghana and Cote d'Ivoire.

[73] See n 71 above.

[74] Rockhopper Italia SpA, *Rockhopper Mediterranean Ltd and Rockhopper Exploration Plc v Italy*, ICSID Case No. ARB/17/14.

offshore drilling ban, and the subsequent denial of an application for a production concession amounted to a direct expropriation under Article 13 of the ECT. Italy's right to impose and strengthen a drilling ban was not in question, the tribunal found, and so side-stepping the issue of whether the ECT was being used to resist government measures to implement its climate change commitments. Instead, it focused on the expropriation provision of Article 13 ECT, noting the protection it gave to investors was not absolute. However, Italy had failed to pay any compensation for the loss of the right to be granted a concession to produce hydrocarbons.[75] Further, when Italy tried to rely upon the police powers doctrine and the precautionary principle in taking action to prohibit drilling so near its coast, the tribunal found that when the Ministry accepted the validity of the EIA in 2015, Italy could no longer rely upon the precautionary principle. More likely its action in rejecting the application was influenced by 'political and civic engagements'. While probably a reasonable conclusion, it is also very likely that these 'engagements' were themselves driven by environmental concerns. Essentially, the tribunal framed the dispute in institutional terms as a conflict between central government and regional authorities, with the latter focusing in their arguments on the potential risks of oil spills occurring on the local coastline, rather than on environmental aspects, and avoided the Energy Transition or climate-related aspects altogether.[76] In this respect it was helped by the apparent reluctance of the Respondent to make more of these aspects in its argumentation before the tribunal.

In the final award, the claimants were awarded €185 million in lost profits plus decommissioning costs of more than EUR 6 million and interest.[77] Italy subsequently filed for annulment of the award and enforcement was stayed provisionally. Sadly, the case does not tell us anything about whether ISDS or the ECT can or do act as potential blocks to legislative measures taken by states to meet their climate mitigation commitments.

In Canada, there have been several examples of Energy Transition-related measures by state entities, leading to arbitral claims by foreign investors. However, these have been more concerned with the operation of renewable energy regimes that have been put in place and their environmental impacts. For example, a decision by the Ontario Power Authority (OPA) to delay the award of permits and authorisations to Windstream Energy led to the company filing a claim under NAFTA,[78] which Canada ultimately lost.[79]

[75] Final Award, 23 August 2022, para 199.

[76] ibid paras 111–14.

[77] ibid para 335. This point is made by Paolo Mazzotti in an interesting article: 'Rockhopper v Italy and the Tension between ISDS and Climate Policy' (*voelkerrechtsblog.org*, 21 December 2022) voelkerrechtsblog.org/de/rockhopper-v-italy-and-the-tension-between-isds-and-climate-policy/.

[78] *Windstream Energy LLC v Government of Canada*, 27 September 2016, PCA Case No 2018- 54. A second arbitration has arisen with Windstream making the claim that its expectations of proceeding with the project after the first arbitration were breached by subsequent actions by the Ontario state company.

[79] See also the renewable energy case, *Tennant Energy LLC v Government of Canada*, PCA Case No. 2018-54, Notice of Arbitration (1 June 2017) (about administration of the FiT programme and grid

However, Canada found itself the respondent in a fossil fuels-related claim arising from the decision by the Provincial government of Alberta to phase out greenhouse gas emissions (GHG) and air pollutants produced by coal-fired power generation by 2030 and make transition payments to certain companies in relation to this policy.[80] The decision to phase out coal-fired electricity was part of Alberta's Climate Leadership Plan and addressed its circumstances as the second highest GHG emitting sector in Alberta. Six of the existing coal-fired power plants were expected to operate beyond 2030, so the Provincial Government agreed to pay the operators around US$1 billion in transition payments, as a form of compensation, between 2016 and 2030. It did not propose to pay suppliers of coal, only the generation units.

In 2019, Westmoreland Mining Holdings (WMH), a US coal mining company, initiated arbitration proceedings under NAFTA Chapter 11. The allegation by WMH was that it suffered discrimination by the policy and the lack of payments made to it (as a supplier of coal). Most of the recipients of payments were in fact customers of WMH. It argued that its investment in 2014 in two Canadian entities, which directly or indirectly owned three coal mines located adjacent to power generators, had been made at a time when a federal regulatory scheme contemplated a 50-year term for coal-fired power plants. Its losses were to include revenue from early closure on or before 2030 and accelerated costs arising from the rehabilitation of land after closure. In fact, the dispute arose from an investment made by Westmoreland Coal Company (WCC), which in late 2018 filed for bankruptcy and sent a notice of arbitration to Canada soon after. Some of its assets were transferred to WMH, the claimant in the arbitration, which had been incorporated in early 2019. WCC withdrew its NAFTA claim and WMH filed its notice of arbitration on its own behalf and under NAFTA.

In its Award of January 2022, the tribunal found that it lacked jurisdiction since the claimant had to have owned or controlled the relevant investment at the time of the alleged treaty breach to bring a NAFTA claim. Since the claimant did not exist when the underlying measures were adopted, it did not qualify as a successor of an entity that owned the investment at the relevant time. No assignment of the right to bring a NAFTA claim could have taken place, so WMH did not qualify as a protected investor. The tribunal also upheld Canada's objection that the challenged measures did not relate to the claimant or its investment in the terms of NAFTA.[81] The claimant had not – in the tribunal's view – undertaken any investment risk since the coal phase-out was widely known at the time when the claimant was incorporated and had even been factored into the purchase price that the claimant paid for the assets of Westmoreland Coal Company.

access). All claims were dismissed after the tribunal found that the claimant was not a qualifying investor under NAFTA: Final Award (25 October 2022).

[80] *Westmoreland Mining Holdings LLC v Government of Canada*, ICSID Case No. UNCT/20/3. See also *Lone Pine Resources Inc. v Government of Canada*, discussed at n 83 below.

[81] Final Award, 31 January 2022. A third arbitral proceeding was subsequently initiated and was ongoing at the time of writing.

IV. The Sun Sets Slowly, Fossil Fuels and Disputes in the Energy Transition

To the extent that an Energy Transition has already begun, it is already clear that it does not mean that investments in fossil fuels will cease. Indeed, there is reliable evidence to the contrary.[82] For many Asian countries, these will be in coal rather than oil and gas. According to Rystad Energy, a specialist consulting firm, the amount of investment estimated to go into the global oil and gas industry in 2022 was around US$628 billion. All of that will be based on contracts that provide extensive forms of legal protection, and all of these have been tried and tested over decades. Many, if not most, of these contracts will contain stabilisation clauses. How might the Energy Transition affect these protections?

So far, there have been examples of arbitrations arising out of attempts by governments to adjust the energy mix in their countries, involving mandatory closures and phase-outs, and eroding the value of assets already created or investments already made. These are alleged to have become stranded assets: infrastructure and assets created that no longer serve a commercial purpose. Compensation claims have followed in the German cases discussed, and were sought in the two Dutch cases, in connection with a government timetable for phasing out coal-fired power plants. In Canada, moratoria on hydrocarbons exploration in Quebec and Alberta have also led to arbitrations.[83] In France a potential arbitration was avoided when proposed legislation constraining hydrocarbons activity was modified, but in Italy legislative restrictions on hydrocarbons activity resulted in a successful claim by an investor.

However, the impacts of the Energy Transition on the international oil industry are potentially much greater than this. The short-term impacts may be limited but need to be weighed up against the creation of a new, unfamiliar set of risks in the investor-state relationship:

(1) For example, possible decisions not to develop a discovery due to projected falls in demand, leading to potential disputes with host governments and/or national oil companies (NOCs). Such disputes may be initiated by host states or by co-venturers for a failure to develop proven reserves.

[82] UNEP et al, Production Gap Report 2023. Governments are planning to produce more than double the amount of fossil fuels in 2030 than would be consistent with limiting warming to 1.5 degrees C.

[83] *Lone Pine Resources Inc v Government of Canada*, ICSID Case No UNCT/15/2; *Westmoreland Mining Holdings LLC v Government of Canada*, ICSID Case No UNCT/20/3. In the former case, the claims – concerning rights to hydraulic fracturing for gas in Quebec – were dismissed on the merits in an award on 21 November 2022 when the majority decided that the claimant's investment had not suffered from 'substantial deprivation' (Final Award, paras 490–528). The test for expropriation had to be applied to the investment as a whole and when all the rights were considered here, the test was not met. In the latter case, examined above in Section III(B), the third set of proceedings is ongoing, but previous attempts by Westmoreland have failed to overcome jurisdictional obstacles.

(2) Similarly, there may be a failure on the part of the hydrocarbons company or consortium to develop reserves in an expeditious manner, with contractual obligations that could well include a duty to do so 'with the utmost diligence'.
(3) Attempts to secure an early exit or terminate the agreement with the host state.
(4) Changes in decommissioning timing and reviews of existing contract terms in the light of national contributions under the Paris Agreement. Decommissioning has already led to investor-state disputes in SE Asia.
(5) Ironically, the stabilisation clauses used to protect the investments of internationally operating companies may be invoked by host states when they can be interpreted as mutual or when they pertain to the host government's legitimate expectations.

Thousands of long-term contracts are in place with terms that predate the arrival of the Energy Transition phenomenon and envisage – even if only implicitly – an endless horizon of demand for fossil fuels. Since the Energy Transition is supposed to be a just transition, we might expect to see several public organisations such as development banks, international NGOs and aid agencies, to line up to assist governments, especially in the newer producing countries, in carrying out a review of their contract terms, prospectively at least. With respect to existing contracts, of which there are very many, such reviews may be a source of future disputes between states and investors.

For the international oil and gas industry, there is also a question to consider that has been asked by tribunals in some of the recent renewable energy cases. At the time you took the decision to invest, a tribunal may ask the claimants, were there no signals that a prudent investor would or could have interpreted as giving a warning that the host state might make significant changes to its laws at some future date in relation to climate mitigation commitments? This is also a question that might well arise in connection with the allocation of decommissioning costs. For this category of investors, it may be timely to carefully scrutinise any public documents that could be construed by a cautious tribunal as conveying such an early warning signal, especially if the investment is of high value, and damages are being calculated.

A final comment concerns the sole energy sector international treaty, the ECT. It has figured in many of the cases considered in Section III above. Its provision on Withdrawal in Article 47 includes a stipulation that the treaty provisions shall continue to apply to investments made in a withdrawing host state by foreign investors or to investments made by investors from a withdrawing host state for a period of 20 years after that state has registered its notification of withdrawal. The importance of this continuing application of the ECT was evident in the *Rockhopper v Italy* case since the Respondent state had registered its withdrawal in 2016, before the claim was commenced. For many states that have recently denounced it, the ECT will be applicable in their territories for many key years when the Energy Transition is ongoing, irrespective of the decision to withdraw.

V. Concluding Remarks, Energy Disputes will Flourish

The Energy Transition heralds an era of sudden policy shifts by governments and a new concern about how to apportion liability for the costs of mitigation or adaptation to climate change. Of course, not all energy disputes in the coming years will be related to the Energy Transition, but a growing number will be. The 'rollercoaster' notion in the title of this chapter was intended to convey not only the pace of change, but also the unexpected pathways of energy disputes in an 'Energy Transition'. However, unlike the rollercoaster analogy, the process will not be guided by some controlling body. It will be a multi-speed process, with different countries taking different actions according to different timetables and using different methods to achieve a common set of targets. Given the long-term character of most energy investments, and the seriousness of the problem which the Energy Transition addresses, this is not a good sign. However, in terms of dispute potential and the future of international arbitration, the dynamics of the group of cases I have called Energy Transition Disputes 1.0 – whether treaty- or contract-based – do not appear to justify any deep-seated concerns about the system itself, or its procedures, or indeed the engagement of claimants and respondents with it. Nor does it yield clear evidence of a 'regulatory chill' in relation to climate change measures: the evidence in the French case is circumstantial, and in Germany the Government decided to explore a contractual route to achieving its policy goals, adapting its method but not its overall objective, in the face of possible investor claims. The claimants themselves seem to be motivated by potentially discriminatory treatment and the lack of (in their view) an appropriate level of compensation offered by the respondent. Moreover, the claims in the cases against The Netherlands were withdrawn under state pressure when the business environment of the claimants required state assistance, due to circumstances unrelated to Transition phenomena. Nor, in those cases where there were outcomes, were they indicative of a bias in procedure or application of the law towards the claimant, whether in the Vattenfall settlement with Germany or the dismissal of the claims in the Canadian Westmoreland case on jurisdictional grounds.

If we were to ask how, in relation to such cases, a tribunal would be likely to understand the protections offered by international treaties, such as the notion of legitimate expectations,[84] the cases considered here remind us of some basic, continuing facts of life. If, indeed, the claimants can prove that they had an

[84] As a way of limiting the potentially broad scope of this notion, tribunals are likely to ask whether specific written statements have been made or promises given to the claimant/(s) by the host state or an authorised agency or official.

investment within the terms of the relevant treaty, the tribunal will then proceed to consider how much was invested and when, under what legal circumstances, with what kind of due diligence, and with what professional or commercial judgement. All these are familiar hurdles, but as the Energy Transition rolls forward, they are ones that an unprepared investor/claimant may not find easy to prove in a dispute arising from a transition measure taken by a state that adversely affects their investment.

An observation can be offered here from the published awards in arbitrations concerning renewable energy in Spain, Italy, and the Czech Republic, even though they have not been examined in this chapter. The available awards have emphasised the differences of view that can arise between and within arbitral tribunals around the notion of Fair and Equitable Treatment and particularly around its constituent notion, an investor's legitimate expectation. Among the uncertainties to which the Energy Transition gives rise, the state's 'right to regulate' and its limits seems likely to continue this trend towards arbitrator scrutiny of what sort of expectation can be considered legitimate as a defence for investors against an adverse state measure. Questions that are likely to be asked will surely include: are the expectations based on contractual commitments or on the host state's legal order? Are they based on representations, circumstances, or context? Separately, but linked to this, there will be questions about possible negligence on the part of the claimant. Article 39 of the ILC Articles on the Responsibility of States for Internationally Wrongful Acts, adopted by the International Law Commission of the United Nations in 2001, notes that the extent to which the claimant's own willful or negligent actions or omissions contributed to the alleged injury are a matter to be considered in the determination of reparation.[85]

The sample of cases in Section III above may indeed suggest a reassuring conclusion about the adequacy of existing dispute resolution mechanisms – and especially arbitration. However, this needs to be supplemented by two caveats. The first is the abundant evidence of an interplay between arbitral tribunals and national courts, and, in the European setting, the supra-national judicial bodies. Arbitrators may need to be more alert to this interplay than usual when addressing Energy Transition disputes, especially if – as seems very likely – there is a continued increase in climate litigation in national courts. The second caveat is that the reassuring conclusion applies 'only insofar as these early disputes are concerned'. The number of disputes arising from Transition-related phenomena is still modest but growing and a broader sample may soon become available. That

[85] See UN Doc. A/56/83 12 December 2001. The Tribunals in *MTD v Chile and Occidental v Ecuador* decided that damages should be reduced because of the claimants' failings. Another example of an arbitral tribunal reducing damages due to contributory fault is *Yukos v Russian Federation*. In this context, see the arguments made in P Bekker and F Bello, 'Reimagining the Damages Valuation Framework Underlying Fair and Equitable Treatment Standard Violations through a Three-Stage Contextualized Approach' (2021) 36 *ICSID Review* 339–65.

sample, Energy Transition Disputes 2.0, may generate different and less reassuring conclusions for the status quo of international investment law.

On a positive note, it should be recalled that the underlying relationship between investors and host states is a cooperative one, aimed at achieving mutual benefits and mitigating the risk of disputes that may arise later, and the adversarial relationships that may result. This cooperative spirit is going to be needed more than ever in the coming years as this Energy Transition unfolds.

7

Future Developments in Investor-State Disputes in the Renewable Energy Sector: From Fair and Equitable Treatment to the Rise of Protectionism and Sovereign Supply?

PENELOPE CROSSLEY

I. Introduction

Renewable energy will become the largest source of electricity by 2025, surpassing coal-fired generation.[1] However, in order to reach net zero emissions by 2050, clean energy investment will have to more than triple by 2030 to approximately $US 4 trillion per annum.[2] This investment promises to create a boon for both the origination of new renewable energy projects and the development and commercialisation of clean technologies. At the same time, a confluence of factors, including the COVID-19 pandemic, and Russia's invasion of Ukraine, has increased both the uncertainty and risk for investors investing in renewable energy technologies and national energy markets. This has led to increased complexity in the legislative responses adopted by national governments to correct the market failures that have historically acted as a barrier to investment.

Over the past 15 years, these legislative responses have shown that they are not sufficiently agile to respond to the rapidly changing market, geopolitical and budgetary conditions, often resulting in blunt responses by host states when the legislative incentives must be changed. If these responses breach the applicable bilateral and/or multilateral agreements that protect the investors from the arbitrary actions of the host state, this leads to investor-state disputes. Most of the pending disputes in the renewable energy sector follow this traditional dispute

[1] International Energy Agency, 'Renewables 2022: Analysis and forecast to 2027' (December 2022) 10.
[2] International Energy Agency, 'World Energy Outlook 2022' (October 2022) 23.

pathway, claiming a breach of the relevant bilateral investment treaty or multilateral agreement, such as the Energy Charter Treaty (ECT).[3] These renewable energy disputes can be worth up to $USD 115.3 million[4] and can take years to be resolved by the international arbitral bodies, such as the World Bank's International Centre for the Settlement of Investment Disputes (ICSID) or the Arbitration Institute of the Stockholm Chamber of Commerce.

The burden imposed by investor-state disputes has prompted several host governments, including the United States, to become more innovative in their design of preferential trade laws. This includes using human rights laws such as the Uyghur Forced Labor Protection Act (2021) (US) for the dual purpose of preventing the use of forced prison labour, and to enable the United States to legally impose trade barriers on manufacturers from their key competitor in the clean technology manufacturing sector, China.[5] Measures such as these have already spread to other jurisdictions, with the European Union recently releasing draft laws designed for similar effect.[6] A further development in investor-state disputes relates to the subject matter of the disputes in question. Traditionally, investor-state disputes in the renewable energy sector focused on the local content clauses used to develop high value manufacturing expertise and markets. In the future, due to the high market concentration in the renewable technology sector, these disputes are likely to shift to securing access to the critical minerals and raw materials that are essential inputs in advanced electronic technologies. This will be critical to enabling other countries to enter the technology manufacturing sector and/or secure their own domestic supply chains.

This chapter will continue in Section II by examining the current global market context within which the renewable energy sector and the clean energy technology manufacturing sector operate. In Section III, the current status of investor-state disputes within the sector will be analysed, with a focus on the Spanish investor-state disputes and the lessons learnt by other countries from the resulting arbitrations. Section IV of the chapter will shift to examining recent developments in protectionist trade practices by the major clean energy economies. In this Section, the nature of the legislative and policy incentives contained in the Inflation Reduction Act (2022) (US),[7] and the Uyghur Forced Labor Protection Act (2021) (US) will also be critically evaluated to understand how

[3] The Energy Charter Treaty, opened for signature 17 December 1994, 2080 UNTS 95 (entered into force 16 April 1998).

[4] *Infrastructure Services Luxembourg S.à.r.l. and Energia Termosolar B.V. (formerly Antin Infrastructure Services Luxembourg S.à.r.l. and Antin Energia Termosolar B.V.) v Kingdom of Spain (Decision on the Rectification of the Award)* (ICSID Arbitral Tribunal, Case No. ARB/13/31) at [40].

[5] M Flacks and M Songy, 'The Uyghur Forced Labor Prevention Act Goes into Effect' (*Center for Strategic and International Studies*, 27 June 2022) www.csis.org/analysis/uyghur-forced-labor-prevention-act-goes-effect.

[6] European Commission, 'Proposal for a Regulation of the European Parliament and of the Council on prohibiting products made with forced labour on the Union market' COM (2022) 453 final.

[7] Inflation Reduction Act of 2022, Pub.L. No.117-169, 136 Stat. 1818 (2022).

countries are now shifting to more protectionist trade practices to support their domestic renewable energy sectors. The chapter will conclude in Section V with an assessment of the likely future direction of investor-state disputes in the sector, with a particular discussion of how laws may be used to protect an investor's access to critical minerals and rare earth metals.

II. The Current Global Market Context

A confluence of factors globally has complicated clean energy investments. First came the COVID-19 pandemic in 2020, which resulted in mass global supply chain disruption throughout many industries as stringent lockdowns were imposed to stop the spread of the virus.[8] Due to the heavy concentration of renewable energy technology manufacturing in China, one of the countries most affected by the pandemic, these disruptions hit the global renewable energy technology sector particularly hard.[9] Manufacturers experienced difficulties in sourcing raw materials and componentry inputs, there were shortages of skilled labour to manufacture these technologies, and there were substantial delays affecting the transportation to final export markets.[10] The severe supply constraints experienced during this period led many of the major renewable energy technology markets to rethink their national strategies with respect to clean energy technologies. In particular, the US, Japan, India, the European Union, and Australia, all announced plans to diversify their supply chains, develop sovereign manufacturing capabilities and enhance their security of supply for renewable energy technologies.[11] This has had an impact in the race to secure supplies of the rare earth metals and critical minerals used in advanced electronics manufacturing.[12]

[8] J Moosavi, A Fathollahi-Fard and M Dulebenets, 'Supply chain disruption during the COVID-19 pandemic: Recognizing potential disruption management strategies' (2022) 75 *International Journal of Disaster Risk Reduction* 102983, 1, www.sciencedirect.com/science/article/pii/S2212420922002023?via%3Dihub.

[9] International Energy Agency, 'A New Era of Shared Clean Energy Leadership Begins in China' (*Commentary*, 14 February 2022) www.iea.org/commentaries/a-new-era-of-shared-clean-energy-leadership-begins-in-china; M Shahid Mastoi et al, 'A Critical Analysis of the Impact of Pandemic on China's Electricity Usage Patterns and the Global Development of Renewable Energy' (2022) 19(8) *Int J Environ Res Public Health* 4608.

[10] See n 8.

[11] See eg The White House, *Inflation Reduction Act Guidebook* (January 2023) www.whitehouse.gov/wp-content/uploads/2022/12/Inflation-Reduction-Act-Guidebook.pdf; Ministry of New and Renewable Energy, 'National Hydrogen Energy Mission: Draft Concept Note' (*Government of India*, 30 September 2022); European Commission, 'REPowerEU Plan' (Communication) COM (2020) 230 final; Australian Energy Market Commission, 'Renewable Energy Zones Discussion Paper' (Discussion Paper, 2019) www.aemc.gov.au/sites/default/files/2019-10/EPR0073%20-%20Renewable%20Energy%20Zones%20Discussion%20Paper.pdf.

[12] W Filho, R Kotter, P Gökçin Özuyar, I Rimi Abubakar, J Henrique Paulino Pires Eustachio, and NR Matandirotya, "Understanding Rare Earth Elements as Critical Raw Materials" (2023) 15(3) *Sustainability* 1919.

Then just as the world was starting to recover from the COVID-19 pandemic, on 24 February 2022, Russia invaded Ukraine. While the advent of any land war on mainland Europe would be likely to trigger energy market disruptions, Russia was the world's largest exporter of natural gas, as well as a major exporter of both petroleum and coal, particularly to European energy markets.[13] Indeed, prior to the invasion, some European countries such as Finland and the Czech Republic were dependent on Russian imports for 100 per cent of their domestic supply of natural gas.[14] The resulting fossil fuel supply disruptions led to significantly higher fossil fuel prices worldwide and deep energy security concerns regarding Europe's ongoing dependence on Russia for its energy supply.[15] Many European nations responded to this conflict by adopting a war footing with respect to their energy laws and policies,[16] with some senior government officials from European nations privately expressing very real concerns about: (i) being able to meet their national peak energy demand during the European Winter in 2022/2023; and (ii) consumers being able to afford rapidly rising energy prices.

A consequence of the cumulative impacts caused by COVID-19 and the invasion of Ukraine on global markets, was high levels of inflation on a wide range of products and services.[17] This has in turn led to a global economic slowdown, with the World Bank predicting that there will be a deep global recession in 2023.[18] As shown in Figure 1 (below), this confluence of factors and the resulting impact on household expenditure on energy bills prompted governments around the world in 2022 to grant almost double the 2021 levels of fossil fuel subsidies provided to industry and consumers to over $US 1 trillion. This represented the highest level of fossil fuel subsidies in more than a decade. It was also a significant

[13] International Energy Agency, 'Energy Fact Sheet: Why Does Russian Oil and Gas Matter?' (19 July 2022) www.iea.org/articles/energy-fact-sheet-why-does-russian-oil-and-gas-matter.

[14] P Crossley, *Renewable Energy Law: An International Assessment* (Cambridge University Press, 2019) 116; K Pohjanpalo, 'Baltic Gas Supply Cut as Russia Turns Off Taps to Finland' (*Bloomberg*, 20 May 2022) www.bloomberg.com/news/articles/2022-05-20/finland-loses-main-gas-supply-as-russia-will-turn-off-taps#xj4y7vzkg; 'Reliance of Finland on Russian Fossil Fuels by Sector from 2015 to 2021' (*Statista*) www.statista.com/statistics/1320270/finland-reliance-on-russian-fossil-fuels-by-sector/; Czech Statistical Office, 'Foreign trade statistics' (code KN8 for gas is 27112100) apl.czso.cz/pll/stazo/STAZO.STAZO; Heinrich Böll Stiftung European Union, 'How to Break Czechia's Dependence on Russian Gas' (21 April 2022) eu.boell.org/en/2022/04/21/how-break-czechias-dependence-russian-gas.

[15] International Energy Agency, 'How to Avoid Gas Shortages in the European Union in 2023' (*IEA*, 2022) iea.blob.core.windows.net/assets/96ce64c5-1061-4e0c-998d-fd679990653b/HowtoAvoidGasShortagesintheEuropeanUnionin2023.pdf.

[16] ibid; J Borrel, 'The war in Ukraine and its implications for the EU' (*European External Action Service*, 14 March 2023) www.eeas.europa.eu/eeas/war-ukraine-and-its-implications-eu_en.

[17] J-D Guénette, P Kenworthy and C Wheeler, 'Implications of the War in Ukraine for the Global Economy' World Bank Group (*EFI Policy Note*, April 2022) thedocs.worldbank.org/en/doc/5d903e848db1d1b83e0ec8f744e55570-0350012021/related/Implications-of-the-War-in-Ukraine-for-the-Global-Economy.pdf.

[18] World Bank Press Release, 'Risk of global recession in 2023 rises amid simultaneous rate hikes' (15 September 2022) www.worldbank.org/en/news/press-release/2022/09/15/risk-of-global-recession-in-2023-rises-amid-simultaneous-rate-hikes; J Guénette, A Kose, and N Sugawara, 'Is a Global Recession Imminent?' (Policy Note, September 2022) 31 openknowledge.worldbank.org/server/api/core/bitstreams/63d145cf-b17d-59fc-aa15-0b14e6512e5a/content.

uptick away from the general downward trend in fossil fuel subsidies that had resulted from agreements between OECD Member States and other countries to phase out fossil fuel subsidies as a strategy to mitigate climate change. This growth in fossil fuel subsidies is even more extraordinary when compared to 2020 levels, with the fossil fuel subsidies provided in 2022 a five-fold increase.[19]

Figure 1 Fossil Fuel Consumption Subsidies by Fuel, 2010–2022

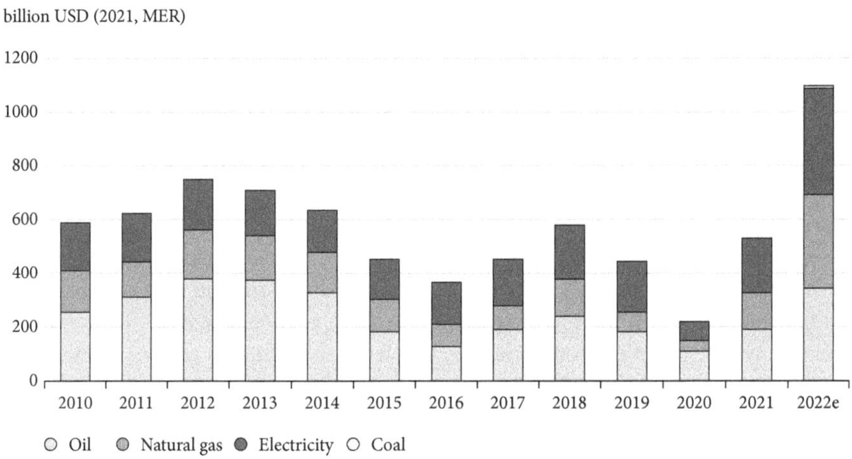

Source: *IEA, 2022 International Energy Agency, 'Fossil Fuel Consumption Subsidies 2022' (IEA, 2022)* www.iea.org/reports/fossil-fuels-consumption-subsidies-2022, *License: CC BY 4.0.*

The combination of these factors strengthened the impetus for countries to rapidly transition to renewable energy sources and use their indigenous energy resources as an effective strategy to reduce fossil fuel costs. Governments around the world have used a range of regulatory support mechanisms in national and state laws, including feed-in tariffs, subsidies, tax credits, tenders/reverse auction bidding and preferential grid access to accelerate the transition. By 2023, some 166 countries had renewable energy targets for their power sector, 164 countries had national policies supporting accelerated deployment, and over 140 countries had national renewable energy laws in place.[20] These laws are designed to provide a predictable and certain regulatory and policy environment to help attract private capital into the sector and to help new renewable energy projects meet their high upfront costs. Increasingly, these government incentives are also being used to help offset the costs associated with rising inflation which have also beset renewable energy projects. Prior to 2020, solar PV and wind technologies had

[19] International Energy Agency, 'Fossil Fuel Consumption Subsidies 2022' (*IEA*, 2022) www.iea.org/reports/fossil-fuels-consumption-subsidies-2022.

[20] Renewable Energy Policy Network for the 21st Century (REN21), 'Global Status Report 2023' (*REN21*, 2023), www.ren21.net/wp-content/uploads/2019/05/GSR2023_Demand_Modules.pdf.

seen significant decreases in costs, due to the impact of learning effects and ever-increasing economies of scale.[21] However, since 2020 the technology costs for solar PV and wind have increased between 10 and 20 per cent, due to ongoing supply constraints and skilled labour shortages.[22] These incentives are also being used to help renewable energy compete in the market with increased fossil fuel subsidies, which distort the market signals around the need for the energy transition, in a vicious cycle of subsidies for fossil fuels creating a need for more subsidies to support renewable energy generation.

III. The Current Status of Investor-State Disputes in the Renewable Energy Sector

In order to attract private capital to invest in a country's renewable energy sector, an important pre-condition is that the regulatory and market environment must protect private investments. This can be achieved by states entering into bilateral or multilateral investment agreements or treaties, such as the ECT. These agreements have the effect of protecting investors from the arbitrary actions of the state, which are especially important in the context of energy infrastructure assets, due to them being effectively stranded following the construction phase of a project. The protections for investors provided by these agreements and treaties include:

(1) fair and equitable treatment;[23]
(2) protections against expropriation,[24] and fair and adequate compensation when expropriation does occur;[25]
(3) protections from unreasonable or discriminatory treatment;[26] and
(4) most constant protection and security.[27] (Article 10.1 ECT)

Given the instability in global markets which has been present since the Global Financial Crisis (GFC), and the compounding effects of the COVID-19 pandemic and the invasion of Ukraine, government interventions to correct the market failures present in the energy sector have become far more complex. These government

[21] A Elia, M Kamidelivand, F Rogan and B Gallacgoir, 'Impacts of innovation on renewable energy technology cost reductions' (221) 138 *Renewable and Sustainable Energy Reviews* 110488, 14 www.sciencedirect.com/science/article/pii/S1364032120307747.

[22] International Energy Agency, 'What is the impact of increasing commodity and energy prices on solar PV, wind and biofuels? '(*IEA*, 2022) www.iea.org/articles/what-is-the-impact-of-increasing-commodity-and-energy-prices-on-solar-pv-wind-and-biofuels; J Anton, 'Labor and materials: Shortages drive costs higher' (*S&P Global*, 5 April 2022) www.spglobal.com/marketintelligence/en/news-insights/research/labor-and-materials-shortages-drive-costs-higher.

[23] The Energy Charter Treaty (n 3) Article 10(1).

[24] The Energy Charter Treaty (n 3) Article 13(1).

[25] ibid.

[26] The Energy Charter Treaty (n 3) Article 10(1).

[27] ibid.

interventions have typically taken the form of legislated regulatory support mechanisms to provide investors with a sufficiently certain and predictable regulatory environment. However, regulatory support mechanisms have time and again proven not to be flexible enough to rapidly respond to changing market, geopolitical and budgetary conditions.[28] Historically, these incentives to invest have often lacked time limits or sunset clauses, and provisions have been abruptly ended when the law has been amended rather than grandfathering the previous legislative incentives for existing projects (now referred to as 'legacy provisioning').[29] Further, the lack of budgetary caps specified in legislation hosting the legislative incentives has caused crippling budgetary blowouts, such as those seen in Spain following the GFC.[30] As a result, renewable energy disputes have grown substantially over the past decade, as the value of sectoral investment has increased.

Arbitration is the preferred method of dispute resolution for investor-state disputes in the renewable energy sector. The World Bank's International Centre for the Settlement of Investment Disputes (ICSID) has traditionally been the favoured venue to host the arbitration within the sector,[31] relying on either bilateral investment treaties, or at least prior to the Achmea decision in 2018,[32] the ECT.[33] Indeed, in 2022, the ECT was invoked as the basis of consent to establish the ICSID jurisdiction in ICSID in 22 per cent of claims.[34] Indeed, despite its comparatively recent rise, investor-state disputes involving the renewable energy sector make up 64 of the total 942 cases brought in ICSID's 57-year long history.[35] When the 284 pending cases are considered, renewable energy disputes represent over 15 per cent of the current caseload with 44 cases still pending.[36]

[28] Crossley (n 14) 167–249.

[29] ibid. See also P Crossley, 'Designing sustainable development? The effectiveness of PV solar regulation in Australia and China' (2013) *Asia Pacific Journal of Environmental Law* 15, 1–15.

[30] P del Río and P Mir-Artigues, 'A Cautionary Tale: Spain's solar PV investment bubble' (*International Institute of Sustainable Development*, February 2014) www.iisd.org/gsi/sites/default/files/rens_ct_spain.pdf.

[31] G Tondapu, 'International Institutions and Dispute Settlement: The Case of ICSID' (2022) 22(1) *Bond Law Review* 81; International Centre for Settlement of Investment Disputes, 'About ICSID' icsid.worldbank.org/about.

[32] Case C-284/16 *Slowakische Republik (Slovak Republic) v Achmea BV* EU:C:2018:158, [2018] 2 CMLR 40 at [31]–[60]. In this decision the European Court of Justice (ECJ) held that an arbitration clause in the Dutch-Slovak bilateral investment treaty undermined the autonomy of, and was incompatible with, EU law.

[33] Energy Charter Treaty (n 3) Articles 26–28.

[34] The International Centre for Settlement of Investment Disputes, 'The ICSID Caseload – Statistics' (2023) 1, 23 icsid.worldbank.org/sites/default/files/Caseload%20Statistics%20Charts/The_ICSID_Caseload_Statistics.1_Edition_ENG.pdf.

[35] Author's own calculations based on International Centre for Settlement of Investment Disputes 'Search Cases' (ICSID) icsid.worldbank.org/cases/case-database. See also, United Nations Trade and Development, 'Treaty-based Investor-State Dispute Settlement Cases and Climate Action' (*IIA Issues Note*, September 2022) investmentpolicy.unctad.org/publications/1270/treaty-based-investor-state-dispute-settlement-cases-and-climate-action.

[36] ibid.

Further, 85 of the 150 disputes instituted under the ECT, a Treaty originally established to facilitate cross-border cooperation in the fossil fuel sector, relate to renewable energy.[37]

A. The Spanish Investor-State Disputes

More than half of the renewable energy disputes instituted under the ECT and brought before ICSID arbitration involve investors bringing claims against the Kingdom of Spain for changes that the Spanish Government made to their renewable energy laws during, and in the immediate aftermath of, the GFC.[38] In the mid-2000s, Spain was not on track to meet its share of the EU renewable energy target. In 2007, this prompted the Spanish government to pass Royal Decree 661/2007.[39] This Royal Decree established a 25-year feed-in-tariff scheme which provided substantial subsidies to the renewable energy sector in an effort to attract new renewable energy projects to the country. This scheme saw Spain pay '… a premium of $556 per megawatt-hour for electricity that rooftop solar panels supplied to the electric grid, compared with an average $52 paid to competing coal- or gas-fired power plants.'[40] Following the introduction of the Royal Decree 661/2007, the capacity of solar PV installed annually increased more than 26-fold when compared to 2005/2006.[41] Various scholars have identified the reasons for this,[42] with Bárcena and Flues noting:

> … [T]he Spanish government had targeted an internal rate of return for solar projects of 5-9%, the actual rate for some large solar installations was closer to 10–15% … The incentive system also lacked a built-in mechanism that allowed it to reduce feed-in-tariffs in line with falling costs of solar projects or to limit costs above a certain threshold.

[37] Author's own calculations based on International Energy Charter, 'List of Cases' (*International Energy Charter*, 2022) www.energychartertreaty.org/cases/list-of-cases/.

[38] ibid; International Centre for Settlement of Investment Disputes 'Search Cases' (ICSID) icsid.worldbank.org/cases/case-database.

[39] Real Decreto 661/2007, de 25 de mayo, por el que se regula la actividad de producción de energía eléctrica en regimen especial, num. 126, de 26.05/2007; see English Translation Royal Decree 661/2007, of 25 May, which regulates the activity of product ion of electrical energy in Special Regime (*Global Regulation*, 2007) www.global-regulation.com/translation/spain/1445573/royal-decree-661-2007%252c-of-may-25%252c-which-regulates-the-activity-of-production-of-electrical-energy-in-special-regime.html.

[40] W Pentland, 'No End in Sight for Spain's Escalating Solar Crisis' (*Forbes*, 16 August 2013) www.forbes.com/sites/williampentland/2013/08/16/no-end-in-sight-for-spains-escalating-solar-crisis/?sh=13d2055f6d39.

[41] L Bárcena and F Flues, 'From solar dream to legal nightmare' (*Transnational Institute*, May 2022) 9 www.tni.org/files/publication-downloads/english_from_solar_dream_to_legal_nightmare_online.pdf; del Río and Mir-Artigues (n 30).

[42] ibid.

These factors saw the investment returns made by investors in the Spanish solar sector increase over time, making Spain an attractive investment destination for foreign investment.[43]

However, in late 2007, the sub-prime mortgage crisis precipitated the Global Financial Crisis, which in turn triggered a deep worldwide recession.[44] Spain was hit particularly hard by the GFC. This is evident from a range of the key economic indicators:

(1) Spain's official national unemployment rate rapidly increased from 8.2 per cent of the eligible population in 2007 to over 18 per cent by 2009, before reaching a peak of 26.1 per cent in 2013;[45]
(2) Spain's youth unemployment rate more than doubled to over 55 per cent of the eligible population by 2013;[46]
(3) Sovereign debt exceeded 100 per cent of gross domestic product (GDP)[47] and exceeded the European Union's 'Eurozone' parameters set to protect Member States from economic risk;[48] and
(4) Property prices declined over 40 per cent from their pre-crisis peak.[49]

At the same time, the costs associated with the Spanish feed-in-tariff scheme continued to grow considerably. Indeed, between 2007 and 2009, the feed-in-tariffs paid to renewable energy projects increased 13-fold from €194m to €2.6bn.[50] As the financial difficulties in Spain grew, its renewable energy support scheme increasingly became financially and politically unviable. As a result, Spain urgently amended and then effectively halted their existing renewable energy subsidies to rapidly reduce their budgetary expenditure and stabilise their economy.

Between 2010 and 2014, a series of regulatory reforms placed increasingly more stringent constraints on both the availability of the Spanish subsidy scheme,

[43] A Mahalingam and David Reiner, 'Energy Subsidies at Times of Economic Crisis: A Comparative Study and Scenario Analysis of Italy and Spain' Energy Policy Research Group (University of Cambridge, 2016); P Voosen, 'Spain's Solar Market crash Offers a Cautionary Tale' (*New York Times*, 2009) archive.nytimes.com/www.nytimes.com/gwire/2009/08/18/18greenwire-spains-solar-market-crash-offers-a-cautionary-88308.html?pagewanted=2#.

[44] A Jose, N Sugawara and M Terrones, 'Global Recessions' (2022) World Bank Policy Research Working Paper 9172, 11 documents1.worldbank.org/curated/en/185391583249079464/pdf/Global-Recessions.pdf.

[45] World Bank, (2023) 'Unemployment – Spain, % of total labor force' data.worldbank.org/indicator/SL.UEM.TOTL.NE.ZS?locations=ES.

[46] J Miguel Verd, O Baranco and M Bolíbar, 'Youth unemployment and employment trajectories in Spain during the Great Recession: what are the determinants?' (2019) 53(4) *Journal for Labour Market Research* 1.

[47] World Bank, 'Central Government Debt, total (% of GDP) – Spain' data.worldbank.org/indicator/GC.DOD.TOTL.GD.ZS?locations=ES.

[48] Council of the European Union, 'Conditions for joining the euro area: convergence criteria' www.consilium.europa.eu/en/policies/joining-the-euro-area/convergence-criteria/; Consolidated Version of the Treaty on the Functioning of the European Union [2012] OJ C 326/47, Article 140; Protocol (No 13) on the convergence criteria (Treaty on the Functioning of the EU) [2012] OJ C 326/281.

[49] International Monetary Fund, 'Spain: Selected Issues' (2015) IMF Country Report No. 15/233, 64.

[50] del Río and Mir-Artigues (n 30) 11.

particularly for photovoltaic solar, and on renewable energy generators more broadly. These modifications included:

(1) reducing the number of operating hours that were eligible for the feed-in-tariff;
(2) introducing new technical obligations;
(3) imposing a new grid access fee;
(4) reducing the feed-in-tariff rate;
(5) removing all economic incentives for improperly registered photovoltaic facilities;
(6) the imposition of taxes on the revenues of renewable generators; and
(7) taxing grid access.

The impact of these reforms was so significant that some scholars have argued that by 2014, 'there was no longer an appreciable difference between the special regime for solar energy and the general regime for conventional energy.'[51]

The various iterations of regulatory changes to the Spanish legislative incentive led to the long series of legal claims referred to above, including *Charanne and Construction Investments v Spain*;[52] *Infrastructure Services Luxembourg S.à.r.l. and Energia Termosolar B.V. (formerly Antin Infrastructure Services Luxembourg S.à.r.l. and Antin Energia Termosolar B.V.) v Kingdom of Spain* (*Antin*),[53] *Eiser Infrastruture Limited and Energía Solar Luxembourg S.à.r.l. v Kingdom of Spain*[54] and *Masdar Solar & Wind Cooperatief U.A. v Kingdom of Spain*.[55]

i. Case Study: Infrastructure Services Luxembourg S.à.r.l. and Energia Termosolar B.V. (formerly Antin Infrastructure Services Luxembourg S.à.r.l. and Antin Energia Termosolar B.V.) v Kingdom of Spain, *ICSID Case No. ARB/13/31*

Antin[56] provides an illustrative example of one of these investment disputes. In 2011, the Claimants had acquired shareholdings in two concentrated solar plants, the Andasol-1 Plant and the Andasol-2 Plant located in Granada in Spain. These plants had benefited from the generous RD 661/2007 and RD 1614/2010 feed-in-tariff schemes, providing a guaranteed return on investment. Following the 2013 amendments to the scheme, the feed-in-tariffs for the Andasol Plants were removed and a tax was imposed on the value of electrical energy produced (TVPEE).

[51] See eg T St John, *Not Easy Being Green: Examining Potential Liability in Legislative Reform to Regulatory Support Mechanisms in the Australian Renewable Energy Sector* (Dissertation, University of Sydney).

[52] *Charanne and Construction Investments v Spain*, SCC Case No. V 062/2012.

[53] *Infrastructure Services Luxembourg S.à.r.l. and Energia Termosolar B.V. (formerly Antin Infrastructure Services Luxembourg S.à.r.l. and Antin Energia Termosolar B.V.) v Kingdom of Spain*, ICSID Case No. ARB/13/31.

[54] *Eiser Infrastructure Limited and Energía Solar Luxembourg S.à.r.l. v Kingdom of Spain*, ICSID Case No. ARB/13/36.

[55] *Masdar Solar & Wind Cooperatief U.A. v Kingdom of Spain*, ICSID Case No. ARB/14/1.

[56] See n 53.

The Claimants argued that they had invested in the Spanish renewable energy sector in reliance of the regulatory framework set forth under RD 661/2007 and reinforced by RD 1614/2010. They stated that they expected that the Andasol Plants would remain subject to the FIT regime for their entire operational life and that any future changes to RD 661/2007 would apply only to new installations.[57] The Claimants' further argued that their expectations regarding the stability of the RD 661/2007 economic regime, and specifically of the fee-in-tariff were legitimate, based on an offer made by the Spanish Government under a 'Royal Decree' (RD 661/2007). The Claimants relied on their own detailed due diligence process, the Respondent's campaign to promote investments in the Spanish renewable energy sector, the adoption of RD 1614/2010, and assurances made by Spain's public officials, which they stated confirmed their expectations were legitimate.[58] Following their investment in the Andasol Plants, the Spanish Government made substantial regulatory changes to the schemes. The Claimants contended that these changes eviscerated all of the key features of the RD 661/2007 regime, frustrating their legitimate expectations and breaching the Spanish Government's obligation to provide Fair and Equitable Treatment under Article 10(1) of the ECT.[59] The Respondents countered that it was not reasonable to expect that laws would not be amended from time to time for public policy reasons and that investors should only expect a reasonable return on their investment.

The Tribunal in their decision stated that:

> … the obligation under Article 10(1) of the ECT to provide FET to protected investments comprises an obligation to afford fundamental stability in the essential characteristics of the legal regime relied upon by the investors in making long-term investments. This does not mean that the legal framework cannot evolve or that a State Party to the ECT is precluded from exercising its regulatory powers to adapt the regime to the changing circumstances in the public interest. It rather means that a regulatory regime specifically created to induce investments in the energy sector cannot be radically altered – i.e., stripped of its key features – as applied to existing investments in ways that affect investors who invested in reliance on those regimes.[60]

The Tribunal found that the Spanish Government had established the legitimate expectation that the 2007 regime would continue in its original application. Therefore, by radically altering the 2007 regime, the Respondents had breached Article 10(1) of the ECT, and awarded the Claimants €112 million in damages.[61]

Antin is just one of the many renewable energy investor-state dispute cases brought against the Kingdom of Spain. In 2023, a further 51 renewable energy sector investor-state disputes are pending against the Spanish state seeking €8 billion in compensation. In addition to the Spanish cases, there are also claims pending against a further 10 other countries (Bulgaria, Costa Rica, France,

[57] ibid 138 at [509].
[58] ibid at [510].
[59] ibid at [511].
[60] ibid 143–44.
[61] ibid 197.

Germany, Italy, Panama, Peru, Romania, Sri Lanka, Türkiye and Ukraine). These disputes also generally relate to previous iterations of their national regulatory support mechanisms.

B. The Lessons Learnt from the Spanish Investor-State Disputes

Countries around the world have learnt from the Spanish investor-state disputes. This has seen countries:

(1) introduce time-limits and in some cases, financial caps, to the subsidies they provide to the sector;
(2) remove guarantees about the continuance of subsidy schemes;
(3) introduce legacy provisions for existing investments, enabling the continued enjoyment of the regulatory support mechanism for the full entitlement period that they made the investment decision under; and
(4) insert their incentive schemes and the associated levels of support to be provided into regulations rather than legislation. This regulation-based approach has been designed to enable more responsiveness to rapidly changing market conditions rather than having to wait for parliament to sit to amend the relevant law.[62]

Despite these changes, for the reasons detailed in Section IV (below), investment disputes continue to grow in the sector. This trend is likely to continue with the Ashurst Energy Transition Survey of 1000 Senior Leaders in the Energy Sector, finding that 91 per cent of senior leaders within the energy sector believe that their company's current approach to the energy transition is likely to lead to disputes with a third party.[63] Disputes with individuals and pressure groups were seen as most likely (cited by 64 per cent), closely followed by disputes with governments and other authorities (57 per cent). Interestingly, just 33 per cent of respondents anticipated disputes with other companies.[64]

[62] See also, I Reynoso, 'Spain's Renewable Energy Saga: Lessons for international investment law and sustainable development' (*International Institute for Sustainable Development*, 27 June 2019) www.iisd.org/itn/en/2019/06/27/spains-renewable-energy-saga-lessons-for-international-investment-law-and-sustainable-development-isabella-reynoso/; M Schmidl, 'The Renewable Energy Saga from Charanne v Spain to the PV Investors v Spain: Trying to See the Wood for the Trees' (*Kluwer Arbitration Blog*, 1 February 2021) arbitrationblog.kluwerarbitration.com/2021/02/01/the-renewable-energy-saga-from-charanne-v-spain-to-the-pv-investors-v-spain-trying-to-see-the-wood-for-the-trees/; Bárcena and Flues (n 41) 9; L Mehranvar and S Sasmal, 'The Role of Investment Treaties and Investor-State Dispute Settlement in Renewable Energy Investments' (*Columbia Centre on Sustainable Investment*, December 2022) ccsi.columbia.edu/sites/default/files/content/ccsi-investment-treaties-isds-renewable-energy.pdf; F Dias Simoes, 'When green incentives go pale: investment arbitration and renewable energy policymaking' (2017) 45(2) *Denver Journal of International Law and Policy* 251.

[63] Ashurst LLP, 'Energy Transition Investment Report 2021' www.ashurst.com/en/news-and-insights/hubs/energy-transition/energy-transition---investment/.

[64] ibid.

IV. A New Wave of Protectionism in Response to the Rise of China?

For over a decade, China has been accused of using its renewable energy regulations to promote its clean technology industry, which has been identified as a strategic 'key growth' industry for the twenty-first century.[65] In 2009, Premier Wen Jiabao explicitly stated:

> We will accelerate the development of a low-carbon and green economy so as to gain an advantageous position in international industrial competition.[66]

This ambition has only intensified over the years, with the 2018 'Made in China 2025 Report' stating that China aims to produce 80 per cent of the global supply of 'basic core components and important basic materials' for renewable energy equipment by 2025.[67] These ambitions are also evident in the 14th Chinese Five Year Plan, which has defined new energy, new materials, new energy vehicles and bio energy as 'key strategic industries,' and hydrogen and battery storage as 'future industries.' This plan makes clear that China is seeking to leverage its:

> … industrial scale advantages, … and first-mover advantages, [to] consolidate and enhance the competitiveness of the entire production chains in … power equipment, new energy, … and other fields, and build strategic and comprehensive production chains starting from complete machine products that conform to the direction of future industrial changes.[68]

Indeed, the current Five Year Plan expresses the ambition that these strategic industries should make up 17 per cent of China's GDP by 2027.[69] A further development of note is that new energy is identified as an area that is necessary to simultaneously increase both China's national defence strength and its economic strength,[70] this reflects the importance of renewable energy to China for its energy and hence, national security. For these reasons, the Chinese Government has been unwavering in its commitment to dominate the renewable energy industry in the twenty-first century. As recently as March 2023, at the National People's Congress, President Xi Jinping emphasised the need for China to further its technological

[65] Chien-Huei Wu and Kuei-Chih Yang, 'Aggressive Legalism: China's Proactive Role in Renewable Energy and Trade Disputes? (2015) 12(3) *Transnational Dispute Management* 1–28; D Yergin, *The Quest: Energy, Security and the Remaking of the Modern World* (Penguin Press, 2011) 544–45.

[66] Wen Jiabao, 'Strengthen Confidence and Work Together for a New Round of World Economic Growth' (Speech delivered at the World Economic Forum, Switzerland, 28 January 2009) quoted in Yergin (n 65) 544.

[67] L Kuo, 'Made in China policy at centre of tariff war with US' *The Guardian* (4 April 2018) www.theguardian.com/world/2018/apr/04/made-in-china-policy-at-centre-of-tariff-war-with-us.

[68] R Creemers et al, 'Translation: China's 14th Five-Year Plan – Dec. 2021' (*DigiChina Stanford Policy Institute*, 24 January 2022) 20, digichina.stanford.edu/work/translation-14th-five-year-plan-for-national-informatization-dec-2021/#:~:text=The%20"14th%20Five-Year%20Plan"%20period%20is%20an%20important,of%20industry%20chains%2C%20promote%20the.

[69] ibid 23–34.

[70] ibid 131–33.

independence and boost domestic manufacturing to enable the ongoing dominance of the global new energy industry.[71]

This approach, when combined with the local content provisions that were prominent features of previous iterations of Chinese wind and solar regulatory support mechanisms,[72] and annual investment in the renewable energy sector, which in 2022, reached $546 billion,[73] has been highly successful. China now boasts 39 per cent of the renewable energy technology jobs globally, and 58 per cent of photovoltaic solar energy jobs.[74] Further, as shown in Figure 2 (below) China is the critical technology supplier that much of the rest of the world will have to rely on if they are to effectively transition their energy sectors to clean energy.

Figure 2 Regional Shares of Manufacturing Capacity for Selected Mass-Manufactured Clean Energy Technologies and Components (2021)

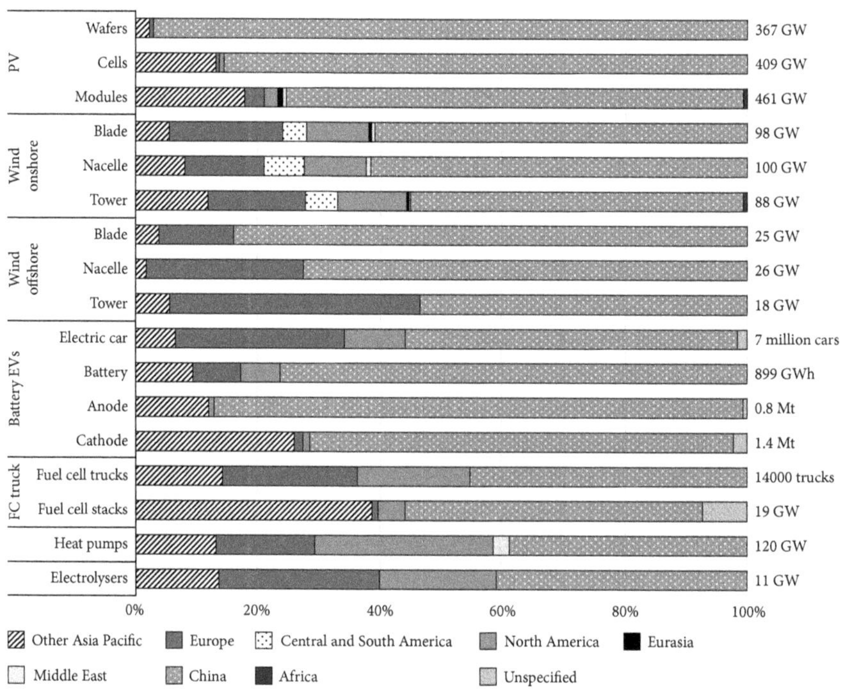

Source: IEA (2023) Energy Technology Perspectives 2023, Figure 2.7, p.96, License: CC BY 4.0.

[71] 'Report on President Xi Jingping's visit to the National People's Congress' *Chinese People's Daily Online* (7 March 2023) cpc.people.com.cn/n1/2023/0307/c64094-32638352.html.

[72] Crossley (n 14).

[73] 'Global Low-Carbon Energy Technology Investment Surges Past $1 Trillion for the First Time' (BloombergNEF, 26 January 2023) about.bnef.com/blog/global-low-carbon-energy-technology-investment-surges-past-1-trillion-for-the-first-time/.

[74] IRENA and ILO, Renewable Energy and Jobs – Annual Report 2021 (2021) 3, www.irena.org/-/media/Files/IRENA/Agency/Publication/2021/Oct/IRENA_RE_Jobs_2021.pdf.

While some key clean energy technology manufacturing economies, namely China, Korea, Japan, India, the United States, and some larger European countries such as Germany, are likely to continue their support for their domestic manufacturing sectors, it is predicted that many other countries will give up. Many countries are rapidly realising that they simply cannot compete with the existing scale of the manufacturing industries, and the size of the government grants being made by these clean technology manufacturing powerhouses. Further, it has become evident that the jobs in the renewable energy sector are primarily focused on the manufacturing and project construction phases, with few far fewer jobs in the operational and maintenance phases than in traditional fossil fuel generation.[75] Given the scale of the renewable energy industry and comparatively cheap cost of labour in countries such as China and India, it is often not economically viable for countries to seek to compete in the export markets for clean energy technology manufacturing. Thus, unless a country views the renewable energy industry as a strategic investment which is necessary for the security of their critical supply chains and sovereign manufacturing capability, it is unlikely that they will continue to manufacture clean energy technologies.

Among the clean energy economies that have strategically decided to compete with China or maintain sovereign manufacturing capability in the renewable energy sector, there has been a new wave of regulatory support mechanisms introduced over the last couple of years. This reflects the realisation of the vulnerability of global supply chains to physical or trade related disruptions during the COVID-19 pandemic. It is also emblematic of growing global geopolitical tensions, the need for countries to meet their Nationally Defined Contributions under the Paris Agreement, and the increasing use of renewable energy laws as an outward expression of national industry policy.

These regulatory support mechanisms can be divided into traditional industrial supports, such as the Inflation Reduction Act (2022) (US), the Green Transformation Strategy (Japan), the Indian Solar PV Incentive II and the European Union's REPowerEU Plan; and more novel interventions such as the Uyghur Forced Labor Protection Act (2021) (US).[76] This Section will examine the recent shift in approach of the United States towards a more protectionist and sovereign supply orientated approach. Two pieces of recent legislation will be used to highlight this shift in approach. First, the Uyghur Forced Labor Protection Act (2021) will be studied to highlight how the United States has effectively used the forced prison labour exemption under WTO law to impose an effective trade barrier on Chinese renewable technology manufacturers. Then, the Inflation Reduction Act (2022) and the associated secondary materials, will be critically

[75] ibid.

[76] See eg Inflation Reduction Act of 2022, Pub.L. No.117-169, 136 Stat. 1818 (2022); Japan GX (Green Transformation) Policy 2022, グリーン・イノベーション戦略", www.meti.go.jp/shingikai/energy_environment/green_innovation/pdf/gi_008_03_00.pdf; Creemers et al (n 68); Ministry of New and Renewable Energy (n 11). European Commission, 'REPowerEU Plan' (n 11).

analysed to highlight how more protectionist trade practices are being adopted in an attempt to stimulate a domestic renewable energy manufacturing sector in the United States.

A. The Uyghur Forced Labor Protection Act (2021)[77]

In 2021, China manufactured over 80 per cent of the world's high-grade polysilicon used in the manufacture of photovoltaic solar cells, with ambitions to increase that level to over 90 per cent in 2022.[78] The majority of polysilicon manufacturing occurs in Xinjiang, due to its cheap power supply (largely sourced from coal fired generation) and labour source.[79] However, following growing international concerns about the use of modern slavery in renewable energy supply chains, on 23 December 2021 President Biden signed the Uyghur Forced Labor Protection Act 2021 into law. This Act, which had passed US Congress 428 votes to 1, came into force on 1 July 2022.

The Uyghur Forced Labor Protection Act was designed to target China's alleged human rights violations in Xinjiang, and in particular, the use of forced prison labour in the manufacture of specified products, including the high-grade polysilicon used in the manufacture of photovoltaic solar cells. This law relies on the exemption to the imposition of trade barriers in Article XX(e) of the General Agreement on Tariffs and Trade (GATT) for products manufactured using forced prison labour.[80] It imposes an effective import ban into the United States of all Chinese solar products by creating the presumption that, unless proved to the contrary through very detailed supply chain tracing, any product or raw material from the Xinjiang Uyghur Autonomous Region has used forced prison labour.[81] While not explicitly cited in the legislation, representatives of the US Government explicitly stated when discussing the draft Bill outside of Congress that US energy policies must prioritise domestic manufacturing and job creation.[82] This law effectively serves two purposes for the US Government. First it enables the United States to block the vast majority of Chinese solar imports and impose additional tracing costs and time delays on those made without the use of forced prison labour, thereby making US manufactured renewable technologies a comparatively easier and more cost competitive option. Indeed, in the first year of operation of the Uyghur Forced Labor Protection Act over $US 1.2 billion worth of shipments

[77] An act to ensure that goods made with forced labour in the Xinjiang Uyghur Autonomous Region of the People's Republic of China do not enter the United States market, and for other purposes., Pub. L. No. 117-78 (2021).

[78] IEA, (August 2022) Special Report on Solar PV Global Supply Chains, Executive Summary.

[79] ibid.

[80] General Agreement on Tariffs and Trade, Oct. 30, 1947, 61 Stat. A-11, 55 U.N.T.S. 194.

[81] See, ss 3, 4, 5 and 9 of the Uyghur Forced Labor Prevention Act 2021.

[82] See eg US Congress Ways and Means House Committee (10 June 2021), 'Open Letter to the Acting Commissioner of the US Customs and Border Protections'.

of electronic equipment (the category into which manufactured photovoltaic solar cells are in) and $US 50 million of industrial and manufacturing materials (the category covering many raw material inputs) were stopped at US Ports by US Customs and Border Protections.[83]

The 1999 electronic shipments made up almost 47 per cent of the total shipments captured under the Act.[84] Of those electronic shipments, 42 per cent of them (840 shipments) have been released, with one per cent (26 shipments) denied and a further 57 per cent of shipments, including 3GW of solar panels, remain pending.[85] By comparison, in the industrial and manufacturing materials category, 25 per cent of shipments have been denied.[86] Across both categories, some of these pending shipments have been stuck on US Ports for over 12 months,[87] leading to complaints about product degradation and quality control.

The second benefit of this law is that it enables the United States to act on concerns about serious alleged human rights violations, as detailed in Section Two of the Act. Previous experience with the failed implementation of section 1502 of the Dodd-Frank Wall Street Reform and Consumer Protection Act 2010 (US)[88] which imposed a similar restriction on the use of conflict minerals from the Democratic Republic of the Congo and its neighbouring countries, highlighted the complexities, administrative burden and costs associated with this style of trade barrier. In both the case of the Democratic Republic of the Congo, and in China, it has proven to be very difficult to trace the supply chain of every raw material and component. These problems are exacerbated in China because the Foreign Affairs Committee of the China's National People's Congress responded to the introduction of the Act with the following response:

> The U.S. act fabricates the so-called 'forced labor' issue in China's Xinjiang and grossly interferes in China's internal affairs under the pretext of human rights … Should the United States choose to go down the wrong path, China will take resolute and forceful countermeasures.[89]

These threats are yet to be realised, although (as discussed below) a draft Chinese law prohibiting the export of a wide range of goods and raw materials, including photovoltaic solar panels and critical minerals is currently undergoing public notification and consultation.

[83] US Customs and Border Protections, (2023) 'Uyghur Forced Labor Prevention Act Statistics,' www.cbp.gov/newsroom/stats/trade/uyghur-forced-labor-prevention-act-statistics.

[84] ibid.

[85] ibid.

[86] ibid.

[87] ibid.

[88] Dodd-Frank Wall Street Reform and Consumer Protection Act, Public Law 203, U.S. Statutes at Large 124 (2010): 1376–2223.

[89] Xinhua, (24 December 2021), 'Chinese top legislature opposes U.S. signing of so-called "Uyghur Forced Labor Prevention Act"' english.news.cn/northamerica/20211224/debcd2faa15b4994a95ab5afdcc9a31d/c.html.

B. The Inflation Reduction Act (2022) (US)

Following supply disruptions over COVID-19 and the invasion of Ukraine by Russia, countries are increasingly using renewable energy policy to bolster energy security and enact a significant shift towards more protectionist industrial policies. The most notable example of this global shift is the United States' Inflation Reduction Act (2022), which utilises an estimated $US 369 billion dollars in fiscal incentives and tax mechanisms to advance the deployment of clean energy.[90] The Act is projected to cut 37 per cent of greenhouse gas emissions from the US power sector by 2030.[91] While the overt aim of the Act is to encourage the development of renewables and take affirmative climate action, the rhetoric used in the White House *Inflation Reduction Act Guidebook* makes it clear that this development program has a distinctly protectionist character:

> The Inflation Reduction Act is aimed squarely at building a better America and delivering on President Biden's vision to make sure the United States – powered by American workers – remains the global leader in clean energy technology, manufacturing, and innovation.[92]
>
> The Inflation Reduction Act makes a historic commitment to build a new clean energy economy, powered by American innovators, American workers, and American manufacturers.[93]
>
> … the Inflation Reduction Act prioritises creating shared prosperity, making the nation more resilient to growing threats to health and well-being ….[94]

This rhetoric is backed up with the legislative framework to deliver such outcomes, making use of economic devices such as tax credits, investment incentives, and grants to strengthen domestic industry. An example of a protectionist mechanism contained within the Inflation Reduction Act is the inclusion of domestic content requirements to gain the 'bonus' benefit of green tax credits.[95] The Production Tax Credit for Electricity from Renewables allows facilities which generate electricity from renewable sources to gain 0.3 cents/kW, which is increased by 10 per cent if the project meets '… certain domestic requirements for steel, iron, and manufactured products'.[96] A similar local content bonus regime applies to the Investment Tax Credit for Energy Property,[97] the

[90] US Treasury Department (2022), 'Treasury, IRS Open Public Comment on Implementing the Inflation Reduction Act's Clean Energy Tax Incentives' 1.

[91] Department of Energy (US), (2022) 'Inflation Reduction Act Summary – Energy and Climate Provisions' www.energy.gov/sites/default/files/2022-10/IRA-Energy-Summary_web.pdf.

[92] The White House, 'Building a Clean Energy Economy: A Guidebook to the Inflation Reduction Act's Investments in Clean Energy and Climate Action' (January 2023, version 2) 5, www.whitehouse.gov/wp-content/uploads/2022/12/Inflation-Reduction-Act-Guidebook.pdf (*Inflation Reduction Act Guidebook*).

[93] Inflation Reduction Act Guidebook, 2.

[94] ibid 5.

[95] ibid 10, 12.

[96] ibid 13.

[97] ibid 14.

Clean Electricity Production Tax Credit,[98] and the Clean Electricity Investment Tax Credit[99] established by the Act. The Inflation Reduction Act also creates grants to encourage domestic manufacturing in renewable energy, such as the Domestic Manufacturing Conversion Grants,[100] and the Advanced Manufacturing Production Credit.[101] The outcome of these initiatives is effectively a rebalancing of US clean energy law and policy in favour of a more protectionist agenda rather than adherence to traditional free trade mechanisms.

The United States' policy shift is indicative of a broader global trend in this direction and away from adhering to the strict legal requirements found in the WTO's rules. In May 2023, China flagged concerns that the US Inflation Reduction Act contains subsidy provisions which are inconsistent with the Agreement on Subsidies and Countervailing Measures.[102] This is one of the more recent developments amongst a broader field of trade disputes between the two countries,[103] and increasingly disputes have been waged outside of the multilateral WTO framework.[104]

It would be remiss not to note that other nations have also described the Inflation Reduction Act as 'super aggressive,'[105] and led to concerns about the ability of other countries to secure the clean energy technologies necessary for their energy transition. This in turn has caused the EU to respond with its own Green Deal Industrial Plan,[106] and other countries such as Australia to heavily bolster their investment and support for the clean energy transition.[107]

V. The Next Phase of Investor-State Disputes in the Renewable Energy Sector: Critical Raw Material Inputs

It is likely that as the renewable energy and clean technology sector evolves, and as renewable energy technologies come down and the cost curve and the need for

[98] ibid 18.

[99] ibid 20.

[100] ibid 55.

[101] ibid 30.

[102] World Trade Organisation, 'Members reiterate concerns on lack of transparency with subsidy notifications' (*SCM Committee Meeting*, 2 May 2023) www.wto.org/english/news_e/news23_e/scm_02may23_e.htm.

[103] A Siripurapu and N Berman, 'The Contentious U.S.-China Trade Relationship' (Council on Foreign Relations, 2 December 2022) www.cfr.org/backgrounder/contentious-us-china-trade-relationship.

[104] H Smith Freehills, 'Are we Headed for a Subsidy War? – A New Front has Opened as De-Globalisation Marches on' (30 November 2022) www.herbertsmithfreehills.com/insight/are-we-headed-for-a-subsidy-war---a-new-front-has-opened-as-de-globalisation-marches-on.

[105] L Abboud, 'Emmanuel Macron says US climate law risks 'fragmenting the west' *The Financial Times* (2 December 2022) www.ft.com/content/a1a03af2-831a-433c-8984-b99c84018a13.

[106] European Commission, 'A Green Deal Industrial Plan for the Net-Zero Age' 1.2.2023 COM(2023) 62 final.

[107] Australian Government, 'Budget 2023-24: Building a Clean Energy Future – The Australian Government's Plan to become a renewable energy superpower', see archive.budget.gov.au/2023-24/factsheets/download/factsheet_clean_energy.pdf.

subsidies falls away, that the nature of investor-state disputes in the sector will also evolve. Going forward it is predicted that these disputes will have a greater focus laws using laws to protect an investor's access to critical minerals and rare earth metals required for the manufacture of renewable energy technologies rather than on local content requirements for manufacturing. As shown in Figure 3 below, the global supply of critical raw material inputs such as lithium, cobalt, and rare earth elements are becoming increasingly dominated by a few major players, with the world's top three producing nations for each of those commodities now controlling more than three-quarters of global output.[108]

Figure 3 Market Concentration in Renewable Energy Raw Material Inputs

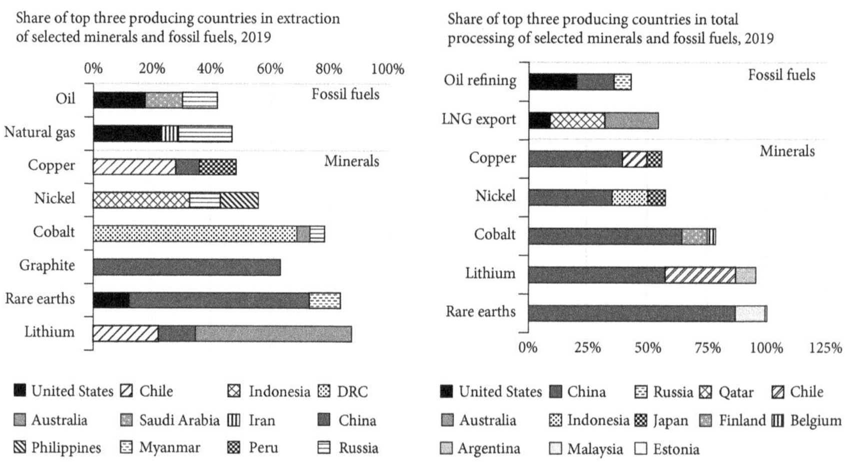

Source: IEA, (2022) 'The Role of Critical Minerals in Clean Energy Transitions' World Energy Outlook Special Report, 13.

Further, in some cases, a single country is responsible for around half of all the total global production.[109] For example, the Democratic Republic of the Congo is responsible for almost 70 per cent of the global production of cobalt, while China produces 60 per cent of rare earths.[110] The level of concentration becomes even higher when the refining and secondary processing of those raw materials, which are necessary for the manufacture of major renewable energy technologies, are examined. Figure 3 highlights that China is currently refining 35 per cent of nickel, 50 to 70 per cent of lithium, and nearly 90 per cent of the earth elements.[111] Further, this refining process often comes at the end of vertically

[108] IEA, (2022) 'The Role of Critical Minerals in Clean Energy Transitions' World Energy Outlook Special Report, 13.
[109] ibid Executive Summary.
[110] ibid.
[111] ibid.

integrated supply chains, with both privately held and state-owned Chinese companies having made substantial overseas investments into mining projects for these critical minerals and rare earths.[112] The location of these strategic investments reflects the geographic distribution of these critical raw materials, with significant Chinese investments in many of the countries identified above, including the Democratic Republic of the Congo, Australia, Chile and Indonesia. The International Energy Agency has stated that the high degree of market concentration, and the complexity of the supply chains to produce, and then refine, these critical minerals, 'increase the risks that could arise from physical disruption, trade restrictions or other developments in major producing countries.'[113]

Concerns about access to critical minerals appear to be justified. In February 2023, the Chinese Government began consultations on revisions to the Catalogue of Technologies Prohibited or Restricted by China from Export.[114] Research by the Hinrich Foundation has found that the critical components for photovoltaic solar systems have been included on the 'export-restricted' list for the first time.[115] This in turn has prompted two further developments, first the European Union released a draft Act, the Critical Raw Materials Act for consultation which, in the words of the President of the European Commission, Urusula von der Leyen, will:

> … significantly improve the refining, processing and recycling of critical raw materials here in Europe. Raw materials are vital for manufacturing key technologies for our twin transition – like wind power generation, hydrogen storage or batteries. And we're strengthening our cooperation with reliable trading partners globally to reduce the EU's current dependencies on just one or a few countries. It's in our mutual interest to ramp up production in a sustainable manner and at the same time ensure the highest level of diversification of supply chains for our European businesses.[116]

The Act also establishes internal EU targets along the strategic raw materials supply chain to diversify the EU supply of critical raw materials by 2030, including:

(1) At least 10% of the EU's annual consumption for extraction,
(2) At least 40% of the EU's annual consumption for processing,
(3) At least 15% of the EU's annual consumption for recycling,
(4) Not more than 65% of the Union's annual consumption of each strategic raw material at any relevant stage of processing from a single third country.[117]

[112] 'How America plans to break China's grip on African minerals' (*The Economist*, 28 February 2023) www.economist.com/middle-east-and-africa/2023/02/28/how-america-plans-to-break-chinas-grip-on-african-minerals.

[113] IEA (n 108) Executive Summary.

[114] KMPG, 'China plans to revise the List of Technologies Prohibited and Restricted from Export of PRC (28 February 2023) kpmg.com/cn/en/home/insights/2023/02/china-tax-alert-08.html.

[115] N Grünber and F Chimits, 'A wake-up call: China threatens a solar trade embargo' (21 March 2023) www.hinrichfoundation.com/research/article/protectionism/china-threatens-a-solar-trade-embargo/.

[116] European Commission, 'Critical Raw Materials: ensuring secure and sustainable supply chains for EU's green and digital future' (16 March 2023) ec.europa.eu/commission/presscorner/detail/en/ip_23_1661.

[117] ibid.

The law also proposes a range of measures to diversify their external supply and make it more secure, including setting up a Critical Raw Materials Club, strengthening the WTO, engaging in more Fair-Trade Agreements covering the sector and stricter enforcement of unfair trade practices.[118] Other nations are also responding to secure their supplies in the wake of China's strategic actions, with the United States, Japan and Australia reaching an agreement at the May 2023 G7 meeting about the supply of critical minerals including rare earths and lithium to the Quad strategic partners.[119]

One of the challenges to responding to this concentration of critical raw materials is that many of these resources are already subject to international long-term supply contracts. Further, as shown in the Spanish investor-state disputes, stabilisation clauses are less common in renewable projects than in other fossil fuel or resources projects. Those countries with an indigenous supply of critical raw material inputs for renewable energy technologies, such as Australia, the Democratic Republic of the Congo, Indonesia, Chile or Argentina, may consider retrospectively imposing domestic reservation policies on existing projects to assist either the country or its strategic partners. If this occurs, as shown in the Spanish examples, investors will likely bring claims against the state for expropriation, a breach of Fair and Equitable Treatment and Legitimate Expectations, and compensation will be required. This is also likely to breach Article XX of GATT, and other Fair-Trade Agreements, not to mention create significant sovereign risk with respect to other foreign investments. For countries that lack access to indigenous resources, either greater capital or creativity is required. As shown with the move by the European Union above, a viable longer-term option is the retention and recycling of these materials to support domestic manufacturing.

To avoid investor-states in the future, countries will need to proactively monitor and investigate their national renewable energy technology supply chains for risks, and investors will have to do the same, but at a corporate level. These audits ought to examine the geographic concentration of the supply of raw materials, the refining of those raw materials and the manufacture of key componentry and other inputs. They also need to consider opportunities to diversify that supply, and they need to understand all the protections available to them from bilateral trade agreements, fair trade agreements, and any other treaties from which they can benefit. Both countries and investors would also benefit from regularly reviewing the risk profile of their supply chains with respect to human rights, climate change, environmental concerns such as water management practices, and corruption.

[118] ibid.

[119] J Hewett, 'Energy, rare minerals to form third pillar of Australia-US alliance' (*The Australian Financial Review*, 21 May 2023) www.afr.com/policy/foreign-affairs/a-third-pillar-of-the-australia-us-alliance-20230521-p5d9z3.

VI. Conclusion

The nature of investor-state disputes within the renewable energy sector has changed over the past decade as countries have learnt the lessons of the Spanish cases about how to structure and then reform their regulatory support mechanisms. However, with the growth of Chinese market dominance, countries are now increasingly incorporating more protectionist trade practices in their renewable energy laws or using novel methods such as the Uyghur Forced Labor Protection Act to achieve a more favourable outcome for their own nationals and support their domestic industry. The significant market concentration in both the supply and processing of critical raw materials such as lithium, cobalt and rare earths for the manufacture of renewable technologies also poses a growing problem for countries and their foreign investors alike. For this reason, it is predicted that the next wave of disputes in the sector is likely to be more focused on securing access to the critical inputs to support market competition and sovereign manufacturing capabilities rather than local content clauses.

8

The Intersection of Human Rights and the Energy Transition: Exploring the Social Dimensions of the Energy Transition and the Potential Impact on Vulnerable Communities

ISLAMBEK RUSTAMBEKOV

I. Introduction

The global energy transition is a profound and revolutionary process that seeks to transfer the world's energy systems from relying on fossil fuels to utilising low-carbon and renewable sources. This transition is crucial in tackling the pressing issue of climate change and attaining the sustainable development goals established by the United Nations.[1] The adoption of the Paris Agreement in 2015 has reinforced the urgency for a swift and extensive shift in energy sources to mitigate global warming.[2] The IPCC has emphasised the significance of the energy transition in reducing greenhouse gas emissions and preventing the severe consequences of climate change.[3]

The energy transition is primarily motivated by environmental considerations, but there is an increasing acknowledgment of its social aspects and the possible consequences for marginalised people. The shift towards a low-carbon economy will have significant consequences for employment, energy accessibility, and social fairness, especially for individuals reliant on fossil fuel sectors or lacking cheap

[1] United Nations General Assembly, 'Transforming our world: the 2030 Agenda for Sustainable Development' (2015) A/RES/70/1.

[2] Paris Agreement (adopted 12 December 2015, entered into force 4 November 2016) 55 ILM 740.

[3] IPCC, 'Global Warming of 1.5°C: An IPCC Special Report on the impacts of global warming of 1.5°C above pre-industrial levels and related global greenhouse gas emission pathways, in the context of strengthening the global response to the threat of climate change, sustainable development, and efforts to eradicate poverty' (2018).

access to clean energy.[4] The notion of a 'just transition' has arisen as a fundamental premise in guaranteeing that the shift towards renewable energy is socially equitable and fair, and that the expenses and advantages of the transition are evenly allocated.[5]

The convergence of human rights and the energy transition is a crucial element of the social aspects of the transition. The internationally recognised human rights framework ensures that the energy transition upholds and advances the fundamental rights of individuals and communities, such as the right to life, health, food, water, and a clean environment.[6] The United Nations Guiding Principles on Business and Human Rights also highlight the obligation of corporations to uphold human rights in their activities and supply chains, particularly in relation to energy transition investments.[7]

This chapter examines the intersection of human rights and the energy transition, specifically analysing the role of international investment law in addressing the social aspects of this shift. International investment law, which regulates the relationship between foreign investors and host states, has significant implications for both the energy transition and the protection of human rights.[8]

The chapter delves into the responsibilities of states and investors under international human rights law and how these responsibilities intersect with the transition to sustainable energy sources. It provides an examination of real-life examples of energy transition initiatives that have successfully integrated human rights considerations, as well as those that have faced challenges or criticism in doing so. Analysis highlights the importance of taking social factors into account alongside economic and environmental ones, and emphasises the need for a just and equitable transition that respects and promotes the fundamental rights of individuals and communities.

By considering the intersection of human rights and the energy transition, valuable insights and recommendations for policymakers, investors, and other stakeholders involved in the shift towards clean energy, will be gained. The chapter contributes to ongoing discussions and debates on the role of international investment law in promoting sustainable development and safeguarding human rights.

The global shift towards cleaner energy sources presents both challenges and opportunities in our quest for a more environmentally friendly and fair future. By incorporating human rights principles into the energy transition process and ensuring a fair and unbiased transition for all, we can build a future that is both

[4] International Labour Organization, 'Guidelines for a just transition towards environmentally sustainable economies and societies for all' (2015).

[5] D McCauley and R Heffron, 'Just transition: Integrating climate, energy and environmental justice' (2018) 119 *Energy Policy* 1.

[6] United Nations Human Rights Office of the High Commissioner, 'Key Messages on Human Rights and Climate Change' (2015).

[7] United Nations Guiding Principles on Business and Human Rights (2011) HR/PUB/11/04.

[8] M Krajewski, 'Human Rights in International Investment Law: Recent Trends in Arbitration and Treaty-Making Practice' (2018) 49 *Netherlands Yearbook of International Law* 63.

ecologically sustainable and socially equitable. This chapter provides a clear roadmap for achieving this vision and encourages readers to actively consider the key arguments and insights presented.

II. The Social Dimensions of the Energy Transition

International legal frameworks and policies increasingly recognise the importance of addressing the social aspects of the energy transition. The United Nations Sustainable Development Goals (SDGs) provide an integrated approach to sustainable development, balancing social, economic, and environmental considerations.[9] The Paris Agreement acknowledges the need to consider the social impacts of climate change and the energy transition, particularly on vulnerable groups and communities.

The International Covenant on Economic, Social and Cultural Rights (ICESCR) recognises the right to an adequate standard of living, including access to affordable and clean energy.[10] The United Nations Guiding Principles on Business and Human Rights (UNGPs) outline the responsibilities of businesses in respecting human rights, including in the context of energy transition investments.[11]

The International Labour Organization (ILO) Declaration on Fundamental Principles and Rights at Work emphasises the need to protect workers' rights during economic transformations, such as the energy transition.[12] The World Bank's Environmental and Social Framework (ESF) requires the assessment of social risks and impacts in investment projects, particularly those related to renewable energy.[13]

The Equator Principles, a risk management framework adopted by many financial institutions, also incorporate social considerations in the assessment of investment projects.[14] Energy transition strategies are increasingly being integrated into national laws and policies, with a growing focus on addressing social and economic factors, as exemplified by the United Kingdom's Climate Change Act (2008) and the European Union's European Green Deal and Just Transition Mechanism.[15]

The concept of a 'just transition' has gained prominence in recent years, emphasising the need to address the social aspects of the shift towards clean

[9] United Nations (n 1).

[10] International Covenant on Economic, Social and Cultural Rights, Dec. 16, 1966, 993 U.N.T.S. 3.

[11] United Nations Guiding Principles on Business and Human Rights, U.N. Doc. A/HRC/17/31 (2011).

[12] International Labour Organization, ILO Declaration on Fundamental Principles and Rights at Work and its Follow-up (1998), www.ilo.org/declaration/lang--en/index.htm.

[13] World Bank, 'The World Bank Environmental and Social Framework' (2017), www.worldbank.org/en/projects-operations/environmental-and-social-framework.

[14] Equator Principles Association, 'The Equator Principles' (2020), equator-principles.com/wp-content/uploads/2020/05/The-Equator-Principles-July-2020-v2.pdf.

[15] Climate Change Act 2008, c. 27 (UK).

energy, particularly the impacts on workers and communities. The International Labour Organization (ILO) has developed Guidelines for a Just Transition towards Environmentally Sustainable Economies and Societies for All, which provide a framework to ensure that the transition is socially fair and equitable. These guidelines prioritise social dialogue, the protection of workers' rights, and the creation of decent work opportunities during the transition towards a low-carbon economy.[16]

Investors and organisations are increasingly recognising the importance of incorporating social factors into energy transition projects, as evidenced by the rise of environmental, social, and governance (ESG) investing.[17] ESG investing considers these factors when analysing and making investment decisions to promote sustainable and responsible investment. Investors and organisations are using ESG criteria to assess the social and environmental impacts of their investments and operations, as well as to identify opportunities to advance sustainable development.

The significance of considering social factors in the energy transition is also reflected in the growing body of research on energy justice and just transition. Energy justice highlights the need for a fair and equitable distribution of the benefits and burdens of energy systems, as well as the importance of inclusive decision-making processes that involve all relevant stakeholders.[18] The literature on just transition emphasises the importance of a transition that is both socially fair and equitable, taking into account the concerns and interests of workers and communities affected by the shift away from fossil fuels.[19]

To successfully navigate the complex challenges of transitioning to cleaner and more sustainable energy sources, we must recognise the importance of addressing the social dimensions of this process. This means involving a wide range of stakeholders, including governments, businesses, civil society organisations, and the communities that will be directly affected. At every step of the energy transition, it is crucial to consider the social implications. This starts with designing policies and programs that take into account the needs and concerns of all stakeholders. It also means conducting thorough social impact assessments to understand how the transition will affect different communities and individuals.

Engaging with stakeholders is key to ensuring that everyone's voice is heard. This can involve consulting with affected communities, seeking input from experts and organisations, and fostering open dialogue between all parties involved. By doing so, we can build trust, address concerns, and develop targeted policies and investments that meet the specific needs of impacted communities.

[16] International Labour Organization (n 4).

[17] Principles for Responsible Investment, 'What is responsible investment?' (2021), www.unpri.org/an-introduction-to-responsible-investment/what-is-responsible-investment/4780.article.

[18] K Jenkins et al, 'Energy justice: A conceptual review' (2016) 11 *Energy Research & Social Science* 174–82.

[19] F Mey and C Britten, 'Just Transition: Implications for the Corporate Sector and Financial Institutions' (2021) *UNEP Finance Initiative*.

The recognition of the social dimensions of the energy transition is growing, and this is reflected in international and national legal and policy frameworks. Investors and companies are also increasingly integrating social considerations into their practices. However, there is still much work to be done. We need further research and proactive efforts to fully understand and address the social impacts of the energy transition, especially for vulnerable and marginalised populations. By taking a multi-stakeholder approach and prioritising social considerations, we can ensure a just and inclusive energy transition that benefits everyone. This means not only focusing on the environmental and economic aspects, but also on the social well-being of all individuals and communities involved.

The inclusion of social factors in the energy transition is also evident in the growing number of legal cases related to the human rights impacts of energy projects. Cases such as *Social and Economic Rights Action Centre (SERAC) and Centre for Economic and Social Rights (CESR) v Nigeria*[20] and *Saramaka People v Suriname*[21] highlight the importance of incorporating human rights considerations into the development and implementation of energy policies and projects, as well as the need for effective remedies and accountability mechanisms to address human rights violations and their impacts.

To effectively address the social dimensions of the energy transition, it is essential to develop appropriate indicators and metrics to measure and monitor the social impacts of energy policies and projects.[22] While there are well-established indicators and metrics for measuring the economic and environmental aspects of the energy transition, such as greenhouse gas emission reductions or renewable energy capacity, there are fewer established indicators and metrics for assessing the social aspects. Several indicators and metrics have been proposed, including job creation and quality, energy access and affordability, health and well-being impacts, and social inclusion and participation. However, challenges remain in developing and implementing these indicators and metrics, such as limited data availability and comparability, the subjective nature of some social impacts, and the need to balance quantitative and qualitative measures.

The energy transition, while essential for tackling climate change and achieving sustainable development goals, may have significant impacts on vulnerable communities. These impacts can be both positive and negative, varying depending on the specific context and characteristics of the affected communities. Communities that rely on fossil fuel industries for employment may face substantial challenges due to job losses and economic disruption as the shift towards

[20] *Social and Economic Rights Action Center (SERAC) and Center for Economic and Social Rights (CESR) v Nigeria*, Communication No. 155/96, African Commission on Human and Peoples' Rights (2001).

[21] *Case of the Saramaka People v Suriname*, Preliminary Objections, Merits, Reparations, and Costs, Judgment, Inter-Am. Ct. H.R. (ser. C) No. 172 (2007).

[22] BK Sovacool et al, 'Metrics for measuring the social sustainability of renewable and low-carbon energy systems' (2021) 152 *Renewable and Sustainable Energy Reviews*.

renewable energy sources progresses.[23] Low-income households may encounter difficulties in accessing affordable clean energy technologies, resulting in energy poverty, which can have far-reaching consequences on health, education, and economic opportunities.[24]

Access to clean and affordable energy poses a significant difficulty in developing countries, especially in rural and remote regions. The United Nations Sustainable Development Goal 7 seeks to ensure universal access to affordable, reliable, and modern energy services by 2030, but achieving this goal will require significant investments and policy support.[25] Energy transition initiatives can have a greater impact on indigenous populations, particularly when their lands and resources are altered without obtaining their free, prior, and informed consent (FPIC). The practical implementation of FPIC has proven to be challenging, as many energy projects have proceeded without adequate consultation or consent from indigenous communities.[26]

Within the framework of the energy transition, social protection measures encompass various strategies such as providing targeted financial support to low-income households, offering retraining programs and employment assistance to workers in fossil fuel industries, and establishing social safety nets to support communities experiencing economic disruption. However, the process of designing and implementing social protection measures can be challenging, particularly in developing countries with limited financial resources and institutional capacities.[27]

International investment law plays a crucial role in shaping the social aspects of the energy transition. International investment agreements (IIAs) provide legal protections and guarantees to foreign investors operating in host countries.[28] There is growing recognition of the need to integrate sustainable development and human rights considerations into IIAs. Recent IIAs, such as the Morocco-Nigeria BIT and the Brazil-Malawi BIT, have included provisions related to sustainable development and human rights.[29]

In conclusion, it is important to consider social factors, along with economic and environmental factors, when transitioning to sustainable energy. This means taking into account the impact on people and communities, not just the planet and the economy. To do this effectively, we need to work together and include everyone in the decision-making process. We also need to create laws and policies

[23] International Labour Organization, 'World Employment and Social Outlook 2018: Greening with jobs' (2018).

[24] BK Sovacool, *Energy & Ethics: Justice and the Global Energy Challenge* (Palgrave Macmillan, 2013).

[25] United Nations (n 1).

[26] United Nations Declaration on the Rights of Indigenous Peoples (adopted 13 September 2007) UNGA Res 61/295 (UNDRIP).

[27] A Atteridge and C Strambo, *Seven principles to realize a just transition to a low-carbon economy* (Stockholm Environment Institute, 2020).

[28] R Dolzer and C Schreuer, *Principles of International Investment Law* (Oxford University Press, 2012).

[29] Brazil-Malawi Cooperation and Investment Facilitation Agreement (25 June 2015).

that protect people's rights and ensure that everyone is held accountable for their actions.

While there has been some progress in recognising the importance of social factors in the energy transition, there are still challenges to overcome. We need to make sure that vulnerable and marginalised communities are not left behind and that they have a say in the decisions that affect them. We also need to develop ways to measure and monitor the social impacts of energy policies and projects, so that we can make informed decisions.

Ultimately, we need to change the way we think about energy. It's not just about the economy and technology, but also about the well-being and rights of people. We need to transform our energy systems to prioritise the needs of communities and citizens, and to recognise that energy, climate, and social justice are all connected.

A. The Importance of Addressing Social Aspects in the Energy Transition Process

The Energy Charter Treaty (ECT), a multilateral investment agreement that pertains exclusively to the energy sector, is presently undergoing a process of modernisation in order to more accurately include principles of sustainable development and climate change.[30] The objective of the modernisation process is to synchronise the ECT with the Paris Agreement and the United Nations Sustainable Development Goals, while enhancing the provisions pertaining to sustainable development, environmental protection, and human rights.[31]

Investor-state dispute resolution (ISDS) is a crucial instrument in international investment law that can effectively tackle the social aspects of the energy transition. ISDS enables international investors to file complaints against host countries for alleged violations of investment agreements, which may include breaches of human rights commitments.[32]

In recent years, there have been numerous ISDS lawsuits pertaining to investments in renewable energy. In the *Windstream Energy LLC v Canada* case, a US investor filed a claim against Canada under the North American Free Trade Agreement (NAFTA) for claimed violations of fair and equitable treatment and national treatment obligations.[33] The investor contended that Canada's legislative

[30] Energy Charter Secretariat, 'Decision of the Energy Charter Conference' (27 November 2019).

[31] R Leal-Arcas and F Morelli, 'The Modernization of the Energy Charter Treaty: An Opportunity to Enhance Legal Certainty in Investor-State Dispute Settlement' (2021) 12 *Indian Journal of International Economic Law* 59.

[32] J Hepburn and LD Ortiz-Blanco, 'Investor-State Arbitration' in J Chaisse and L Choukroune (eds), *Handbook of International Investment Law and Policy* (Springer, 2021).

[33] *Windstream Energy LLC v Government of Canada*, PCA Case No. 2013-22, Award (27 September 2016).

environment for offshore wind energy development lacked stability and predictability, resulting in the abandonment of their proposed project. The tribunal ultimately ruled in favour of the investor and granted damages amounting to CAD 25 million.

In the *Eiser Infrastructure Limited and Energía Solar Luxembourg S.à r.l. v Spain* case, a consortium of international investors filed a lawsuit against Spain under the ECT for purported violations of responsibilities related to fair and equal treatment.[34] The investors contended that Spain had modified its renewable energy subsidy system retroactively, resulting in substantial financial losses for their solar energy investments. The tribunal ruled in favour of the investors and granted damages amounting to EUR 128 million.

These instances demonstrate the capacity of ISDS to serve as a mechanism for holding states responsible for breaching their commitments to foreign investors, particularly in regards to the advancement of investments in renewable energy. Nevertheless, ISDS has faced criticism for its potential to restrict the abilities of nations to regulate in the interests of the public, particularly in regards to the energy transition and social protection measures.[35]

ISDS claims initiated by fossil fuel companies are raising worries about their potential to impede states' endeavours to phase out fossil fuels and shift towards renewable energy. In the *Vattenfall AB and others v Germany* case, a Swedish energy firm filed a claim against Germany under the ECT for purported violations of responsibilities related to fair and equal treatment.[36] The company argued that Germany's choice to gradually eliminate nuclear energy in the aftermath of the Fukushima catastrophe in Japan had resulted in substantial financial setbacks for its investments in nuclear power stations. Ultimately, the dispute was resolved in a settlement, in which Germany agreed to provide compensation to the investors.

In response to these concerns, there have been initiatives to revise the international investment system in order to achieve a more equitable distribution of rights and responsibilities between investors and states. The UNCITRAL Working Group III is currently engaged in deliberations over proposed revisions to the ISDS system. These revisions encompass the creation of a multilateral investment court and the incorporation of provisions pertaining to sustainable development and human rights.[37]

Collaborative endeavours, such as the Principles for Responsible Investment (PRI) and the Equator Principles, can also contribute to making social factors a common and integral part of energy transition investments. The PRI is an

[34] *Eiser Infrastructure Limited and Energía Solar Luxembourg S.à r.l. v Kingdom of Spain*, ICSID Case No. ARB/13/36, Award (4 May 2017).

[35] L Johnson L et al, 'Alternatives to Investor-State Dispute Settlement' (Columbia Center on Sustainable Investment, 2019) Working Paper.

[36] *Vattenfall AB and others v Federal Republic of Germany*, ICSID Case No. ARB/12/12.

[37] United Nations Commission on International Trade Law, 'Report of Working Group III (Investor-State Dispute Settlement Reform) on the work of its thirty-seventh session' (9 April 2019) A/CN.9/970.

international consortium of investors dedicated to integrating environmental, social, and governance (ESG) criteria into their investment choices and ownership strategies. The PRI has formulated a series of six principles for responsible investment, which encompass the integration of ESG factors into investment analysis and decision-making procedures, as well as the pursuit of adequate transparency regarding ESG matters from the entities in which they invest.

Investment agreements between investors and states may also have explicit conditions pertaining to social performance and the sharing of benefits. These contracts may necessitate investors' adherence to specific social and environmental criteria, the establishment of community development funds or other mechanisms for sharing benefits, and the creation of procedures for addressing concerns or complaints from impacted communities.[38]

To ensure that international investment law effectively addresses the social aspects of the energy transition, several challenges need to be overcome. These include the specific terms of IIAs and investment contracts, their interpretation by dispute resolution bodies, and the willingness of states and investors to prioritise social factors in their investment decisions and activities.[39]

Implementing social and environmental provisions in IIAs and investment contracts can be difficult due to their broad language, lack of specific requirements, and inconsistencies between agreements. To address these issues, it is necessary to develop model clauses, establish monitoring and implementation systems, and provide capacity building and technical assistance to states, particularly developing countries.[40]

Transparency and accountability in the negotiation and implementation of IIAs and investment contracts should be enhanced through the public disclosure of agreements and related documents, as well as the creation of mechanisms for public participation and oversight.

Developing countries face specific challenges in attracting foreign investment for renewable energy projects, such as limited institutional capacity, weak regulatory frameworks, and high-perceived risks.[41] International investment law should promote renewable energy investments in these countries, focusing on sustainable development and poverty reduction through technology transfer, capacity building, and financial support.[42]

[38] L Cotula, 'Investment Contracts and Sustainable Development: How to Make Contracts for Fairer and More Sustainable Natural Resource Investments' (International Institute for Environment and Development, 2010).

[39] V Kube and EU Petersmann EU, 'Human rights law in international investment arbitration' (2016) 11(1) *Asian Journal of WTO & International Health Law and Policy* 65.

[40] United Nations Conference on Trade and Development, 'UNCTAD's Reform Package for the International Investment Regime' (UNCTAD, 2018).

[41] R Leal-Arcas, A Filis and ES Abu Gosh, *International Energy Governance: Selected Legal Issues* (Edward Elgar, 2014).

[42] C Rees, 'Mediation in Business-Related Human Rights Disputes: Objections, Opportunities and Challenges' (John F Kennedy School of Government, 2010) Working Paper No. 56.

International investment law should take into account the needs and challenges faced by marginalised and disadvantaged groups when it comes to investments in clean energy. This means including specific rules that promote gender equality, protect the rights of indigenous peoples and persons with disabilities, and encourage their participation and empowerment. To effectively address the social aspects of the shift towards clean energy, international investment law needs to be reformed. This reform should prioritise the integration of social and environmental considerations, promote transparency, accountability, and participation, and give priority to the needs and rights of communities affected by these investments and sustainable development. Achieving these reforms will require a significant change in how investment agreements are negotiated and implemented. It will also require collaboration between states, investors, and other stakeholders.

III. Human Rights and the Energy Transition

A. The Intersection of Human Rights and the Energy Transition

The intersection of human rights and the energy transition is a crucial matter that has garnered more scrutiny in recent years. In the context of the global movement towards reduced carbon emissions, it is crucial to guarantee that the change is not only environmentally sustainable, but also socially fair and impartial. This necessitates the adoption of a human rights-centred strategy that will give priority to the needs and rights of marginalised communities and guarantee their active involvement in decision-making procedures.

The human rights framework offers a potent instrument for promoting a fair and impartial transition towards sustainable energy. The connections between energy availability and the achievement of other human rights are firmly established. Access to clean and inexpensive energy is crucial for the realisation of the rights to health, education, and gender equality. Women and girls in many poor nations are disproportionately affected by the lack of access to modern energy services. They are generally responsible for gathering firewood and other traditional fuels for cooking and heating.[43] Not only does this subject children to health hazards caused by indoor air pollution, but it also restricts their chances for education and economic advancement.

Within the framework of the energy transition, the UNGPs mandate that corporations must uphold human rights in all aspects of their operations and supply chains. This entails performing human rights due diligence to identify,

[43] L Benería, G Berik and M Floro, *Gender, Development and Globalization: Economics as if All People Mattered*, 2nd edn (Routledge, 2015).

prevent, mitigate, and report on how they handle their effects on human rights, as well as facilitating or collaborating in the rectification of negative human rights consequences to which they have contributed or caused.[44]

The convergence of human rights and the energy transition underscores the necessity of adopting a rights-oriented approach to energy transition policies and investments. A rights-based approach acknowledges that the capacity to obtain clean and reasonably priced energy is not solely a matter of technical and economic factors, but also a fundamental human entitlement that is crucial for the fulfilment of other entitlements, such as the entitlements to health, education, and gender equality.[45]

The intersection of human rights and the energy transition is a pressing matter that demands immediate attention and action from all parties involved. The human rights framework offers a potent instrument for promoting a fair and impartial shift towards sustainable energy that gives priority to the requirements and rights of susceptible and marginalised people, while guaranteeing their active involvement in decision-making procedures.

B. Obligations of States and Investors under International Human Rights Law

According to international human rights legislation, states are primarily responsible for upholding, safeguarding, and ensuring the fulfilment of human rights. States have an obligation to not interfere with or limit the enjoyment of human rights in order to respect them. Within the framework of the energy transition, it is imperative for states to guarantee that their policies and initiatives do not infringe upon fundamental human rights, including the right to life, the right to health, the right to housing, and the right to a clean environment. States are obligated to guarantee that the development of renewable energy infrastructure, such as wind farms or solar arrays, does not result in the involuntary removal or relocation of populations without their voluntary, prior, and well-informed agreement.[46]

International human rights law acknowledges the entitlement of indigenous peoples to exercise self-determination and to provide their consent freely, prior to, and with full knowledge of the consequences, in regards to initiatives and regulations that impact their lands, territories, and resources. The United Nations Declaration on the Rights of Indigenous Peoples (UNDRIP), which was approved by the General Assembly in 2007, states that indigenous peoples have the authority

[44] United Nations Office of the High Commissioner for Human Rights, 'The Corporate Responsibility to Respect Human Rights: An Interpretive Guide' (2012) UN Doc HR/PUB/12/02.
[45] United Nations Development Programme, 'Integrating human rights into energy and environment programming: a reference paper' (2005).
[46] UN Committee on Economic, Social and Cultural Rights, 'General Comment No. 7: The right to adequate housing (Art.11.1): forced evictions' (20 May 1997) UN Doc E/1998/22.

to decide and establish priorities and plans for the development or utilisation of their lands and resources. It also mandates that states must engage in sincere consultation and collaboration with indigenous peoples, and obtain their free, prior, and informed consent (FPIC) before authorising any project that impacts their lands or territories.[47]

Investors, which can be companies and financial organisations, are also required to follow international laws that protect human rights. In 2011, the United Nations created the United Nations Guiding Principles on Commercial and Human Rights (UNGPs) to set a standard for preventing and addressing any harm to human rights caused by business activities. These principles are based on three important ideas: the government's responsibility to protect human rights, the accountability of companies to respect human rights, and the need for victims of human rights abuses related to business activities to be able to seek justice. Businesses have a duty to respect human rights, as outlined in the UNGPs. This means they must avoid violating people's human rights and take steps to address any negative impacts on human rights in which they may be involved. It doesn't matter how big or small a business is, what sector it operates in, where it is located, who owns it, or how it is structured – all businesses have a responsibility to uphold internationally recognised human rights.

Businesses have a responsibility to respect human rights within the context of the energy transition by implementing appropriate policies and procedures, conducting human rights due diligence, and engaging with potentially affected groups and stakeholders. This includes assessing and addressing the potential human rights impacts of their investments and operations, such as those related to land acquisition, resettlement, labour rights, community health and safety, and environmental protection. Businesses should also seek the Free, Prior, and Informed Consent (FPIC) of affected communities before undertaking projects that may impact their rights and interests.[48] Furthermore, businesses have a responsibility to respect human rights not only within their own operations, but also throughout their supply chains and business relationships, working proactively to prevent or mitigate adverse human rights impacts directly linked to their operations, products, or services.

The Organisation for Economic Co-operation and Development (OECD) Guidelines for Multinational Enterprises offers voluntary principles and standards for ethical business practices. These guidelines also cover the human rights obligations of companies in relation to the energy transition. The Guidelines advise enterprises to uphold human rights, refrain from producing or contributing to negative human rights consequences, and take action to resolve such consequences when they arise, including by facilitating or collaborating in their resolution.[49]

[47] UNDRIP (n 26) Articles 19, 32(2).

[48] UN Global Compact, 'Business Reference Guide to the UN Declaration on the Rights of Indigenous Peoples' (UN Global Compact, 2013).

[49] Organisation for Economic Co-operation and Development (OECD), 'OECD Guidelines for Multinational Enterprises' (OECD, 2011).

Notwithstanding these global standards and efforts, corporations engaged in the energy transition have frequently failed to meet human rights expectations. There have been multiple accounts of renewable energy initiatives, such as hydroelectric dams and wind farms, causing the relocation and deprivation of local communities, the devastation of ecosystems and means of living, and the infringement upon the rights of indigenous peoples.[50]

The responsibilities of countries and investors when it comes to international human rights law during the energy transition are clear and compelling. It is the basic duty of countries to protect and fulfill human rights. This means they must make sure that companies and investors behave responsibly and ensure that people affected by their actions have a way to seek justice. Companies and investors also have a duty to respect human rights by carefully examining the impact of their actions on people, involving and listening to those affected, and taking action to fix any harm caused.

C. Interaction between Human Rights Obligations and the Energy Transition Process

The process of transitioning from fossil fuels to clean and renewable energy sources, known as the energy transition, has important consequences for the realisation of human rights. The shift towards a low-carbon economy is essential for mitigating the effects of climate change and fostering sustainable development. However, it can also have varying effects on the rights of individuals and communities, depending on the manner in which it is planned, executed, and regulated.

Transitioning to clean energy can positively help in the achievement of the right to a sufficient and sustainable standard of living, which includes affordable access to energy services. The primary objective of the United Nations Sustainable Development Goal 7 (SDG 7) is to guarantee universal access to reasonably priced, dependable, environmentally friendly, and up-to-date energy sources by the year 2030.[51] Access to clean and inexpensive energy is crucial for the fulfilment of other fundamental human rights, including the rights to health, education, and employment. For instance, the utilisation of clean cookstoves and fuels can diminish indoor air pollution and enhance the well-being of women and children, who are disproportionately impacted by the adverse effects of conventional biomass cooking.[52]

The energy transition can also contribute to the mitigation of air and water pollution, positively affecting the rights to health and a clean environment.

[50] Business & Human Rights Resource Centre, 'Renewable Energy & Human Rights Benchmark: Key Findings from the Wind & Solar Sectors' (BHRRC, 2020).

[51] United Nations (n 1).

[52] World Health Organization, 'Household Air Pollution and Health' (8 May 2018) www.who.int/news-room/fact-sheets/detail/household-air-pollution-and-health.

Adopting renewable energy sources like wind and solar power can effectively mitigate greenhouse gas emissions and enhance air quality, especially in urban regions.[53] The shift can also contribute to the mitigation of water pollution and safeguard the entitlements of communities reliant on uncontaminated water for their sustenance and welfare.[54]

Nevertheless, if not well controlled, the process of transitioning to clean energy can also result in infringements of human rights and worsen pre-existing disparities. One significant peril is the compulsory relocation of communities to accommodate renewable energy initiatives, such as hydroelectric dams, wind farms, and solar arrays. The hasty pursuit of these projects, frequently lacking sufficient consultation or compensation, can result in the infringement of the rights of impacted populations, encompassing their rights to land, housing, food, and culture.[55]

For example, in Honduras, the establishment of the Agua Zarca hydroelectric dam on the Gualcarque River resulted in the compelled displacement of indigenous Lenca communities and the murder of human rights advocate Berta Cáceres, who had been actively opposing the initiative.[56] The establishment of wind farms in the Isthmus of Tehuantepec in Mexico has resulted in land seizures, social disputes, and the infringement of the rights of indigenous groups. These communities have not been properly consulted or remunerated for the utilisation of their lands.[57]

The rapid pursuit of renewable energy initiatives may potentially result in the infringement of the rights of indigenous communities, namely their entitlement to freely, priorly, and knowledgeably give consent (FPIC) for projects that impact their territories and resources. The United Nations Declaration on the Rights of Indigenous Peoples (UNDRIP) states that indigenous peoples possess the authority to establish and advance their own priorities and strategies for the development or utilisation of their lands and resources. It also mandates that states engage in sincere consultation and collaboration with indigenous peoples, ensuring their FPIC is obtained before authorising any project that impacts their lands, territories, and other resources.[58]

However, in practice, the implementation of FPIC has been restricted and irregular, as numerous renewable energy initiatives have advanced without the complete and meaningful involvement of indigenous communities. For instance, in Kenya, the development of the Lake Turkana Wind Power project, which is the largest wind farm in Africa, has faced criticism due to its failure to get the FPIC

[53] International Renewable Energy Agency, 'Renewable Energy: A Key Climate Solution' (IRENA, 2017).

[54] United Nations Environment Programme, 'The Emissions Gap Report 2018' (UNEP, 2018).

[55] Business & Human Rights Resource Centre (n 50).

[56] Interamerican Association for Environmental Defense (AIDA) and others, 'Informe sobre la situación de los derechos humanos en el contexto de la construcción del proyecto hidroeléctrico Agua Zarca y el asesinato de la defensora lenca Berta Cáceres Flores' (AIDA, 2016).

[57] R Peñaloza et al, 'Winds of change, socio-environmental conflicts and mitigating actions in the Isthmus of Tehuantepec, Mexico' (2021) 278 *Journal of Cleaner Production* 123625.

[58] UNDRIP (n 26).

of indigenous pastoralist groups. Additionally, it has been accused of causing the displacement of grazing grounds and cultural sites.[59]

The transition away from fossil fuels may result in job reductions and economic upheaval for communities reliant on these sectors, thereby adversely affecting the rights to employment and a satisfactory quality of life. The coal sector has been an important source of employment in several locations, and the discontinuation of coal-fired power stations and mines can result in substantial job reductions and societal disruption.[60]

In Germany, the government's plan to gradually eliminate the use of coal for electricity generation by 2038 has sparked demonstrations and labour strikes by coal workers and unions. These groups are concerned about the impact on their jobs and the long-term prospects of their towns.[61] According to certain estimates, South Africa's shift away from coal, which currently contributes to over 90 per cent of the country's electricity production, may result in the elimination of up to 120,000 jobs in the coal mining and power industries by 2050.[62]

The substantial initial expenses associated with renewable energy technology, such as solar panels, wind turbines, and electric vehicles, might further worsen energy poverty and disparities, especially among low-income and marginalised populations. Although the expenses associated with these technologies have been decreasing quickly in recent years, they are still unaffordable for some people and communities, especially in developing countries.[63] This disparity can result in an increasing disparity between individuals who possess the ability to obtain clean and reasonably priced energy and those who lack such access. Consequently, this discrepancy can adversely affect the ability to fully enjoy other fundamental human rights, including the rights to health, education, and employment.

In order to tackle this dilemma, it is crucial to implement policies and initiatives that encourage the affordability and availability of clean energy technology, specifically targeting low-income and marginalised groups.

The correlation between human rights commitments and the energy transition process underscores the necessity for a governance and management approach to the transition that is rooted in human rights principles. A human rights-based approach prioritises the involvement, empowerment, and responsibility of all individuals involved, especially those who are most impacted by the change, such as indigenous populations, women, and marginalised communities.[64]

[59] Danish Institute for Human Rights, 'Scoping Study: Human Rights in Wind Turbine Supply Chains' (DIHR, 2019).

[60] International Institute for Sustainable Development, 'The End of Coal: Alberta's coal phase-out' (IISD, 2018).

[61] S Eckert and I Witt, 'Just Transition for Whom? Social Challenges of Energy Transitions in the German Ruhr Area' (2021) 13(9) *Sustainability* 5217.

[62] J Burton et al, 'The Risks of a Just Energy Transition for South Africa: Insights from the Mpumalanga Coalfields' (2022) 66(4) *Africa Today* 47.

[63] International Renewable Energy Agency, 'Renewable Power Generation Costs in 2020' (IRENA, 2021).

[64] Infrastructure Development Company Limited, 'Solar Home System Program', idcol.org/home/solar.

Human rights impact assessments (HRIAs) are an essential component of a human rights-based strategy for evaluating the effects of renewable energy projects and policy. HRIAs are a methodical procedure used to identify, anticipate, and address the potential effects on human rights caused by a proposed project or policy, with the goal of maximising beneficial outcomes and minimising adverse ones.[65] HRIAs should be carried out in a way that involves active involvement and clear communication, ensuring that impacted communities and stakeholders are fully and effectively engaged.

In 2019, the Danish Institute for Human Rights carried out a Human Rights Impact Assessment (HRIA) of the Lake Turkana Wind Power project in Kenya. The assessment revealed that the project had both beneficial and detrimental effects on the human rights of the local populations, particularly in relation to their rights to land, livelihoods, and culture.[66] The HRIA provided several suggestions to the project developers and the Kenyan government. These recommendations included enhancing community participation and consultation procedures, establishing a community development fund, and offering compensation and resettlement aid to households affected by the project.

Another crucial aspect of a human rights-based approach involves creating efficient channels for impacted groups and parties to address their grievances. Grievance mechanisms refer to established procedures, whether formal or informal, that enable individuals or groups to voice their concerns or file complaints over the effects of a project or policy on their rights and interests.[67] Efficient grievance systems must be easily reachable, clear, and autonomous, and should ensure the timely and equitable settlement of grievances.

In Mexico, the National Human Rights Commission (CNDH) has created a specific role called the special rapporteurship on human rights and the environment. This role is responsible for receiving and examining a large number of complaints from indigenous communities who have been impacted by renewable energy projects, specifically wind farms located in the Isthmus of Tehuantepec.[68] The CNDH has issued several recommendations to the Mexican government and project developers. These recommendations include enhancing consultation and FPIC (Free, Prior, and Informed Consent) procedures, ensuring equitable compensation and benefits for impacted communities, and upholding the cultural and environmental rights of indigenous peoples.

[65] Columbia Center on Sustainable Investment, Danish Institute for Human Rights, and Sciences Po Law School, 'A Collaborative Approach to Human Rights Impact Assessments' (CCSI, 2017).

[66] Danish Institute for Human Rights, 'A Human Rights Impact Assessment (HRIA) of the Lake Turkana Wind Power Project, Kenya' (DIHR, 2019).

[67] Office of the United Nations High Commissioner for Human Rights, 'Guiding Principles on Business and Human Rights' (OHCHR, 2011).

[68] Comisión Nacional de los Derechos Humanos, 'Informe Especial sobre el Derecho a la Consulta Previa de los Pueblos y Comunidades Indígenas de la República Mexicana' (CNDH, 2016).

A human rights-based approach also highlights the significance of holding individuals and entities responsible for human rights violations and ensuring that victims have the means to seek redress for such violations and abuses that are connected to the energy transition. This entails guaranteeing that individuals who are accountable for human rights transgressions, regardless of whether they are affiliated with the government or not, are held responsible through efficient legal and non-legal procedures. Additionally, it involves ensuring that victims have the means to seek redress, such as compensation, restitution, and assurances that similar violations will not occur in the future.[69]

In the case of the Agua Zarca dam in Honduras, the Inter-American Commission on Human Rights (IACHR) issued precautionary measures to the indigenous communities and human rights defenders affected by the dam. The IACHR called upon the Honduran government to ensure the safety and well-being of these individuals and to halt the construction of the dam until proper consultations, which are free, prior, and informed, have taken place.[70]

The relationship between human rights obligations and the energy transition process is complex and varied. It has both advantages and challenges when it comes to achieving human rights. Let's break it down in simpler terms.

We all know that adopting clean and renewable energy is really important for dealing with climate change and promoting sustainable development. However, we have to be careful and make sure that this transition doesn't make things worse for certain groups of people, like indigenous communities, women, and marginalised communities. To make sure that the energy transition is fair and just for everyone, we need to think about human rights. This means giving people a say in the decisions that affect them, empowering them to take part in the process, and making sure that those responsible for the transition are held accountable. However, changing the way we produce and use energy won't be easy. It will require a lot of effort and cooperation from different groups, like governments, businesses, and communities. We also need to provide financial and technical support, especially to developing countries and communities that need it the most. In the global fight against climate change and for sustainable development, it's really important to consider human rights in the energy transition. This will help us make sure that the transition is not only good for the environment, but also fair and inclusive for everyone. By working together, we can make sure that everyone has access to clean, affordable, and reliable energy, while respecting and protecting their rights and dignity.

[69] United Nations General Assembly, 'Basic Principles and Guidelines on the Right to a Remedy and Reparation for Victims of Gross Violations of International Human Rights Law and Serious Violations of International Humanitarian Law' (21 March 2006) A/RES/60/147.

[70] Inter-American Commission on Human Rights, 'PM 112-16 – Members of COPINH, Berta Cáceres' relatives and other, Honduras' (5 March 2016) www.oas.org/en/iachr/decisions/precautionary.asp.

IV. Case Studies and Lessons Learned

It is really important to think about people's rights when we make changes to how we get our energy. We need to make sure that when we switch to clean and renewable energy, everyone is treated fairly and equally. This is because switching to cleaner energy is really important for reducing the effects of climate change and making progress towards a more sustainable future. However, we have to be careful to do this in a way that respects and protects the rights of the communities that are affected, especially those who are already vulnerable and marginalised.

An exemplary instance is the Lake Turkana Wind Power Project in Kenya, renowned as the largest wind farm in Africa, boasting a total installed capacity of 310 MW. A group of foreign and Kenyan investors, comprising the African Development Bank, the European Investment Bank, and the Finnish Fund for Industrial Cooperation, created the initiative, which achieved full functionality in 2018.[71]

From the beginning, the project planners acknowledged the significance of actively involving local communities and attending to their needs and concerns. The project site is situated in Marsabit County, an isolated and disadvantaged region in northern Kenya, which is inhabited by many indigenous pastoralist populations, such as the Rendille, Samburu, and Turkana.[72] These communities have endured persistent poverty, limited access to fundamental services, and the consequences of climate change, such as prolonged droughts and degradation of land.[73]

In order to tackle these difficulties and guarantee that the project would have positive effects on the local communities, the project developers carried out a thorough evaluation of the environmental and social impacts (ESIA) in compliance with globally recognised standards, such as the Equator Principles and the International Finance Corporation's Performance Standards. The ESIA entailed thorough consultations with local people, government officials, and civil society organisations, leading to the creation of a comprehensive environmental and social management plan (ESMP) and a community development plan (CDP).[74]

The CDP, created through collaboration with local communities and stakeholders, has identified several key areas for investment and assistance, including education, health, water and sanitation, and livelihoods.[75] A community development fund has been formed by the project developers. This fund receives a

[71] Lake Turkana Wind Power, 'Project Overview' ltwp.co.ke/overview/.

[72] African Development Bank, 'Lake Turkana Wind Power Project: The largest wind farm project in Africa' (AfDB, 2015).

[73] International Work Group for Indigenous Affairs, 'Kenya: Renewable energy projects and the rights of marginalised/indigenous communities' (IWGIA, 2015).

[74] Lake Turkana Wind Power, 'Environmental and Social Sustainability' ltwp.co.ke/newsite/wp-content/uploads/LTWPESP.pdf.

[75] World Bank, 'Kenya: Bringing sustainable energy to marginalized communities' (World Bank, 2018).

percentage of the project's income and is overseen by a multi-stakeholder committee consisting of representatives from local communities, the government, and the project business.[76]

The fund has provided financial assistance for many community development projects, including the building of educational and medical facilities, granting scholarships to local students, and implementing a livestock insurance programme to safeguard pastoralists from the consequences of droughts. The project has generated employment possibilities for local communities, employing more than 1,500 individuals during the building phase and creating over 200 permanent positions throughout the operational phase. Furthermore, the project developers implemented a grievance process and a community liaison office to promote continuous communication and resolution of disputes with the communities affected.[77]

An additional instance of a prosperous renewable energy initiative owned by the community is the Pikangikum First Nation Solar Project located in Canada. Pikangikum is an isolated indigenous hamlet located in northeastern Ontario that has endured persistent energy poverty and dependence on diesel generators for its electricity needs. In 2018, the town collaborated with the federal government, the Ontario government, and many private sector organisations to establish a 1 MW solar project aimed at delivering environmentally friendly and cost-effective energy to the community.[78]

The project was implemented using a distinctive partnership model that guaranteed the community's active involvement and ownership throughout the whole process. The Pikangikum First Nation, via its economic development organisation, possesses a controlling interest in the project and was engaged in all facets of its conception, building, and functioning. The project further generated employment and training prospects for the local community, employing more than 40 individuals during the construction period and establishing numerous permanent posts for ongoing maintenance and operation.[79]

The Pikangikum Solar Project has not only delivered environmentally friendly and dependable energy to the community, but it has also enabled them to assume authority over their energy prospects and generate local economic advantages. The project has been acclaimed as an exemplary example for the development of renewable energy driven by indigenous communities. It has also served as a source of inspiration for other First Nations communities in Canada, motivating them to undertake similar efforts.[80]

The Isle of Eigg community in Scotland has effectively shifted to a community-owned and run renewable energy infrastructure. Eigg is a tiny island situated on the western coast of Scotland, housing approximately 100 inhabitants. Prior to

[76] Lake Turkana Wind Power, 'Environmental and Social Sustainability' (n 5).
[77] Lake Turkana Wind Power, 'Environmental and Social Sustainability' (n 5).
[78] Natural Resources Canada, 'Pikangikum First Nation'.
[79] Wataynikaneyap Power, 'Pikangikum Power Project' www.wataypower.ca/project/pikangikum-first-nation.
[80] Lumos Energy, 'Pikangikum First Nation Solar Project'.

2008, the island depended on diesel generators to generate energy, a method that was costly, unreliable, and had negative environmental impacts. In 2008, the Isle of Eigg Heritage Trust, a community-owned organisation responsible for the island's land and resources, made the decision to allocate funds towards a renewable energy system. The purpose of this system was to supply clean and cost-effective electricity to all citizens. The system, financed through a blend of grants, loans, and community contributions, consists of three hydropower generators, four wind turbines, and a solar photovoltaic array, with a combined capacity of approximately 184 kW. The Eigg Electric cooperative owns and operates the renewable energy system, with management responsibilities delegated to a board of directors elected by the community.[81]

All residents of Eigg are members in the cooperative and everyone has the ability to influence the management of the system and the allocation of the generated income. The cooperative has implemented a maximum limit on electricity usage to guarantee the long-term viability and affordability of the system for all members. Additionally, they have created a fund to promote energy efficiency initiatives and community development endeavours.

The Eigg renewable energy system has not only supplied the community with environmentally friendly and dependable energy, but it has also given them the ability to determine their energy future and generate local economic advantages. The project has been showcased as a case study in numerous studies and publications on community energy, serving as a source of inspiration for other communities in Scotland and beyond to undertake comparable endeavours.[82]

The Renewable Energy Independent Power Producer Procurement Programme (REIPPPP) in South Africa has effectively included social and economic development criteria into its auctions for renewable energy. The Renewable Energy Independent Power Producer Procurement Programme (REIPPPP), initiated in 2011, has the objective of acquiring 17.8 GW of renewable energy capacity by 2030. Currently, it has granted contracts for more than 6.4 GW of capacity through 92 projects. An outstanding characteristic of the REIPPPP is its focus on social and economic advancement, which is incorporated into the assessment and selection of bids. As a part of the programme, project developers must provide contributions to the development of the local community, provide training for skills, and create job opportunities. Their commitments and plans in these areas are assessed and evaluated.[83]

The Renewable Energy Independent Power Producer Procurement Programme (REIPPPP) has yielded substantial socio-economic advantages for local communities, with a total investment of ZAR 1.2 billion (USD 83 million) in community

[81] Isle of Eigg Heritage Trust, 'Eigg Electric' isleofeigg.org/eigg-electric/.

[82] Friends of the Earth Scotland, 'The Isle of Eigg: Building a Sustainable Community' (FoE Scotland, 2017).

[83] Department of Mineral Resources and Energy, 'Independent Power Producers Procurement Programme (IPPPP): An Overview' (DMRE, 2020).

development initiatives as of 2020. These endeavours have encompassed the erection of educational institutions, medical facilities, and communal hubs, the allocation of financial aid and educational grants to indigenous pupils, and the formation of small enterprises and cooperative ventures. The programme has generated more than 52,000 job years, which is comparable to providing employment for one person for one year. These jobs have been produced in both construction and operations, and a considerable number of them have been allocated to local communities.[84]

The REIPPPP, or Renewable Energy Independent Power Producer Purchase Programme, has gained significant recognition for its successful integration of social and economic development into the purchase of renewable energy. This programme has been extensively studied and replicated by other nations in Africa and beyond. The programme has been acknowledged for its role in reducing the cost of renewable energy in South Africa and fostering a more competitive and dynamic market for renewable energy investment.[85]

These case studies provide evidence that research has shown how energy transition projects can take into account human rights considerations. This means that when planning and implementing renewable energy projects, it is important to involve communities, share the benefits, and include them in decision-making processes. By doing so, these projects not only provide clean and affordable energy, but also empower communities to have a say in their energy future and create economic opportunities for themselves.

However, it is important to note that not all renewable energy projects have successfully incorporated human rights considerations. Some projects have had negative effects on communities, such as displacing them from their homes, violating the rights of indigenous peoples, or worsening existing inequalities and vulnerabilities. In order to replicate the successful models and overcome these challenges, it is necessary to establish strong laws and policies that encourage and enforce the integration of human rights into renewable energy projects. This includes creating guidelines for community involvement, benefit-sharing, and mechanisms to address grievances. It is also important to monitor and hold accountable those who are involved in these projects to ensure that they adhere to these standards.

In addition, broader changes are needed in the governance and financing of the energy transition at both national and international levels. This means incorporating human rights into energy policies and plans, ensuring that international agreements align with human rights obligations, and securing fair and balanced financing from public and private sources.

[84] IPP Office, 'Independent Power Producers Procurement Programme (IPPPP): An Overview – March 2020' (IPP Office South Africa, 2020).

[85] A Eberhard and R Naude, 'The South African Renewable Energy Independent Power Producer Procurement Programme: A Review and Lessons Learned' (2020) 3(4) *Journal of Energy in Southern Africa* 1.

To ensure a successful energy transition, it is not only important to adopt renewable energy technologies, but also to establish a system of energy governance that is inclusive, participatory, and accountable. This system should prioritise the needs and involvement of individuals and communities. By studying and expanding upon the successful examples of human rights integration in renewable energy projects, and addressing the obstacles and disparities that hinder a fair and equal transition, we can create a more sustainable and resilient energy future for everyone.

The case studies mentioned in this section highlight projects that have effectively incorporated human rights considerations. For example, the Lake Turkana Wind Power Project in Kenya, the Pikangikum First Nation Solar Project in Canada, the Isle of Eigg community energy project in Scotland, and the Renewable Energy Independent Power Producer Procurement Programme (REIPPPP) in South Africa are all examples of projects that have not only provided clean energy, but have also empowered communities and brought economic benefits.

It is crucial to prioritise human rights in energy transition projects in order to achieve a sustainable, resilient, and equitable energy future. The case studies presented here offer valuable insights and examples of how to successfully integrate human rights considerations, with a focus on community engagement, benefit-sharing arrangements, and participatory decision-making processes. However, it is important to acknowledge that there have been instances where energy transition projects have faced opposition and criticism for their alleged violations of human rights and inadequate consultation and compensation for affected communities, particularly indigenous peoples. This Section will explore various case studies of such projects and the challenges they have encountered.

An example that stands out is the Agua Zarca hydroelectric project in Honduras. It encountered strong opposition from local indigenous communities who argued that the project posed a threat to their ancestral lands, livelihoods, and cultural heritage. The project, being developed by the Honduran company Desarrollos Energéticos S.A. (DESA) with funding from international investors, was planned to be built on the Gualcarque River, which holds great cultural significance for the indigenous Lenca people.[86]

The Lenca communities, under the leadership of activist Berta Cáceres and the organisation she co-founded, the Civic Council of Popular and Indigenous Organisations of Honduras (COPINH), have consistently opposed the project. They argue that they were not adequately consulted or given their free, prior, and informed consent (FPIC) as required by international human rights law. Additionally, they argued that the project would have significant negative impacts

[86] N Lakhani, 'Berta Cáceres: seven men convicted of murdering Honduran environmentalist' *The Guardian* (29 November 2018) www.theguardian.com/world/2018/nov/29/berta-caceres-seven-men-convicted-conspiracy-murder-honduras.

on the environment, lead to the displacement of communities, and jeopardise their access to vital resources such as water.[87]

Despite these objections, the project was approved by the Honduran government in 2010, and construction commenced in 2012. As a response, the Lenca communities initiated a campaign of peaceful resistance by organising blockades and protests to impede the project's advancement. Nevertheless, they encountered harsh repression and violence from state security forces and private security contractors hired by DESA, who were accused of employing threats, intimidation, and attacks to suppress opposition.[88]

In 2013, the conflict reached a boiling point when Tomás García, a respected leader of the Lenca community, tragically lost his life at the hands of a soldier during a peaceful protest.[89] In the subsequent year, Berta Cáceres and fellow COPINH members faced a barrage of death threats and harassment, believed to be linked to their opposition to the Agua Zarca project.[90] In spite of pleas for protection from various international human rights organisations, the Honduran authorities did not take sufficient steps to guarantee their safety.[91]

In March 2016, Berta Cáceres was tragically killed in her own home by armed intruders. This act was widely seen as a politically motivated assassination, connected to her activism against the Agua Zarca project.[92] The murder caused widespread international outrage and condemnation, leading to demands for an independent investigation and the cancellation of the project.[93] As a result, FMO and Finnfund halted their funding for the project, and the Chinese state-owned company Sinohydro, which had been hired to construct the dam, pulled out of the project.[94]

Nevertheless, the Honduran government and DESA persisted with the project, disregarding the protests and legal battles initiated by the Lenca communities. In 2018, a Honduran court convicted seven individuals for the murder of Berta Cáceres, which included two ex-DESA employees and two former members of

[87] International Rivers, 'The Struggle to Protect the Gualcarque River' archive.internationalrivers.org/resources/the-struggle-to-protect-the-gualcarque-river-17092.

[88] Global Witness, 'Honduras: The Deadliest Country in the World for Environmental Activism' (2017).

[89] N Lakhani, 'Honduran human rights activists survive attack by gunmen' *The Guardian* (6 December 2013).

[90] Frontline Defenders, 'Case History: Berta Cáceres' www.frontlinedefenders.org/en/case/case-history-berta-cáceres.

[91] Inter-American Commission on Human Rights, 'IACHR Condemns the Killing of Berta Cáceres in Honduras' (4 March 2016) www.oas.org/en/iachr/media_center/PReleases/2016/024.asp.

[92] N Lakhani, 'Berta Cáceres, Honduran human rights and environment activist, murdered' *The Guardian* (4 March 2016) www.theguardian.com/world/2016/mar/03/honduras-berta-caceres-murder-enivronment-activist-human-rights.

[93] UN experts, 'UN experts urge Honduras to ensure independent and impartial investigation into death of human rights defender' (11 March 2016) www.ohchr.org/en/press-releases/2016/04/honduras-murders-un-expert-urges-independent-investigation-killings-rights.

[94] Bank Track, 'Agua Zarca Hydro Project' www.banktrack.org/project/agua_zarca_dam.

the Honduran military.[95] Nonetheless, the trial faced criticism from COPINH and other human rights organisations for its failure to thoroughly investigate the masterminds behind the crime and the involvement of state authorities in facilitating and concealing the assassination.[96]

The Agua Zarca case underscores the significant human rights concerns linked to academic energy projects that lack the involvement of affected indigenous communities and fail to provide sufficient safeguards for their rights and well-being. It emphasises the importance of increased responsibility and carefulness from project developers, investors, and state authorities to prevent violence, displacement, and environmental damage caused by such projects.

Yet another instance of an energy transition project that has encountered human rights obstacles is the Eólica del Sur wind farm in Mexico. The project is situated in the Isthmus of Tehuantepec in the southern state of Oaxaca, an area rich in indigenous communities such as the Zapotec and Huave peoples. It is one of the largest wind farms in Latin America, boasting an impressive capacity of 396 MW.[97]

The project was created by a collaboration of academic and industry leaders from around the world, including renowned companies like EDF Renewables, Mitsubishi Corporation, and Zuma Energía.[98] It started operating in 2019 following a lengthy period of construction and controversy.

The indigenous communities in the project area have expressed their concerns about the wind farm, stating that they were not adequately consulted or compensated for the use of their lands. They also believe that the project could have adverse effects on their environment, health, and cultural heritage. The consultation process has faced criticism for its rushed and superficial nature, as well as the division it has caused among community members. There have been allegations of pressure and bribery to secure agreement signatures.[99]

Communities have expressed their concerns regarding the project's potential environmental and social impacts. These concerns include the clearing of forests, changes to local ecosystems, displacement of traditional agricultural and fishing activities, as well as the effects of noise and visual pollution from the turbines. They have raised multiple legal concerns regarding the project, presenting their case in Mexican courts as well as international human rights bodies. They claim that their rights to consultation, FPIC, land, and culture have been violated.[100]

[95] Lakhani (n 86).

[96] Civic Council of Popular and Indigenous Organizations of Honduras (COPINH), 'Statement on the Conviction of Sergio Rodríguez, Mariano Díaz, Douglas Bustillo, Elvin Rápalo, Edilson Duarte, Oscar Torres and Emerson Duarte for the Murder of Berta Cáceres' (1 December 2018) copinh.org/2018/11/comunicado-ante-el-fallo/.

[97] D Simonelli, 'Eólica del Sur wind farm, Mexico' (*Environmental Justice Atlas*, 25 February 2020) ejatlas.org/conflict/eolica-del-sur-wind-farm-mexico.

[98] Business & Human Rights Resource Centre, 'Eólica del Sur wind farm' www.business-humanrights.org/en/companies/mare%C3%B1a-renovables-joint-venture-macquarie-mitsubishi-corp-pggm/.

[99] ProDESC, 'The Consultation Process for the Eólica del Sur wind park project' (November 2015).

[100] PODER, 'Eólica del Sur: The Power of Wind in the Hands of Indigenous Peoples' (14 November 2018).

Land rights and compensation have been a major source of disagreement. The project developers assert that they possess legal titles to the land and have provided fair compensation to the landowners. Nevertheless, there is a dispute among communities regarding the ownership of the land. Some argue that the land is collectively owned under indigenous customary law, questioning the validity of individual land titles due to alleged fraud or coercion. They insist on halting the project until a thorough study on land tenure is conducted, and they argue that any compensation should be given to the entire community rather than individual landowners.[101]

The Mexican government has been a strong advocate for the project, emphasising its importance in the country's shift towards clean energy and fulfilment of climate change obligations. Furthermore, it has been asserted that the consultation process was sufficient and that the project has yielded economic advantages for the region, including employment opportunities and infrastructure growth.[102]

However, the government's handling of the case has faced criticism from human rights organisations and independent experts. They argue that the government has not adequately protected the rights of indigenous communities or ensured a fair and transparent consultation process. They have requested a temporary halt to the project while a thorough investigation is conducted into the reported human rights violations. Additionally, they are advocating for changes to the country's energy development and indigenous rights laws and policies.[103]

The Eólica del Sur case highlights the intricate difficulties of implementing extensive renewable energy projects in regions with indigenous communities and conflicting land rights. It emphasises the importance of thorough consultation and FPIC processes that uphold the rights of indigenous peoples to self-determination and collective ownership. Additionally, it calls for the establishment of impartial and easily accessible grievance mechanisms to resolve disputes or address any violations.

Yet another prominent example of an energy transition project grappling with human rights issues is the Belo Monte hydroelectric dam in Brazil. The dam, a massive structure with a capacity of 11,233 MW, is situated on the Xingu River in the heart of the Amazon rainforest. Since its establishment in the 1970s, it has been a source of intense debate and opposition.[104]

The project was revitalised in the 2000s as a component of Brazil's efforts to boost its renewable energy production and decrease its reliance on fossil fuels. It was created through a collaboration between Brazilian and international companies,

[101] ProDESC, 'The Consultation Process for the Eólica del Sur wind park project' (n 15).

[102] J Carrasco, 'Empresa de parque eólico dio más de 30 mdp a ejidatarios para operar: ASF' (*Proceso*, 21 February 2019) www.proceso.com.mx/nacional/2019/2/21/empresa-de-parque-eolico-dio-mas-de-30-mdp-ejidatarios-para-operar-asf-220616.html.

[103] Simonelli (n 97).

[104] F Del Bene, 'Belo Monte dam: Electricity or Life?' (*Environmental Justice Atlas*, 25 June 2020) ejatlas.org/conflict/belo-monte-dam-brazil.

with funding from the Brazilian National Development Bank (BNDES) and various public and private sources.[105]

However, the project has encountered significant opposition from indigenous communities in the Xingu basin. These communities have expressed concerns that the dam would result in the flooding of their ancestral lands, disruption of their livelihoods, and irreversible harm to the region's ecosystem and biodiversity. Critics have raised concerns about the consultation and compensation processes, arguing that they are insufficient and exclusive. They are calling for the recognition of their right to Free, Prior, and Informed Consent (FPIC).[106]

The indigenous communities, along with environmental and human rights organisations, have actively opposed the project through legal and political means, both in Brazil and internationally. They have taken various actions, including filing lawsuits and petitions, organising protests and blockades, and lobbying governments and investors to cancel or modify the project. An important concern regarding the Belo Monte dam is its effect on the Xingu River and its tributaries. These waterways support a wide range of fish species and other aquatic life that are crucial for the well-being and traditions of indigenous communities. The dam has had a significant impact on the river's natural flow and flooding cycles, resulting in the creation of canals and reservoirs. These changes have affected the water quality and temperature, rendering it inhospitable for numerous species.[107]

The construction of the dam has resulted in the forced relocation of numerous individuals, both indigenous and non-indigenous, who have not been adequately compensated or provided with assistance to resettle.[108] The increase in workers and migrants at the construction site has caused social and cultural disruption, as well as added strain on local services and resources.[109]

The Brazilian government and the project developers have consistently argued that the Belo Monte dam is a crucial and advantageous undertaking for the country's energy security and economic growth. It has been stated that the project has undergone thorough environmental and social impact assessments, and that the affected communities have been adequately consulted and compensated.[110]

However, the government's claims have faced criticism from independent experts and international human rights bodies, who argue that the project infringes upon the rights of indigenous peoples and violates international environmental

[105] PM Fearnside, 'Brazil's Belo Monte Dam: Lessons of an Amazonian resource struggle' (2017) 148 *Die Erde* 2–3.

[106] International Rivers, 'Belo Monte Dam' archive.internationalrivers.org/campaigns/belo-monte-dam.

[107] Del Bene (n 104).

[108] Instituto Socioambiental (ISA), 'Belo Monte: 5 years of impunity and destruction in the Amazon' (5 May 2021) www.socioambiental.org/en/noticias-socioambientais/belo-monte-5-years-of-impunity-and-destruction-in-the-amazon.

[109] PM Fearnside, 'Impacts of Brazil's Madeira River Dams: Unlearned lessons for hydroelectric development policy and the environment in Amazonia' (2014) 9(2) *Environmental Science & Policy* 164.

[110] Del Bene (n 104).

and human rights standards. In 2011, the Inter-American Commission on Human Rights (IACHR) granted precautionary measures to the indigenous communities affected by the dam. The IACHR called on Brazil to suspend the project until it had conducted consultations with the communities and taken measures to protect their rights and mitigate the impacts of the dam.[111]

The Brazilian government initially rejected the decision made by the IACHR, but eventually agreed to engage in consultations with the indigenous communities. Nevertheless, the consultations faced extensive criticism for their lack of depth and formality, and failed to bring about any substantial alterations to the project's design or compensation measures.[112]

In 2016, the Belo Monte dam started operating fully, despite facing legal challenges and protests from affected communities and civil society organisations. The dam has encountered various challenges, such as technical and financial issues, including increased costs, delays in construction, and reduced energy generation caused by drought and the effects of climate change.[113]

The Belo Monte case is like a puzzle that shows the challenges and conflicts that can happen when building big hydroelectric projects in important places like the Amazon rainforest. It reminds us how important it is to conduct better assessments of the impact these projects have on the environment and the people who live there. We need to make sure that the rights and well-being of indigenous communities and local people are taken into account and protected.

The case also makes us worry about how these projects will hold up in the face of climate change and other environmental problems. It shows us that when we focus on transitioning to cleaner energy sources, we can't forget about the rights and concerns of the communities that are affected, especially indigenous people. We have to be more careful and make sure we do thorough assessments, listen to the communities, and include them in the decision-making process.

The case also shows us that when communities' rights are violated by energy projects, they often have to fight for justice in courts. However, they face a lot of obstacles like limited access to justice, corruption, and impunity. This is why it's so important for the people and organisations financing and executing these projects to be transparent and accountable, and to follow human rights and environmental standards. They need to use their power to prevent any harm to communities and make things right if harm does occur.

The cases also tell us that the problems with these projects go beyond just the specific impacts they have. They bring up bigger concerns like land rights, self-determination, and the unfair treatment of indigenous and local communities. To solve these problems, we need to take a comprehensive and inclusive approach

[111] Inter-American Commission on Human Rights, 'Indigenous Communities of the Xingu River Basin, Pará, Brazil' (1 April 2011) PM 382/10.

[112] Instituto Socioambiental (ISA), 'Belo Monte: 5 years of impunity and destruction in the Amazon' (n 35).

[113] M Anderson, 'The Belo Monte Dam: An Environmental Crime' (*Amazon Watch*, 15 June 2019).

to transitioning to cleaner energy. We have to prioritise the needs and dreams of the communities affected by the transition and find fair and sustainable ways to develop. This could mean changing land ownership rules, making agreements to share the benefits of the projects, requiring that local people are involved in the work, and supporting community-led energy projects, for example.

In conclusion, the case studies in this chapter teach us a lot about how human rights and energy transition projects are connected. Some projects have done a good job of including communities in the process and respecting their rights, but many others have caused harm and faced criticism for not doing enough. The cases of the Agua Zarca hydroelectric project in Honduras, the Eólica del Sur wind farm in Mexico, and the Belo Monte hydroelectric dam in Brazil show us how these projects can violate the rights of indigenous communities, like their right to have a say in what happens to their land and culture. These projects have been criticised for not talking to the communities enough and not giving them fair compensation. They have also harmed the environment and the local economy.

The challenges faced by these projects tell us that we need to conduct better assessments, listen to the communities, and make sure their rights are protected. We also need to have good ways for communities to complain and get help if their rights are violated. We need to be more open and honest about how these projects are paid for and carried out.

In the end, this chapter shows us that we have to take a big-picture approach when transitioning towards cleaner energy. We have to think about the needs and dreams of the communities affected and find ways to develop that are fair and sustainable. This might mean changing land ownership rules, making agreements to share the benefits of the projects, requiring that local people are involved in the work, and supporting community-led energy projects. By learning from both the successes and failures of past projects, and by addressing the underlying factors that contribute to conflict and inequality in the development of energy transition projects, we can work towards a more sustainable, fair, and strong energy future for everyone.

V. Strategies for a Socially Just and Equitable Energy Transition

A. Participatory Decision-making Processes in Energy Transition Policies and Investments

Participatory decision-making processes are essential for ensuring that energy transition policies and investments are fair, equal, and considerate of the needs and priorities of affected communities. In order to ensure a comprehensive and inclusive approach to energy transition strategies, it is crucial to take into account the viewpoints and needs of all stakeholders, especially those who are most vulnerable and marginalised.

Participatory decision-making is based on democratic principles, emphasising transparency and accountability. It acknowledges the importance of including those most impacted by a decision in the decision-making process, and recognising the value and respect for their knowledge, experiences, and aspirations.[114] Participatory decision-making is strongly connected to the idea of procedural justice, highlighting the significance of fair, inclusive, and transparent processes in distributing benefits and burdens in society.[115]

When it comes to energy transition policies and investments, participatory decision-making means creating open and inclusive channels for consultation and dialogue. This ensures that everyone has a say, including local communities, civil society organisations, and marginalised groups. These mechanisms should be designed to foster trust, promote information sharing, and facilitate the collaborative creation of solutions that consider the interests of various stakeholders.

To ensure inclusive decision-making in energy transition policies and investments, governments and investors must actively facilitate and encourage the participation of local communities and civil society organisations at every stage of the project, from planning and design to implementation, monitoring, and evaluation. This involves providing the necessary resources and support, defining stakeholder roles and responsibilities, and establishing channels for continuous communication, feedback, and adjustments based on the input and concerns of impacted communities.

During the planning and design stages, involving the community can ensure that energy transition policies and investments are in line with their needs and priorities. It also helps identify and address potential impacts and risks at an early stage. One approach to consider is the use of participatory impact assessment tools, like community-based environmental and social impact assessments (CBIAs). These tools allow communities to evaluate the potential effects of projects on their livelihoods, cultures, and environments.[116]

During the implementation phase, involving the community in decision-making processes can ensure that energy transition projects are carried out with transparency, accountability, and responsiveness to community input. This may require the creation of community monitoring and evaluation committees that oversee project progress and offer consistent feedback to project developers and investors.[117]

[114] SR Arnstein, 'A Ladder of Citizen Participation' (1969) 35(4) *Journal of the American Institute of Planners* 216.

[115] D Schlosberg, 'Reconceiving Environmental Justice: Global Movements and Political Theories' (2004) 13(3) *Environmental Politics* 517.

[116] KH Kenyon and M Holden, 'Exploring the Social and Participatory Processes of Community-Based Impact Assessment' (2021) 44 *Environmental Impact Assessment Review* 106560.

[117] J Hicks et al, 'Community-Owned Renewable Energy: A How to Guide' (2020) Community Power Agency.

During the monitoring and evaluation phase, participatory processes can be utilised to assess the impacts and outcomes of energy transition policies and investments, as well as to identify lessons learned and areas for improvement. One approach to consider is the use of participatory evaluation methodologies, like the most significant change (MSC) techniques. These techniques allow communities to share their stories and experiences of change.[118]

In order to build social licence, legitimacy, and ownership of energy transition policies and investments, it is crucial to have participatory decision-making processes. This ensures that the benefits of these policies and investments are distributed to all members of society, especially those who are most vulnerable to the impacts of climate change and the energy transition.

Recognising the significance of participatory decision-making processes in establishing social licence, legitimacy, and ownership, international and national energy and climate policies are placing greater emphasis on this aspect. As an illustration, the Paris Agreement on climate change highlights the significance of involving the public in developing and executing national climate plans and strategies.[119] The United Nations Sustainable Development Goals (SDGs) also acknowledge the significance of involving all stakeholders in decision-making processes to achieve sustainable development.[120]

Many countries at the national level have implemented policies and frameworks to encourage inclusive decision-making in energy transition policies and investments. As an illustration, in the United States, the Biden administration is dedicated to ensuring that 40 per cent of the benefits of federal climate and clean energy investments reach disadvantaged communities. To gather input and recommendations on these investments, they have set up an Environmental Justice Advisory Council.[121]

The European Union places great emphasis on citizen and stakeholder engagement in the design and implementation of climate and energy policies. To mobilise citizens and communities to take action on climate change, the European Green Deal has established the European Climate Pact.[122] The EU has also created various tools and methods for participation, including the Climate-KIC Transitions Hub. This platform allows different stakeholders to collaborate and work together on climate and energy matters.[123]

In Singapore, the government has implemented various public participation mechanisms in environmental and energy decision-making, including public

[118] R Davies and J Dart, 'The "Most Significant Change" (MSC) Technique: A Guide to Its Use' (2005) CARE International.

[119] Paris Agreement (adopted 12 December 2015, entered into force 4 November 2016) 55 ILM 740.

[120] United Nations (n 1).

[121] The White House, 'Fact Sheet: President Biden Takes Executive Actions to Tackle the Climate Crisis at Home and Abroad, Create Jobs, and Restore Scientific Integrity Across Federal Government' (27 January 2021).

[122] European Commission, 'The European Green Deal' (2019) COM/2019/640 final.

[123] Climate-KIC, 'Transitions Hub' https://transitionshub.climate-kic.org/.

consultations and stakeholder engagement platforms.[124] The government has also created various participatory tools and methodologies, like the Smart Nation Initiative, to encourage citizen engagement and collaboration on sustainable development and climate change concerns.[125]

Despite recent policy advancements, there remain substantial obstacles to successfully implementing participatory decision-making in energy transition policies and investments. Some challenges in the academic realm include limited capacity and resources for community engagement, lack of access to information and technical expertise, power imbalances between communities and project developers, and inadequate legal and institutional frameworks for public participation.[126]

Participatory decision-making processes are crucial in ensuring that energy transition policies and investments are fair, inclusive, and aligned with the needs and priorities of affected communities. Through the establishment of inclusive and transparent consultation and dialogue mechanisms, the use of participatory tools and methodologies, and the provision of sufficient resources and capacity-building support, governments and investors can facilitate the active involvement of all stakeholders in the development and execution of energy transition strategies.

Engaging all affected communities, especially those who are vulnerable and marginalised, in decision-making processes can foster social acceptance, credibility, and a sense of ownership over energy transition policies and investments. They can also assist in identifying and addressing potential risks and impacts, while collaboratively developing solutions that consider the needs of various stakeholders.

B. Targeted Support Measures for Vulnerable Communities Affected by the Energy Transition

Ensuring that vulnerable communities are not left behind is of the utmost importance as countries worldwide shift towards cleaner and more sustainable energy systems. The transition from fossil fuels to renewable energy sources can bring about substantial social and economic consequences for communities reliant on traditional energy sectors, like coal mining and oil and gas extraction.[127] These impacts can result in negative consequences such as

[124] National Climate Change Secretariat, 'Public Consultation on Singapore's Climate Ambition' (2022) Government of Singapore.

[125] Smart Nation Singapore, 'Pillars of Smart Nation' www.smartnation.gov.sg/about-smart-nation/pillars-of-smart-nation.

[126] S Hanger-Kopp et al, 'Stakeholder Engagement in Integrated Assessment Modeling of Global Climate Change: A Review of Best Practices' (2022) 43 *Environmental Modelling & Software* 105425.

[127] J Cartwright, 'Toward a Just Transition Away from Coal: Identifying Local Priorities in India and South Africa' (World Resources Institute, 2021).

unemployment, decreased earnings and tax revenue, and the gradual loss of social and cultural identity.[128]

In order to address the adverse effects and promote fairness in the distribution of benefits from the energy transition, it is crucial to implement specific support measures for vulnerable communities. It is important to tailor these measures to suit the unique needs and circumstances of each community. This includes considering factors like geographic location, socio-economic status, and cultural and historical context.[129]

It is necessary for governments and investors to collaborate with local communities, civil society organisations, and other stakeholders in order to create and execute support measures that are both effective and sustainable, while also promoting fairness. This necessitates an academic approach that values the input and perspectives of impacted communities.[130]

Community benefit agreements (CBAs) are a promising model for fostering community engagement and partnership. CBAs are contracts that project developers and community organisations enter to outline the benefits that the community will receive from a project. These benefits can include things like job creation, affordable housing, or community infrastructure.[131] CBAs are essential for ensuring that the advantages of renewable energy projects are fairly distributed among local communities and that community issues and priorities are taken into account during project planning and execution.

It is important for governments, investors, and other stakeholders to actively participate in creating and executing focused assistance measures that are efficient, fair, and enduring. This necessitates a dedication to continuous involvement and collaboration with impacted communities, along with the utilisation of inventive funding methods and inclusive assessment methods.

The magnitude and intricacy of the issues confronting vulnerable communities in the energy transition necessitate a united and synchronised endeavour from all parties involved. Collaboration among governments at various levels is crucial for the development and execution of policies and programmes that promote a fair and balanced transition.[132]

The United Kingdom has been at the forefront of promoting a fair transition to a low-carbon economy, implementing various policies and programmes to assist workers and communities impacted by the energy shift. The UK's Industrial

[128] I Heffron and D McCauley, 'The Concept of Energy Justice Across the Disciplines' (2017) 105 *Energy Policy* 658.

[129] C Zinecker et al, 'Just Transition for All – Analytical Evidence' (European Commission, 2021) 19.

[130] D Farrell and M Petersen, 'Beyond Inclusion: Equity-Centered Community Engagement for Clean Energy' (2022) 6(3) *One Earth* 225.

[131] J Konisky et al, 'The Use of Community Benefits Agreements in the Energy Transition: Implications for Energy Law, Policy, and Justice' (2022) 91 *Energy Research & Social Science* 102768.

[132] A Michaelowa, 'Ensuring Additionality Under Art. 6 of the Paris Agreement' (Harvard Project on Climate Agreements, 2021).

Strategy features a Clean Growth Grand Challenge, which seeks to optimise the benefits for UK industry from the worldwide transition to clean growth.[133]

The strategy involves implementing various measures, including investing in low-carbon technologies and infrastructure, supporting businesses to develop and adopt clean technologies, and ensuring that the workforce possesses the necessary skills and knowledge for the low-carbon economy. The UK has also set up a Just Transition Commission to provide guidance to the government on achieving a fair transition to a net-zero economy. The commission's main focus is assisting workers and communities in high-carbon industries like oil and gas.[134]

Singapore has also taken proactive steps to support a fair and inclusive energy transition, implementing various measures to assist low-income households and vulnerable communities. The Energy Market Authority (EMA) has set up an Energy Assistance Package to offer financial support to low-income households in paying their electricity bills.[135]

The package offers a $50 credit for eligible households, along with a monthly $20 credit for households with a member who is elderly, disabled, or critically ill. The EMA has also introduced a Community Energy Masterplan to involve local communities in creating sustainable energy solutions. The plan aims to enhance energy efficiency and lower energy expenses for low-income households.[136]

These examples show different ways through which we can make sure the switch to cleaner energy is fair and balanced. We can do this by implementing plans at a national level, by supporting local community projects, and by providing financial help. However, there's still more work to do to make sure that everyone benefits from this transition and that no one is left behind.

It's really important to give specific help to communities that might be affected by the switch to cleaner energy. We want to make sure that everyone has a fair chance to be a part of a low-carbon economy. To do this, we need to listen to the people who are directly affected and include their ideas and knowledge. This will help them thrive in the future and make sure that the transition is fair for everyone.

C. Human Rights Influence Assessments in Energy Transition Projects

Human rights impact assessments (HRIAs) are now seen as essential in identifying, preventing, and mitigating potential human rights risks and impacts of energy transition projects. In the pursuit of a low-carbon future, it is important

[133] HM Government, 'The Clean Growth Strategy: Leading the Way to a Low Carbon Future' (HM Government, 2017).

[134] Just Transition Commission, 'Just Transition Commission: A National Mission for a Fairer, Greener Scotland' (Scottish Government, 2021).

[135] Energy Market Authority, 'Energy Assistance Package' (Government of Singapore, 2022).

[136] Energy Market Authority, 'Community Energy Masterplan' (Government of Singapore, 2022).

to prioritise human rights and avoid marginalising vulnerable communities when developing and implementing renewable energy projects.

HRIAs involve a methodical evaluation of the real and potential human rights effects of a project at every stage, using global human rights standards and best practices.[137] They require a thorough examination of the human rights context in which a project is being developed, including the legal and policy framework, the socio-economic and cultural context, and the specific human rights risks and vulnerabilities of affected communities.

The process of conducting an HRIA usually includes multiple stages, such as scoping, data collection and analysis, impact assessment, and the creation of mitigation and management measures. In the scoping stage, it is important to identify the main human rights issues and stakeholders related to the project, and to define the assessment's scope and methodology.

Collecting and analysing data requires gathering information from different sources, such as desk-based research, stakeholder consultations, and field visits. This may involve reviewing relevant laws, policies, and reports, as well as conducting interviews and focus group discussions with affected communities, civil society organisations, and other stakeholders.[138]

During the impact assessment stage, the data collected is carefully analysed to identify the human rights impacts of the project, whether they are positive or negative. This may involve evaluating the severity, extent, and probability of various impacts, as well as the particular groups and individuals who may be impacted.[139]

After analysing the impact assessment results, the HRIA should create a plan of action to deal with the risks and impacts that have been identified. This may involve implementing strategies to mitigate negative effects and maximise opportunities for promoting human rights.

The results of an HRIA should be utilised to guide the development and execution of the project, which involves recognising and addressing any potential human rights violations through preventive, mitigative, and remedial measures. This may require the creation of a human rights action plan, which details the necessary steps and resources to tackle the identified risks and impacts, along with the roles and responsibilities of various stakeholders.

Some countries at a national level have also established legal and policy frameworks for conducting HRIAs in relation to energy projects. As an illustration, in the United States, the National Environmental Policy Act (NEPA) mandates that federal agencies carry out environmental impact assessments for significant

[137] Danish Institute for Human Rights, 'Human Rights Impact Assessment Guidance and Toolbox' (2016) www.humanrights.dk/tools/human-rights-impact-assessment-guidance-toolbox.

[138] E Wilson and J Harrison, 'Human rights impact assessment: A review of current practice' (2015) pubs.iied.org/sites/default/files/pdfs/migrate/16529IIED.pdf.

[139] S McInerney-Lankford et al, 'Human Rights Impact Assessments: A Review of the Literature, Differences with other Forms of Assessments and Relevance for Development' (2011) World Bank documents1.worldbank.org/curated/en/834611524474505865/pdf/125557-WP-PUBLIC-HRIA-Web.pdf.

projects, such as energy projects, which must also take into account the potential effects on human rights and vulnerable communities.[140]

Within the European Union, the EIA Directive mandates the performance of environmental impact assessments for specific projects, such as energy projects. In regards to the EIA Directive, it does not specifically state the need to consider human rights impacts.[141] However, the European Commission has provided guidance on incorporating human rights into environmental impact assessments. This guidance emphasises the significance of assessing potential impacts on vulnerable groups and the importance of engaging stakeholders in a meaningful way.[142]

Furthermore, there are various voluntary initiatives and standards that encourage the utilisation of HRIAs in energy projects, in addition to the legal and policy frameworks. As an illustration, the Equator Principles, a risk management framework widely embraced by financial institutions, necessitate the performance of human rights due diligence and impact assessments for projects that may pose human rights risks.[143]

Human rights impact assessments have become essential in identifying, preventing, and mitigating potential human rights risks and impacts of energy transition projects. Ensuring that the development and implementation of renewable energy projects will not lead to human rights violations and the marginalisation of vulnerable communities is crucial as the world moves towards a low-carbon future.

D. The Role of International Investment Law in Promoting a Socially Just and Equitable Energy Transition

International investment law is vital in shaping the global energy transition and its social and environmental impacts. When countries aim to attract foreign investment for renewable energy projects and infrastructure development, the legal frameworks that govern these investments can greatly impact the rights and well-being of local communities, as well as the achievement of sustainable development goals.[144]

In the past, international investment law has faced criticism for favouring the protection of foreign investors' rights and interests at the expense of the social and environmental concerns of host states and communities.[145] Numerous

[140] National Environmental Policy Act of 1969, as amended (Pub L 91-190, 42 US C 4321-4347, 1 January 1970).

[141] Directive 2011/92/EU of the European Parliament and of the Council of 13 December 2011 on the assessment of the effects of certain public and private projects on the environment [2011] OJ L 26/1.

[142] European Commission, 'Guidance on Integrating Human Rights into Environmental Impact Assessments' (2013) ec.europa.eu/environment/eia/pdf/EIA%20Guidance.pdf.

[143] Equator Principles (n 14).

[144] M Hodgson, 'Reconciling Investment and Climate Policy: A Role for International Investment Agreements?' (2022) 36(2) *Journal of International Arbitration* 141.

[145] K Tienhaara, 'Regulatory Chill in a Warming World: The Threat to Climate Policy Posed by Investor-State Dispute Settlement' (2018) 7(2) *Transnational Environmental Law* 229.

international investment agreements (IIAs), including bilateral investment treaties (BITs) and free trade agreements (FTAs), aim to offer extensive safeguards for foreign investors against actions taken by host states that could impact their investments, such as expropriation, discrimination, and unfair treatment.[146]

Enforcing these protections has commonly involved the use of investor-state dispute settlement (ISDS) mechanisms, which enable foreign investors to file claims against host states in international arbitral tribunals.[147] Critics have raised concerns about the lack of transparency, accountability, and legitimacy surrounding ISDS. They argue that it may restrict host states' abilities to regulate in the interests of the public, particularly in areas such as environmental protection, human rights, and climate change mitigation.[148]

Take the case of *Vattenfall v Germany*, where the Swedish energy company Vattenfall filed an ISDS claim against Germany. They challenged Germany's choice to phase out nuclear power plants after the Fukushima disaster in 2011.[149] Vattenfall claimed that the phase-out was a form of indirect expropriation of its investments and a breach of its legitimate expectations. It requested compensation of more than €4.7 billion. The case sparked worries regarding the impact of ISDS on countries' energy transition policies and their capacity to address public concerns and democratic pressures.[150]

Similarly, in the *Lone Pine v Canada* case, the US oil and gas company Lone Pine filed an ISDS claim against Canada under the North American Free Trade Agreement (NAFTA), contesting Quebec's fracking moratorium in the St. Lawrence River Valley.[151] Lone Pine contended that the moratorium constituted an illegal seizure of its investments and a breach of its rights under NAFTA, leading it to pursue compensation exceeding US$100 million.[152] The case brought attention to the conflicts between the rights of foreign investors and the regulatory authority of host states, especially when it comes to environmental and health issues.[153]

There has been an increasing demand for the reform of international investment law to be better aligned with sustainable development and human rights

[146] J Viñuales, 'Energy Charter Treaty Reform: A Missed Opportunity for Enhanced Multilateralism in Investment Dispute Settlement' (2019) 34(4) *ICSID Review* 480.

[147] L Johnson and L Sachs, 'The Outsized Costs of Investor-State Dispute Settlement' (2016) 16(1) *Academy of International Business*.

[148] G Van Harten, 'The European Commission's Push to Consolidate and Expand ISDS: An Assessment of the Proposed Canada-Europe CETA and Europe-Singapore FTA' (2015) Osgoode Hall Law School Legal Studies Research Paper No. 23/2015.

[149] *Vattenfall AB and others v Federal Republic of Germany*, ICSID Case No. ARB/12/12.

[150] C Tietje and F Baetens, 'The Impact of Investor-State-Dispute Settlement (ISDS) in the Transatlantic Trade and Investment Partnership' (2014) Study prepared for Minister for Foreign Trade and Development Cooperation, Ministry of Foreign Affairs, The Netherlands.

[151] *Lone Pine Resources Inc. v The Government of Canada*, ICSID Case No. UNCT/15/2.

[152] N Lobel and M Fermeglia, 'Investment Protection and Unburnable Carbon: Competing Commitments in International Investment and Climate Governance' (2018) 4(4) *Transnational Environmental Law* 1.

[153] K Tienhaara, 'Investor-State Dispute Settlement in Trade and Investment Agreements: Implications for Health and the Transition towards Green Energy' (2019) 8(4) *Global Policy* 608.

considerations, in response to these criticisms and concerns. The United Nations Guiding Principles on Business and Human Rights (UNGPs), adopted in 2011, establish a global framework for the responsibilities of states and businesses in upholding human rights during economic activities, including foreign investment.[154]

The UNGPs highlight the importance of states ensuring that their investment policies and agreements do not hinder their ability to fulfil their human rights obligations. Similarly, businesses should carry out human rights due diligence to identify, prevent, and mitigate any negative impacts on human rights. The UNGPs also emphasise the need for efficient grievance mechanisms and avenues for redress for individuals and communities impacted by human rights violations linked to business activities. Expanding on the UNGPs, there have been attempts to integrate human rights and sustainable development factors into IIAs and other investment policy instruments. As an illustration, the United Nations Conference on Trade and Development (UNCTAD) has created the Investment Policy Framework for Sustainable Development (IPFSD), a tool that offers countries guidance on crafting investment policies that support sustainable development and responsible investment.[155]

The IPFSD suggests that IIAs should contain provisions that oblige investors to uphold human rights and support sustainable development. This can be achieved by conducting human rights due diligence and implementing social and environmental safeguards. The document also suggests including provisions that safeguard the ability of states to regulate in the interests of the public, particularly regarding the energy transition and the protection of human rights. This would help prevent any potential investor-state-disputes. Several countries have begun integrating these suggestions into their investment policies and agreements. As an illustration, the Netherlands Model BIT, implemented in 2019, incorporates provisions on sustainable development and responsible business conduct. It also mandates investors to adhere to domestic laws and regulations concerning human rights, labour rights, and environmental protection.[156]

The Dutch Model BIT also includes a provision that upholds the state's authority to implement measures to safeguard important public welfare goals, such as public health, safety, the environment, and labour rights, even if these measures may impact foreign investments. The provision aims to protect against ISDS claims that could potentially challenge measures like indirect expropriation or unfair treatment.[157]

[154] United Nations Human Rights Council, 'Guiding Principles on Business and Human Rights: Implementing the United Nations 'Protect, Respect and Remedy' Framework' (2011) UN Doc A/HRC/17/31.

[155] UNCTAD, 'Investment Policy Framework for Sustainable Development' (2015) UNCTAD/DIAE/PCB/2015/5.

[156] Netherlands Model Investment Agreement (2019), Article 7.

[157] K Tienhaara, 'Is the Netherlands Model Investment Agreement a Step Forward for Sustainable Development?' (*International Institute for Sustainable Development*, 12 June 2019) www.iisd.org/

In a similar vein, the Morocco-Nigeria BIT, signed in 2016, incorporates a section on sustainable development. This section mandates that investors adhere to environmental and social impact assessment requirements, carry out thorough examinations of their human rights impacts, and actively support corporate social responsibility and community development. The BIT also includes a provision that permits the host state to implement measures to safeguard human rights, labour rights, and the environment, without being susceptible to ISDS claims.[158]

In addition to revising current IIAs and investment policy instruments, there have been suggestions to create new models of investment governance that prioritise social and environmental sustainability rather than solely focusing on investor protection. As an illustration, the Model Treaty on Sustainable Investment for Climate Change Mitigation and Adaptation, created by the International Institute for Sustainable Development (IISD), offers a blueprint for modern investment agreements that are in line with the Paris Agreement and the Sustainable Development Goals. The Model Treaty incorporates provisions that necessitate investments to support sustainable development and address climate change. It also mandates assessments of their environmental and social impacts, as well as due diligence on human rights. Additionally, it includes provisions that enable states to implement measures to meet their climate and sustainable development goals, without being vulnerable to ISDS claims.[159]

The Investment Policy Tools propose the implementation of screening and approval processes for foreign investments, with a focus on protecting human rights and the environment. It is also suggested that grievance mechanisms and access to remedy be provided for those impacted by investment-related human rights abuses, in accordance with the UNGPs.[160]

Several countries have begun integrating these suggestions into their own investment policies and regulations. In 2015, the South African government implemented the Protection of Investment Act, replacing the previous BITs with a new domestic legal framework for foreign investment.[161]

These examples demonstrate how domestic legal frameworks and institutions can contribute to responsible investment, sustainable development, and the alignment of international investment law with human rights and climate goals. Nonetheless, the success of these frameworks and institutions relies on their structure, execution, and enforcement, as well as the determination and capability of governments to utilise them for overseeing foreign investment in the best interests of the public. Academic institutions and research organisations should enhance

itn/2019/06/12/is-the-netherlands-model-investment-agreement-a-step-forward-for-sustainable-development-kyla-tienhaara/.

[158] Morocco-Nigeria Bilateral Investment Treaty (2016), Articles 13, 15, 18, 23, 24.

[159] IISD, 'A Model Treaty on Sustainable Investment for Climate Change Mitigation and Adaptation' (2022).

[160] UNDP, 'Investment Policy Tools for Sustainable Development' (2021).

[161] Protection of Investment Act 22 of 2015 (South Africa).

their environmental and social safeguard policies and accountability mechanisms to ensure that their investments are in line with sustainable development and human rights objectives. This includes strengthening mechanisms like the World Bank's Inspection Panel and the IFC's Compliance Advisor Ombudsman (CAO). It is crucial for them to enhance their backing for renewable energy and energy efficiency initiatives, while gradually discontinuing their support for fossil fuel projects, aligning with the Paris Agreement and the Sustainable Development Goals.[162]

The role of international investment law in promoting a fair and equal energy transition is incredibly important. However, there is a need for change and alignment with sustainable development and human rights goals. To tackle this issue, we need a comprehensive strategy.

First, we should include sustainable development and human rights provisions in investment policies. This means making sure that investment treaties and agreements prioritise the well-being of communities and the environment, not just the interests of investors. For example, when a company invests in a renewable energy project, they should also consider how it will benefit the local community and protect the environment.

Second, we need to improve our domestic laws and institutions to encourage responsible investment. This includes having screening and approval processes based on human rights, so that only investments that respect people's rights are allowed. We also need mechanisms to address complaints and provide help for affected communities. We should protect the rights of governments to make decisions in the best interests of the public.

Third, it's really important to involve and empower communities and other stakeholders in investment decisions. This can be done by creating groups where different people can give their opinions and advice. We can also use methods that allow everyone to have a say in how investments will affect them. We should encourage partnerships between communities and investors, so that everyone can benefit from the investments.

Last, international financial institutions and development finance institutions need to do more to protect the environment and people's rights. They should have better policies and procedures to assess and manage the impact of their investments. They should also support projects that promote renewable energy and energy efficiency.

To sum up, there are many challenges and opportunities for international investment law to help us have a fair and balanced energy transition. We need to change investment treaties and how we settle disputes. We need to come up with new ways to make investment decisions. We need to improve our laws and

[162] S Narain et al, 'Investing in a Green Future: Renewables and Energy Efficiency' in H Kharas and J McArthur (eds), *Building Back Better after COVID-19: Pathways to a More Sustainable, Inclusive, and Resilient Global Economy* (Brookings Institution Press, 2022) 55–56.

institutions. We need to involve communities and stakeholders. We need to make sure that international financial institutions do their part. By doing all of this, we can make sure that international investment law can help us in having a more sustainable and fair energy transition.

VI. Conclusion

The transition to clean and renewable energy sources is a major undertaking with profound implications for our planet and its inhabitants. International investment law, which governs the rules and regulations surrounding investments made across borders, plays a critical role in shaping the energy sector's transformation. It can either hinder or facilitate the necessary changes. From a legal perspective, this presents both challenges and opportunities. In promoting a fair and balanced energy transition, the purpose and nature of investment should be reconsidered. Traditionally, investments have been focused solely on economic returns. However, in the context of the energy transition, a more holistic approach that considers the social and environmental impacts of investments should be adopted. This means shifting our focus from profit alone to a broader understanding of investment that takes into account its effects on communities and the environment. Governing investments in the energy sector should be based on transparency, participation, and accountability to ensure that the needs and aspirations of local communities are met, and public interest is protected. This requires involving stakeholders in decision-making processes and holding investors accountable for their actions. Furthermore, it is important to recognise the social dimensions of the energy transition. Often overlooked, these dimensions are crucial in addressing the wider challenges of climate change and achieving sustainable development. It is essential to prioritise social justice and human rights in the planning and implementation of the transition. In conclusion, the energy transition presents both challenges and opportunities from a legal perspective. To ensure a fair and balanced transition, the purpose of investment, rethink investment governance, and prioritise social justice and human rights should be redefined. By doing so, a sustainable future that benefits both the environment and all members of society can be created.

Conclusion: Navigating the Interplay of International Investment Law and the Global Energy Transition

RAHMI KOPAR AND VOLKER ROEBEN

This book analyses the legal rather than political change of IEIL in the era of the energy transition. With this aim, it develops an analytic framework that distinguishes the external and internal systems of this branch of international law.

The external system comprises the treaty and dispute settlement through which new rules are adopted and new interpretations of extant rules are developed. Treaty amendment and convergent practice of the several arbitral tribunals become instruments of change. In terms of a treaty as an instrument of change, the ongoing reform of the ECT, or modernisation, takes centre stage. The process of amending it is governed by the law of treaties, codified in the Vienna Convention on the Law of Treaties. While this law accords Parties a high degree of autonomy, the multilateral nature of the Treaty also limits that autonomy. This may affect what is possible in both directions of the modernisations, that is the reduced protection for fossil fuel investments and the increased protection for low-carbon. As an alternative for explicit treaty change, the instrument of ISDS comes into play. That practice is indeed absorbing the normative impetus of the transition and develops and adapts the existing and accepted standards of the characteristics of low-carbon energy.

Turning to the substance of the matter, these instruments bring about change that is best measured against the unwritten internal system of IEIL. This unwritten internal system provides for the scrutiny of the rationality of host states' policy decisions on investments in new energy. At the same time, it formulates an outer limit to states' policy decisions. In this way, international energy investment law advances the transition by increasing low-carbon investment. Formed initially for the fossil fuel economy, this internal system is robust and flexible enough to absorb the impetus of the transition to a low-carbon energy system, marked by decentralised resources, infrastructure, novel and maturing technologies, strong government involvement, and a supply chain anchored in critical minerals and covering generation, transmission and consumption. The resulting change thus takes place within this system of international energy investment law and brings out doctrinal development to deal with structural features of low-carbon energy investments. This has to do in particular with the balancing between the right of the host states to regulate and the right of the investor to stability of the conditions of the investment.

The delicate balance between investment protection and state sovereignty is a central and recurring theme of the book. The analyses show that there is a necessity for a nuanced approach to the subject whereby on the one hand states are allowed to pursue their sustainable development goals and implement policies toward a cleaner energy system and on the other, international investors are not exposed to undue harm. This balance must be struck well since it is the private investors who will mostly fund this energy transition. Delimitating the concept of right to regulate and weighing legitimate public interests against investor benefits becomes crucial at this point. This is where international investment law and the dispute settlement mechanisms – mostly arbitration – come into play. The dynamic, ever-changing, and unpredictable landscape of the energy industry necessitates an adaptive and effective dispute resolution mechanism. This is imperative to sustain the legitimacy of international investment law. In order to address these emerging issues, there is a need to put creative frameworks in place.

The ECT continues to play a significant role even though there is harsh criticism against its current condition and the proposed modernised versions. At a theoretical level it still provides a good benchmark for the future of international investment law and investment treaties. The pressing need to align international treaties with contemporary environmental objectives cannot be overlooked. 'Can the ECT be flexible enough to address these concerns' is a question which is difficult to answer. However, it is undisputed that modernising investment treaties to address these novel realities is essential. While renegotiating and revising the already existing treaties is one way to tackle this issue, repealing them and signing a whole new set of treaties would be another alternative. However, the dilemma is that the energy transition moves forward at an unprecedented pace whilst it takes much more time for states to take the necessary actions on this legal ground.

ISDS has been an effective mechanism to protect foreign investors against host state interventions and changing conditions. States can also defend their legitimate policy actions before arbitral tribunals. The ISDS has also helped to develop the theoretical portion of international investment law. However, legitimacy concerns have been raised by many stakeholders. It is now much more important to establish a resilient and adaptive dispute resolution mechanism as the investment types and models in the energy sector are evolving rapidly, leading to the nature of disputes to change. Some believe that this new era will bring about a rise in protectionist measures by host states and a new wave of disputes. If the current ISDS mechanism cannot keep up with the new realities of the sector, it would be hard to provide stability and protection to foreign investors, the key players of the whole energy transition phase, and this could decelerate the pace of the transition towards cleaner energy. Arbitral practice also requires aligning with the international commitments towards low-carbon future and adapting a novel interpretative approach.

It is obvious that the energy transition is not only a pure environmental or financial endeavour. Rather, it also includes a social dimension which looms large. While a just and inclusive energy transition principle is the spearhead, there are many social considerations that must be integrated into investment policies and strategies. The success of the energy transition hinges on ensuring that it is socially equitable as well. The burdens and benefits arising from this process must all be shared fairly and all stakeholders, especially the vulnerable communities, must be included.

A low-carbon future necessitates substantial investments in infrastructure and emerging technologies. Mobilising the capital towards these areas is crucial to its success. International investment law plays a significant role in ensuring that the stability and predictability needed is in place and in the event of a dispute, there is an effective resolution to the dispute and efficient protection mechanisms for investors.

As this book reaches its conclusion, it becomes evident that international investment law is integral to the global energy transition. The principles, legal frameworks and mechanisms, and alternative proposals explored throughout this book establish the necessary foundation for attracting and channelling investments, protecting foreign investors' interests, leaving enough space for states for legitimate policy decisions, and ensuring that the transition is just and inclusive. However, since the energy scene changes swiftly, there is an increasing need to employ adaptive and innovative legal and regulatory approaches both on domestic and international levels to overcome any potential hurdles. To keep international investment law relevant during the energy transition era, states, investors, financiers, arbitral tribunals, and all other related stakeholders must set forth a collaborative effort to construct and implement adaptable and resilient legal frameworks that are aligned with global environmental aspirations and international commitments.

INDEX